The
Book
of
The
Continental
Soldier

being a compleat account of the

with three technical contributions by
Detmar H. Finke and Marko Zlatich
and special illustrations by H. Charles McBarron, Jr.,
Clyde A. Risley, and Peter Copeland

The Book of The Continental Soldier

by Harold L. Peterson

uniforms, weapons, and equipment
with which he lived and fought

PROMONTORY PRESS

Library of Congress Catalog Card Number: 74-27880

ISBN 0-88394-033-7

Published by arrangement with Stackpole Books

Printed in the United States of America

Design by **EARL R. BLUST** and associates of **KRONE ART SERVICE**

TO

Mr. and Mrs.
Ralph H. Parker

WHOSE FOREFATHERS FOUGHT THE WAR

Contents

Chapter

Preface

*O*n the morning of September 3, 1783 a small group of men gathered in the Hotel d'York in Paris. Their task was a momentous one for the new United States of America. The treaty ending hostilities and establishing independence was ready for signature, and before noon the representatives of Great Britain and the United States had signed their names to the historic document. Great Britain still had to sign agreements with France and Spain, but as far as America was concerned the war was now officially over. With the final flourish of the last signature the conflict became the province of historians, and they set to work with a will. Within two years David Ramsay brought forth his first book on the war. A steady stream of histories and analyses had begun, and it has seldom slackened since.

For almost two centuries scholars have examined the conflict that brought forth the new nation. They have treated it as a social phenomenon and they have analyzed it politically, economically, and even psychologically. Biographers have studied the great men, and archivists have edited vast collections of documents. Military historians, too, have probed the conflict with studies of tactics, strategy, and command.

Despite all this impressive array of scholarship, however, one area of the subject has been left largely untouched. The Continental soldier and the weapons, uniforms and other tools of his profession have been almost neglected. Some fifty years ago Reginald P. Bolton wrote his pioneering book, *The Private Soldier under Washington,* which offered a lode of interesting data on the enlisted man and his activities. John W. Wright followed with his brief compilation, *Some Notes on the Continental Army,* and more recently the late Lynn Montross produced the popular *Rag, Tag and Bobtail.* All of these volumes have dealt primarily with the men themselves, their activities, attitudes, organization and life, and they have covered the subject well.

Men, however, are just one element of an army. They cannot function without a host of physical objects. They need weapons to fight the enemy, uniforms to clothe themselves and to provide for recognition, equipment to carry food and necessary personal gear, tents or other shelter for protection from the elements, tools to build fortifications and to clear campsites or fields of fire, to name a few of the more obvious requirements. No army could operate without such necessities, and indeed the types, qualities and capabilities of these objects often determined how an army would perform and what it could do. The range and accuracy of firearms, for instance, set the distances at which opposing forces could engage each other. The ability of the individual soldier to carry his personal necessities on his body directly affected the need for a baggage train and consequently the freedom and speed with which a unit could maneuver. And there are dozens of other examples.

It is impossible to understand a war without understanding the armies which fought it, and it is impossible to understand an army without a knowledge of the physical objects with which it functioned. This volume is offered in the hope that it will help promote such an understanding.

Like any book this work represents the thoughts and efforts of many people. Numerous individuals have made their expert knowledge available to me and have contributed generously of their time and effort. It would be impossible to mention all who have offered advice or confirmed fact or theory or who have made their personal collections available for study and photographing. Many of these persons are acknowledged in the captions for the illustrations, but I should especially like to note the great contributions made by the following people and to express my deep appreciation.

To Donald W. Holst, who made his extensive notes on Revolutionary War material readily available, who lent photographs and negatives and who not only has read and criticized this entire work but has also participated in the preparation of three plates for it.

To Detmar H. Finke who has lent research notes and read the manuscript and who has also contributed special sections of technical interest to it.

To Marko Zlatich for his work on the uniform chapter, a subject in which he has done a great amount of primary research.

To H. Charles McBarron, Jr., Peter Copeland, Robert L. Miller, and Clyde Risley, each of whom has prepared special illustrations. Seldom is it possible to find talented artists who are at the same time specialists who have spent years studying the objects they portray.

To S. James Gooding for making his pictures of the important Rudyerd artillery drawings available.

To George P. Carroll, Musick Master-Drum Major at Colonial Williamsburg for generously lending his notes on the bands of the Continental Army and for much sage advice on the subject of fifes and drums.

To Dr. Francis S. Ronalds and Theodore Sowers of Morristown National Historical Park, Col. Frederick P. Todd of the New Windsor Cantonment, Richard E. Kuehne and Gerald C. Stowe of the West Point Museum, Dr. Philip Lundeberg, Craddock Goins, Jr. and Edgar Howell of the U. S. National Museum, Mrs. Alice Starner of the Historical Society of York County, Mr. Theodore Waterbury of the Newport Historical Society, Richard Koke of the New-York Historical Society, and Mrs. Harriet R. Cabot of the Old State House, Boston, all of whom made the resources of their institutions easily accessible and who went out of their way to provide photographs upon request.

To Bluford W. Muir, object photographer extraordinary, who took a number of the finest photographs for this book.

And finally to my patient wife, Dorothy, who typed the manuscript and tolerated all the nonsense that necessarily accompanies the writing of books.

Harold L. Peterson

Arlington, Virginia

Master of

Chapter 1

the Tools of Revolution

Being an introduction to the Continental soldier

Jesse Lukens was surprised. The American force besieging Boston was not quite what he had expected when he journeyed northwards with Colonel William Thompson's battalion of riflemen to help form the new national army. "Such Sermons," he wrote back to a friend, "such Negroes, such Colonels, such Boys, & such Great Great Grandfathers." (1) Lukens was not letting his imagination get the better of him. All of his subjects were to be found, but it was the unusual that caught his eye. Actually, the great majority of the soldiers in camp were men in their youth and middle years. Perhaps the young rifleman had expected this, however, and so did not comment upon it.

Still it was truly a motley host, more a mob than an army. It had sprung into existence almost spontaneously as the various local minutemen, alarm companies, and volunteers had pursued the British troops in their retreat from Concord and Lexington on April 19, 1775 and had then remained to lay siege to the city, and it had grown in size as men from other New England colonies poured in to join the common cause. For the first few weeks chaos was almost complete with no overall command, no definite enlistments, and only such discipline as the natural decency of the men provided. Attempts had been made to bring order by appointing officers and enlisting volunteers under them for the rest of the year, but it had not been enough. Powerful help was needed, and the Massachusetts Provincial Congress had sent an urgent appeal to the Continental Congress in Philadelphia asking it to adopt the new army and to give it direction. With dispatch the Congress had accepted the new responsibility. On June 14 it had authorized the raising of ten companies of riflemen in Virginia, Maryland, and Pennsylvania as the nucleus of a national army, and on June 15 it had appointed George Washington of Virginia Commander in Chief. By July 3 Washington had taken command and started to bring order and organization, and a few weeks later the riflemen, Jesse Lukens among them, had arrived to make the army truly national. *(2)*

Even so the new Continental Army did not spring into being overnight. The volunteer regiments enlisted at Boston were of different sizes, ranging from 500 to 1,000 men each. Terms of enlistment varied, though most ran until the end of the year. Discipline was lax, and to Lukens' shame, this was especially noticeable among his own riflemen who disobeyed orders and openly mutinied on one occasion. Worst of all, there was no overall plan for an army, no table of organization. All these situations had to be corrected as speedily as possible in the face of an enemy and while appealing to the patriotism of the men for further enlistments. *(3)*

Organization of the Continental Army

It was autumn before the new organization was set. In September conferences between Washington and a committee of Congress produced a plan for a Continental Army of 26 regiments or battalions of infantry, each containing 728 men, one regiment of riflemen and one artillery regiment, a total of 20,372 men. Each of the infantry regiments was to be composed of 8 companies of 86 men and 4 officers, and there was to be an 8-man regimental staff. All were to be administered by the Continental Congress and all were to be enlisted for a period running until the end of 1776, some 16 months away. On January 1, 1776 the new organization went into effect, but it was far from complete. Even the short one-year enlistment seemed too long to many. Others hesitated to serve under any officers but those they had selected themselves. Officers who had achieved high rank in the 38 volunteer regiments were reluctant to accept demotion for service in the Continental Army. By March when the spring campaign got under way only 9,170 men had joined the ranks, less than half the desired number. In order to obtain an adequate operating force Washington had to rely on help from local militia units.

Despite many organizational changes, this was to be true throughout the war. The Continental Army increased in size as additional regiments were authorized, the artillery and rifle regiments became a corps and a brigade, respectively, and cavalry, light infantry, and artificer regiments joined the force along with special mixed units called legions. The one factor that remained constant was the Continental Line's inadequacy by itself. It was never large enough to conduct a campaign entirely on its own. The various states organized and outfitted the regular infantry regiments according to a quota system, but they also maintained troops of their own, the so-called state lines, and there were in addition the local militia organizations that could be called out for a short period to meet an emergency in their special vicinity. Almost all major actions and campaigns were fought with a combination of the three types of units, and the American Revolutionary War soldier might be a member of any one. Possibly during his career he

might have served for one enlistment or another in all three, from the elite Continental Line to the irregular and often unreliable militia. His personal and family circumstances would dictate his choice, and the short enlistments made the changes possible. After 1776 Congress began to recruit Continental soldiers for longer periods, usually three years or the duration, but many a man who had served in the first year did not re-enlist, and many new recruits served just one hitch.

The men of these various military units closely resembled modern soldiers in many ways. They came from all walks of life—farmers, artisans, merchants, professional men and politicians, rich men and poor. From the very beginning there were Negroes, as noted by Jesse Lukens. The enlistment of these Negroes caused considerable discussion, especially in the South where slavery was an important factor. It was generally agreed, however, that free men regardless of color were welcome, and many regiments numbered Negroes among their veterans. There were also a few Indians, but not many since there were few inducements for them to enlist and fight for the American cause. (4)

Recruitment Methods

It was this matter of enlistment that offers one of the major differences between the Revolutionary soldier and his modern counterpart. The Revolutionary soldier was a volunteer, at least in the Continental Line. Some states used a quota system requiring either men or money, and there were bounties of money or land offered to induce enlistment or to make it economically possible for a man to sign up. On the whole, however, it was a free-will matter depending primarily on the individual's patriotism or desire for adventure. This was the reason there were never enough soldiers. Congress might authorize 88 battalions totalling 80,000 men, but it was an entirely different matter to put such regiments in the field. Some of the regiments were never raised; others were always under strength. The number of soldiers in the field varied, but the best estimates are that Washington never had as many as 15,000 able-bodied regulars of the Continental Line at his disposal at any one time. The usual number was closer to 10,000. Still, this was an impressive number of pure volunteers. (5)

Jesse Lukens also mentioned another difference in the American army from that of today. This was the spread of ages. Most state militias required the services of almost every able-bodied male between the ages of sixteen and sixty-five. Such men, and some even outside this great spread, pursued the British back to Boston and stayed to form the first army which Lukens saw. There were attempts during the war to eliminate "old men and boys" from the Continental Line, but both groups remained in the militia. Today they would be considered too immature or too decrepit to fight, but many a Revolutionary soldier came from one age extreme or the other.

Young or old, the Revolutionary soldier was a strong individualist. He could be led but not driven. If independence from Great Britain was worth fighting for, he believed a certain amount of personal independence was also his right. He did not take easily to strict military discipline. He talked back to officers. Sometimes he refused to obey, and occasionally he mutinied. The sermons mentioned by Lukens helped convince him of the correctness of the subservient attitude he was asked to take, but most important was the character of the officer who commanded him. In the militia system he had elected his officers. In the volunteer army which surrounded Boston he had selected the officer under whom he would serve, and the same relationship carried over at least to some degree in the Continental Line. One incident related by a New Jersey private enlisting with a new company graphically portrays his attitude towards his officers:

[The men were] sworn to be true and faithful soldiers of the Right Honorable Congress. After this we chose our officers.... When on parade, our 1st lieut. came and told us he would be glad if we would excuse him from going, which we refused; but on consideration we concluded it was better to consent; after which he said he would go; but we said, "You shall not command us, for he whose mind can change in an hour is not fit to command in the field where liberty is contended for." In the evening we chose a private in his place. (6)

How typical of the Revolutionary soldier; how different from his modern counterpart!

Manuals of Military Discipline

Obedience, whether it is forced upon a soldier or won from him, is necessary to any army. So are discipline, order, and a uniformity of drill. A soldier has to know how to handle his weapon in a group, how to march, fight and change position without causing confusion. To achieve this, systems of discipline were developed, and manuals were published. The older veterans at Boston had undoubtedly obtained their first training from a manual prepared by the British general Humphrey Bland and entitled simply *A Treatise of Military Discipline*. It had been almost universally used in the colonies from its first publication in 1727. Then, about 1768, there was a general shift at least in the New England area to a simplified military system that had been prepared for the militia of the county of Norfolk, England in 1759. Timothy Pickering further simplified the "Norfolk Discipline," as it was called, in *An Easy Plan of Discipline for a Militia*, which he published in his home city of Salem, Massachusetts at the outbreak of the Revolution in 1775. Pickering's system was essentially the Norfolk plan, but reduced to its basic essentials and with every step carefully spelled out. Most manuals, for instance, assumed that any fool would know how a cartridge was made. Pickering described one in detail and even provided drawings for the proper position of a soldier's feet in turning or firing. Some colonies also adopted the regular British Army manual of 1764 which was known popularly as the "Sixty-fourth," and an American edition was printed in New Haven. Washington himself owned six copies of this British manual but his copy of Pickering was also very well thumbed. And there were other textbooks as well. Most of these manuals were generally similar, but there were differences that might cause confusion and embarrassment in time of crisis.(7)

Nevertheless the American army limped along for two years with men who had been trained from at least three different manuals. Then, during the cold winter of Valley Forge, a man who called himself Baron Friedrich Wilhelm Ludolf Gerhard Augustin von Steuben arrived to set matters straight. The facts that he was not a baron and that he was only a half-pay captain rather than the lieutenant general he claimed were of no importance. Swearing in German, French (and in English, when he could find a voluble and imaginative interpreter), Von Steuben hammered the Continental soldiers into well-trained units which all fought by the same book. It was a new book, too, prepared by the drillmaster himself with ideas borrowed freely from English, French, and German sources. In 1779 the first of many editions of his *Regulations for the Order and Discipline of the Troops of the United States* came off the press to provide the basic manual for American fighting forces for over a quarter of a century. With keen insight into the needs of the ·men and country, Von Steuben had simplified and sharpened commands. He had reduced the number of motions required for firings and maneuvers, and most important of all, he had shifted the basic formation from a line of battle three ranks deep to one of two ranks, thus achieving even more maneuverability.

Under Von Steuben's guidance the Revolutionary War soldier became a first-class fighting man in the best European tradition. Contrary to popular tradition, he did not hide behind trees and stone walls to pot at enemy formations. With exceptions such as Kings Mountain and various routs, he met the British Army on its own terms in open fields and drawn up in a line of battle. He learned to make savage bayonet charges, and in such famous attacks as Stony Point and the assault on the redoubts at Yorktown, he charged with an unloaded weapon, relying solely on cold steel. By the end of the war the Continental was no longer just the citizen with a gun. He was a hardened campaigner. He knew his weapons and his drill. He could face the enemy under any and all circumstances. He knew how to throw up fortifications and how to obtain shelter. His independent spirit remained but he knew the military hierarchy and how to recognize it by insignia—and he knew the deference due it. He was, in short, the master of all the miscellaneous hardware and gear of military life, the basic tools of the Revolution.

Notes to Chapter 1

1. Jesse Lukens to John Shaw, Jr., September 13-18, 1775, *Historical Manuscripts in the Public Library of the City of Boston*, No. 1, Boston, 1900, p. 27.

2. The history of the Continental Army has been covered in a number of secondary works. Among them are Lynn Montross, *Rag, Tag and Bobtail, the Story of the Continental Army, 1775-83*, New York, 1952, and the standard military history of the Revolution, Christopher Ward, *The War of the Revolution*, 2 vols., New York, 1952. Allen French, *The First Year of the American Revolution*, Boston, 1934, is especially good on the early organizational period.

3. Lukens, *op. cit.*, pp. 24-26.

4. Charles K. Bolton, *The Private Soldier Under Washington*, New York, 1902, pp. 20-25, *et passim*. Benjamin Quarles, *The Negro in the American Revolution*, Chapel Hill, N.C., 1961, *passim*.

5. Bolton, *Private Soldier, passim*. Montross, *Rag, Tag and Bobtail, passim*.

6. Aaron Wright's *Revolutionary Journal*, quoted in Bolton, *Private Soldier*, p. 25.

7. Charles J. Hoadly, ed., *The Public Records of the Colony of Connecticut*, 15 vols., Hartford, 1850-1890, VIII, 568. Bolton, *Private Soldier*, pp. 109-111. John W. Wright, *Some Notes on the Continental Army* (New Windsor Cantonment Publication No. 2), Vails Gate, N.Y., 1963, pp. 2-5.

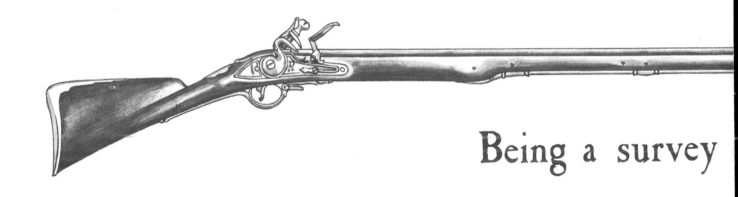

Being a survey

of the shoulder weapons
and hand guns of
the Continental Army

Lock, Stock and Barrel

Chapter 2

Variety was the word for the firearms of the Continental soldier. There were muskets, musketoons, carbines, rifles, fusils, pistols, and wall guns with many variations in each and every type. They reached the soldiers' hands by a variety of routes, and the soldiers used them in a variety of ways. There was no such thing as a single standard. Even calibers varied though attempts were made to keep them as uniform as possible. When it came to supply there was supposedly a system. The individual states were responsible for providing arms to the regiments they supplied for the Continental Line while Congress armed the other Continental troops. Even here, however, there was variety. Both the states and Congress purchased arms from American gunsmiths and dealers. Some states and Congress also purchased arms abroad. There were gifts of arms that found their way into both state-supplied regiments and Congressional troops. Guns were captured from the enemy and confiscated from Tories, and some soldiers, especially in the beginning, brought their own guns with them when they enlisted. If they were sound and serviceable arms, few questions were asked about model or source. All were gratefully received.

The Musket in Use

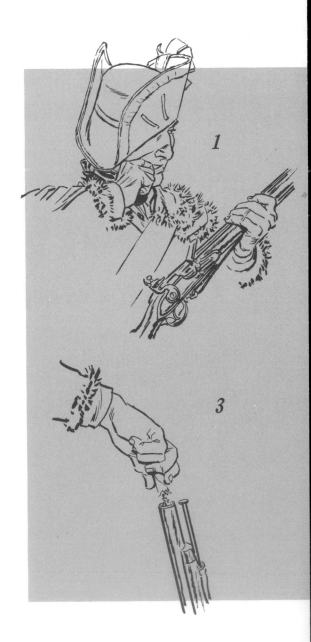

Of all the types of individual fire-arms, the musket was by far the most important. This was the workhorse of the Revolution. The bulk of the troops in the Continental Line were regular infantry. They were the core of the Army. Cavalry and riflemen were spectacular and highly useful in given situations. Artillery was a handy resource, but the major pitched battles were decided by steady lines of infantry, and the musket was their weapon.

During the Revolution the musket was a single-shot smoothbore muzzle-loader. It was 4 1/2 to 5 feet long, had a caliber of .69 to .80, and was fired by a flintlock. This lock was an ingenious device that had been invented in France about 1610. It produced a spark in the same way that the average householder had been lighting his fires for centuries—by striking a piece of flint against a steel. In the flintlock the flint was held in the jaws of a vise on the end of an arm called the cock. When the soldier was ready to shoot he pulled this cock back against a strong spring until it latched in place. When he pulled the trigger it released the latch and the spring threw the cock forward so that the flint in its jaws struck a glancing blow against a piece of steel called the frizzen or hammer. The frizzen flew back and the sparks from the blow dropped down into a small supply of priming powder in a little receptacle called a pan and caused it to flash. Flame from this flash darted through a touchhole in the side of the barrel and set off the main charge inside. It all happened much faster than it can be described. The shooter could notice a slight delay from the time he pulled the trigger until the load inside the barrel went off, but it was only a brief hesitation.

To load a musket the soldier used a cartridge, which consisted of a bullet and a load of powder wrapped in paper. First the

Steps in loading a musket:

1. *Cartridge is bitten open with gun at half cock and pan open.*

2. *Pan is primed.*

3. *Remainder of powder is poured down barrel.*

4. *Ball and wadded cartridge paper are rammed home.*
   Drawing by H. Charles McBarron, Jr.

soldier opened the pan of his lock. Then he bit off the end of the cartridge, poured a little powder into the pan for priming, closed the pan, poured the rest of the powder down the barrel and dropped the bullet still wrapped in the paper after it. Next he drew his ramrod and rammed the ball down the barrel to make sure that it was seated tightly on top of the powder where the paper of the cartridge held it in place. These bullets were always smaller than the bore of the musket so that they could be loaded quickly and easily. Thus they needed the paper to keep them from rolling out if the muzzle were pointed down.

The basic formation for infantry soldiers armed with such muskets was the line of battle. As taught by Von Steuben this consisted of two ranks of men, shoulder-to-shoulder, with a line of file-closers in the rear to take the place of fallen comrades. In this formation the regiments advanced to the attack, and in it they also received the charge of the enemy. Given the single-shot muzzle-loading weapons of the day, it was a practical formation. The usual procedure in an attack was to advance within sure range of the enemy (some theorists recommended thirty yards), fire a volley, then charge to decide the issue with the bayonet hand-to-hand. In receiving a charge the line waited until the advancing enemy was within range, fired a volley, loaded, and if possible fired one or two more volleys before the enemy closed with them. (1)

Volley-firing from a line of battle was a very formal practice. All loading and shooting was done on command. There was little aiming as it is understood today. The volley was delivered directly ahead or to the right or left oblique as commanded. The theory was to lay down a field of fire, and consequently rapidity of fire was prized much more highly than accuracy. (2)

Thus the musket, which could be loaded rapidly, was considered a fine weapon, even though its accuracy left something to

be desired. Some idea of the speed of loading and firing expected of the soldier armed with the musket can be obtained from the following entry in a military treatise of 1768:

No recruit to be dismissed from the drill, till he is so expert with his firelock, as to load and fire fifteen times in three minutes and three quarters. (3)

This would mean a sustained fire of one shot every fifteen seconds, a rate which would assure at least two volleys at an approaching enemy in any average charge.

Thus, if, as was often the case, a charge involved only one regiment on each side, and if each regiment consisted of 500 men, it would mean that the attacking force would have to suffer the effects of 1,000 bullets in two volleys in the 20 or 25 seconds it would take them to negotiate a charge of less than 100 yards. The second volley would be received, if delivered properly, at a range of no more than 30 yards.

If the charge were more than 100 yards, if there were obstacles to be surmounted, if it was necessary to halt and consolidate forces after the effects of one of these volleys, then the attacking force would have to withstand 500, 1,000, or possibly 1,500 more shots. It should be remembered also that this attacking force was not spread out in the manner in which modern infantrymen advance under fire. It was a compact and solid mass of men, a perfect target for fire from another compact body of men at point-blank range. Accuracy would have been superfluous in this type of warfare. Speed was everything. Speed for the defending force to pour as many bullets into the attacking force as possible; speed for the attacking force to close with its adversary before it had been too severely decimated to have sufficient strength to carry the position.

There were some instances, however, in which an accurate weapon was to be desired, and here the musket was weak. Troops detached to act as flankers on a march through hostile territory, pickets, rangers, and other similar small groups where the action was apt to involve only a few men or perhaps single individuals, felt the need of accurate weapons. It was to these troops and in these instances that the rifle later proved a valuable arm.

These men wanted accuracy, and they practiced marksmanship even with the musket. Washington had encouraged such marksmanship since his days as a colonel of the Virginia militia during the French and Indian War. Even British soldiers tried to learn how to shoot their muskets as accurately as possible for those times in which they would need to aim at an individual target. (4)

No matter how they tried, however, they could never become marksmen with the smoothbore musket. It just was not an accurate weapon, primarily because the bullet fit so loosely in the bore. It had a tendency to bounce from side to side as it shot down the barrel, and the nature of the last bounce had a considerable effect on the direction of its flight. The limitations and capabilities of the musket have been well described by Colonel George Hanger of the British Army, one of the most famous marks-

men and authorities on shooting of the day. He maintained:

A soldier's musket, if not exceedingly ill-bored (as many of them are), will strike the figure of a man at eighty yards; it may even at 100; but a soldier must be very unfortunate indeed who shall be wounded by a common musket at 150 yards, provided his antagonist aims at him; and as to firing at a man at 200 yards with a common musket, you may just as well fire at the moon and have the same hopes of hitting your object. I do maintain and will prove, whenever called on, that no man was ever killed at 200 yards by a common soldier's musket, by the person who aimed at him. (5)

It was just such British muskets as these that formed the bulk of the American armament at the beginning of the war. Many an American veteran of the colonial wars still retained his British musket, and he took it with him when he enlisted. Magazines and arsenals in the various colonies contained stores of British arms that had been kept there during the earlier wars, and there were also captured arms here and there. Americans had grown familiar with the British arms during the colonial period, and the British pattern was the natural one for them to select for their own military purposes.

The Brown Bess

Actually there were two models of the British musket in use at the time, both known by the soldiers' nickname of Brown Bess. The first was officially designated the long land musket. It had been adopted back during the reign of George I, and it boasted a barrel 46 inches long. It is often called the first model Brown Bess. The second model, the short land musket, which had only a 42-inch barrel, was introduced about 1740 and officially superseded the long musket about

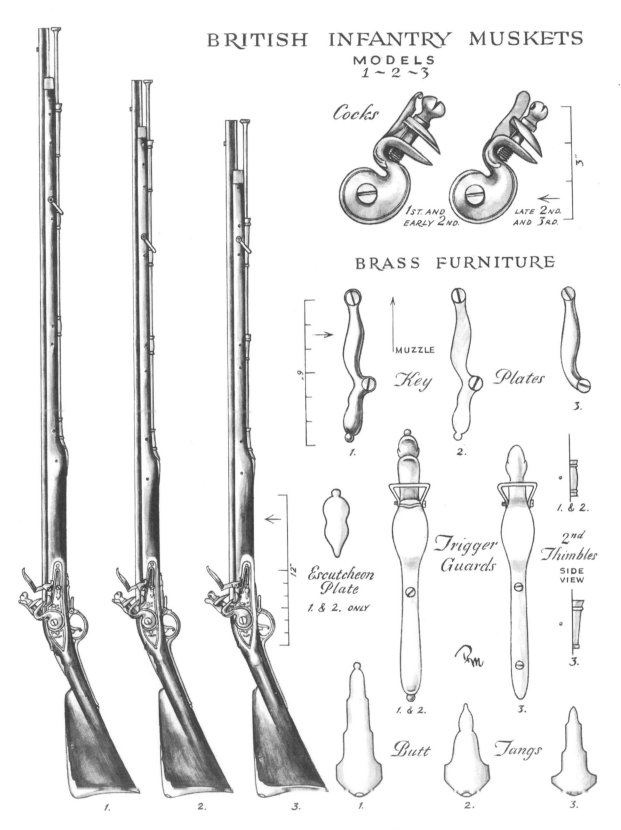

BRITISH INFANTRY MUSKETS
MODELS
1 ~ 2 ~3

Cocks

1ST. AND EARLY 2ND.

LATE 2ND. AND 3RD.

3"

BRASS FURNITURE

MUZZLE

Key *Plates*

1.   2.   3.

Escutcheon Plate

1. & 2. ONLY

Trigger Guards

1. & 2.   3.

2nd *Thimbles*

SIDE VIEW

1. & 2.

3.

12"

Butt *Tangs*

1.   2.   3.

1.   2.   3.

Drawing by Robert L. Miller. Courtesy Company of Military Historians.

1765, though the older pattern remained in use until supplies were exhausted. There was also a still shorter third model known as the India-pattern musket which came along a little later and was not formally adopted by the British Army until the early 1790's. All models were .75-caliber arms with handsome brass mountings and brown finished walnut stocks fastened to the barrels by pins. It was the brown color of these stocks, in fact, that gave the muskets their nickname. Before them, British muskets had had their wooden stocks painted black. (6)

The locks on all these muskets were plainly marked to indicate their British origin. Usually there was engraved the royal monogram, a crown over the letters "GR" (Georgius Rex), and a broad arrow indicating that the piece was government property. These marks appeared in front of the cock. In back of the cock there was an indication of the manufacturer. If the piece had been completely made by one maker, it usually bore his name and the date. If it had been assembled at one of the government arsenals it bore the name of the arsenal, most often "TOWER" for the Tower of London but occasionally "DUBLIN CASTLE" instead.

Light Infantry and Fusils

In addition to these standard infantry muskets there were also lighter weapons designed for the artillery or light infantry. These resembled the bigger muskets in everything but size. In the British Army, officers and occasionally non-commissioned officers also carried a lighter form of musket called colloquially a fusil or fuzee. Most often these are distinguishable from the artillery muskets by their fine

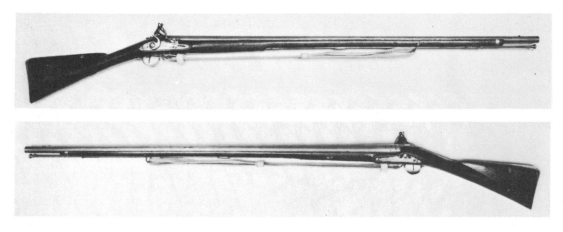

British officer's fusil. The sling is modern. Colonial Williamsburg.

workmanship and by the fact that the mountings are often engraved or otherwise decorated. Such guns were seldom used in the Continental Army, however, for Washington strongly disapproved of his infantry officers' carrying firearms. He believed that guns took too much of an officer's attention and so prevented him from performing at his best. After 1777 he tried to abolish the practice of carrying them. A pistol in a pocket or saddle holster might be permissible, but a shoulder arm never. (7)

Committee of Safety Muskets

Despite the large number of British arms in America there were not nearly enough to equip an entire army. Thus Congress and the individual colonies promptly turned to American gunsmiths and placed orders with them for as many guns as they could produce. During the first years of the war the colonies were governed by committees or councils of safety, and it was these groups which contracted for the production of arms. They let their first contracts in the spring and early summer of 1775 and continued to work actively at procuring weapons and equipment until they were superseded by the new state governments two or three years later. Collectors today tend to call all American-made muskets of the Revolutionary War period "Committee of Safety muskets." Actually the term should apply only to those muskets made under a direct contract to a committee or council of safety during the short period of their existence.

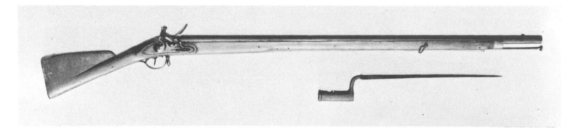

Committee of Safety musket with original British-style bayonet. Robert L. Klinger Collection.

Committee of Safety muskets followed the pattern of British arms. They were, in fact, as close copies of the second model Brown Bess as it was possible for American gunsmiths to make. Congress set the pattern for the various colonies by specifying that model as preferred with two resolutions in July 1775. Then, on November 4, it passed the following detailed resolution:

Resolved That it be recommended to the several Assemblies or conventions of the colonies respectively, to set and keep their gunsmiths at work, to manufacture good fire locks, with bayonets; each firelock to be made with a good bridle lock, 3/4 of an inch bore, and of good substance at the breech, the barrel to be 3 feet 8 inches in length, the bayonet to be 18 inches in the blade, with a steel ramrod, the upper loop thereof to be trumpet mouthed: that the price to be given to be fixed by the Assembly or convention, or committee of safety of each colony.... (8)

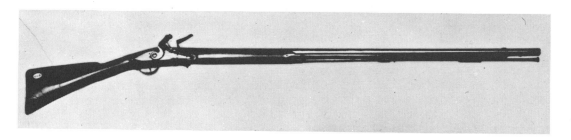

American Revolutionary War musket by Deacon Barrett of Concord, Massachusetts. Claud E. Fuller Collection, National Park Service, U.S. Department of the Interior.

Massachusetts set up its specifications the day before Congress passed its detailed resolution; yet the musket called for is of the same design preferred by Congress:

Resolved, That for every effective and substantial Fire-Arm which shall be manufactured in this Colony with a barrel of three feet and nine inches in length that will carry an ounce ball, a good bayonet with a blade not less than eighteen inches in length, a steel ramrod with a spring to retain the same, two loops for gun strings, and the maker's name stamped or engraved on the lock...and resemble in construction, and, as nearly as may be, equal in goodness with the King's new arms there shall be allowed...the sum of three Pounds. (9)

The maker of the gun was required to prove it at his own risk with four and a half inches of powder and a ball, each topped by a wad. Some of the guns were then to be stamped "MB" (Massachusetts Bay) on the barrel near the lock. (10)

Connecticut set its standards as early as April 1775, when the following bill was passed by the General Assembly:

Resolved, That the three thousand stands of arms to be procured for the use of this Colony be of the following dimensions, to wit: the length of the barrel three feet ten inches, the diameter of the bore from inside to inside three-quarters of an inch, the length of the blade of the bayonet fourteen inches, the length of the socket four inches and one quarter; that the barrels be of a suitable thickness, with iron ramrods, a good substantial lock, and a good stock well mounted with brass and marked with the name or initial letters of the maker's name. (11)

All such arms manufactured in the colony by May 1, 1775 were to be purchased "at a reasonable price." In March 1776, the committee purchased some imported barrels and locks that fitted the specifications and passed them out to local gunsmiths for stocking and mounting. After May 1776 Connecticut also began the practice of impressing needed guns from their owners. These impressed arms were then stamped with the initials of their former owners with the promise that payment would be made in due time. (12)

Rhode Island apparently set up no specifications for its arms. For the most part it relied on the unusually ample supply of public arms which had been built up in the magazines of its various towns throughout the entire colonial period. Beginning in 1776, these guns were supplemented by purchases from individual citizens and dealers and later by imports from foreign countries. One distinguishing characteristic, however, is found in the fact that all arms purchased were ordered to be stamped with the Rhode Island coat of arms and the letters "CR." (13)

Committee of Safety musket by Lewis Prahl of Pennsylvania. The cock is an early replacement. Warren Hay Collection.

New Hampshire, like Rhode Island, let no specific contract for arms. Instead the colony periodically appropriated money and sent out agents to purchase whatever they could find in the line of serviceable firearms. One of the favorite hunting grounds for these agents was the Salem-Marblehead area of Massachusetts. Eventually conditions became so bad that when Washington wrote the colony in 1777 to ask about the possibility of purchasing some muskets for the use of Continental troops, the Committee of Safety was forced to reply: "Fire arms cannot be procured from us that can be depended upon." They added they were also practically without undependable ones. (14)

In New York, the Committee of Safety supplied contracting gunsmiths with a "Brown Bess" and an English lock as patterns and required them to follow them both in design and quality. (15)

Pennsylvania required that its muskets have barrels 3 feet 8 inches long "well fortify'd, the bore of sufficient size to carry 17 Balls to the Pound." The bayonets were to have blades 16 inches long. Contractors were issued a pattern, apparently a "Brown Bess," to guide them in the construction of the desired gun. Since Pennsylvania gunsmiths were so well known, the colony was faced with a particular problem. Buyers from other states were purchasing most of their products. To put an end to this situation, the Pennsylvania Council of Safety passed a law forbidding anyone to take a firearm out of the colony without a specific license. In March of 1776 the Council established a provincial gunlock factory since the main deterrent to the swift production of muskets was a shortage of locks. *(16)*

Complete data on the arms purchases of New Jersey are not available, and nothing at all has been found on those of Delaware. From such records as are obtainable, however, it appears that New Jersey relied more on scattered purchases than on systematic contracts.

Maryland proofmark.

The nearby Pennsylvania gunsmiths were a special temptation until that state forbade the exportation of firearms. *(17)*

Maryland defined its standards on August 30, 1775, when it required:

> ...good substantial proved Musquets, 3 1/2 Feet in the Barrel, and of three Quarters of an Inch in the Bore, with good double Bridle Locks, black walnut or Maple Stocks and plain strong brass mountings, Bayonets with Steel Blades 17 Inches long, steel Ramrods, double Screws, priming Wires, and Brushes fitted thereto, with a pair of brass Molds for every Eighty Musquets to cast 12 Bullets on one Side, and on the other side, to cast Shot of such Size, as the Musket will chamber three of them, for such a Sum not exceeding Ten Dollars and two Thirds of a Dollar in Bills of Credit.... *(18)*

Another statement a short time later indicated that the barrels were pin-fastened. Some barrels were later especially ordered with full-inch bores. The Council appointed Thomas Ewing as an inspector in Baltimore, and there he proved all submitted muskets with an ounce of powder and two balls. He had a proof stamp made at that time. The initials or device that this stamp bore are not definitely known, although two muskets found in Maryland and conforming to that

Committee of Safety musket
bearing the supposed Maryland proofmark.
Author's Collection.

colony's specifications bear a proofmark somewhat resembling a *fleur-de-lys*.

Ewing was a rigid inspector, once rejecting as many as nineteen out of thirty-two muskets presented to him, but the Council was forced to abandon its standards at least to the extent of accepting iron as well as brass mountings and single-bridled as well as double-bridled locks. Which bridle was omitted is not clear, but it was probably the arm from the pan to the frizzen since that was the second of the two

Lock from a Fredericksburg Manufactory musket. Robert L. Miller Collection.

bridles to come into general use. Like Connecticut, Maryland was also forced to import suitable barrels and locks in March 1776 and hire local gunsmiths to stock and mount them. In another move to correct the shortage of locks, the Council established a state gunlock factory at Frederick in 1776. *(19)*

Virginia pursued a path somewhat different from those of the other colonies and established a state manufactory in the very beginning. Under the leadership principally of Fielding Lewis and Charles Dick, the Fredericksburg Manufactory proceeded in the fall of 1775 to repair arms already in the colony and in the late spring of 1776 it began also to manufacture arms, generally following the British pattern but somewhat lighter and often mounted in iron instead of brass. Two complete muskets made in the Fredericksburg Manufactory have survived along with one lock on a repaired musket. The barrel lengths in the two complete specimens measure 39 inches and 37 inches respectively.

Rappahannock Forge musket. Formerly in the Arthur O'Neill Collection.

The Manufactory continued in operation until 1783, but lack of funds and labor after 1780 seriously hampered its work and relegated it primarily to the position of a repair shop. *(20)*

At the same time Virginia contracted with individual gunsmiths and such private establishments as James Hunter's Rappahannock Forge at Falmouth, across the river from the Fredericksburg Manufactory. A typical contract, dated September 28, 1776, called for 200 stands of arms:

> ...to consist each of a Good Musket three feet eight Inches in the Barrel, three quarters of an Inch bore Steel rammers, the upper thimble trumpet mouthed the lower thimble with a spring to retain the ramrod, bridle Lock, brass mounting, a Bayonet eighteen inches blade with a Scabbard, one pair bullet moulds, to mould sixteen Bullets, to every forty guns; a priming wire & brush to each musket. *(21)*

In the southern colonies of North Carolina, South Carolina,

Lock from Rappahannock Forge musket. Formerly in the Arthur O'Neill Collection.

and Georgia an entirely different situation prevailed. The war came more slowly to this area, with only two engagements before 1777. Consequently there was more time in which to procure arms. Also, the West Indies and Bermuda were close at hand and easy to reach. The ports of these islands were soon swarming with war profiteers who possessed large stocks of good and bad European arms. It was natural, therefore, that these colonies should turn to that source for the bulk of their supplies. Even so, some few arms were purchased locally, and in regard to these, the Georgia Council of Safety on January 2, 1776, passed a resolution to the effect that all such guns should conform as nearly as possible to the specifications set forth by the Continental Congress. (22)

With all these specifications available, it would seem reasonable that a student could expect to examine a given specimen and determine immediately whether it was or was not a Committee of Safety musket. This, unfortunately, is not the case. There are very few muskets in existence today which meet all the qualifications established by any colony.

There are two possible explanations for this situation; either practically no Committee of Safety muskets have survived, or individual contractors deviated from the specifications. In regard to the first possibility, it is true that such muskets would be expected to have an unusually low rate of survival. They were made and issued during the early years of the war; they saw severe service and there was no steady supply of replacements. Also, since they were worn out and since they were not of the newer and more popular French pattern and caliber, many of those that remained in government arsenals at the end of the war were weeded out when the "third class" arms were sold or broken up for spare parts. Thus the possibility of almost total destruction is good.

On the other hand, the possibility that individual contractors deviated somewhat from specifications is also good. This possibility is enhanced by the fact that there are muskets in existence today which bear the names of men who had Committee contracts and which, while conforming in general to the Committee pattern, differ in one or two details. The most frequently found variance is in the barrel length, but in some few instances it is the caliber that differs from the specified size. Naturally, the marks on some of these specimens are suspect. On others, however, the marks are apparently genuine, and the piece is obviously American. With these latter pieces, then, the important question is posed: Are these guns Committee of Safety muskets or does the fact that they differ in some degree from the contract specifications disqualify them? In this connection it is known that Maryland was forced to accept iron as well as brass mountings and single-bridled as well as double-bridled locks, and it seems probable that other colonies made similar exceptions as long as the pieces complied with the general specifications.

Imported Muskets

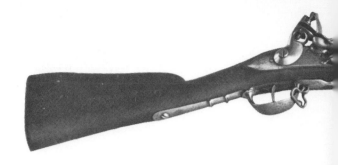

In addition to the arms produced in America, many more firearms were imported from Europe both by individual colonies and by Congress. Benjamin Franklin, who had been a colonial representative in England, left orders for arms with French, Dutch, and even English dealers before returning to America at the outbreak of hostilities. Pliarne Penet *et cie,* a French firm, sent one of their members to Philadelphia in 1775 and contracted with the Secret Committee of Congress for firearms. In the spring of 1776 Congress sent Silas Deane, a merchant and former member of Congress from Connecticut, to France to obtain arms and military equipment as well as to induce the French government to lend money and perhaps to enter the war as an ally. In addition to these contacts, emissaries from various colonies traveled to Europe, purchasing arms in France, Holland, and Prussia; while European concerns sent arms to ports in the West Indies and Bermuda where they made contact with colonial agents. *(23)*

Of all the arms imported from foreign countries, by far the most came from France. The largest number of French arms and the best ones were obtained by Deane from the French government. France had been severely beaten in the series of wars with England for control of the American continent, and the French government was therefore predisposed to help the colonies in their struggle with Great Britain in any way it could. Obviously, one way was to supply arms. To sell arms directly to the colonies, however, could be construed by England as an overt act of war, and so a dummy corporation was set up under the name of Roderique Hortalez *et cie.*

In charge of this corporation was an agent named Pierre Caron de Beaumarchais, who took his orders directly from the French foreign minister. It was with these men that Deane had his dealings, and through this subterfuge arms and equipment were released from the French arsenals and shipped to America. Because of English protests the ships were forced to clear for the French West Indies, and some actually went there and left their stores to be picked up by American ships. Others sailed directly to America. In all, ten ships carried these stores to the colonists, the first arriving in April 1777 and the last in November of that year. Only one was captured by the British. By early 1778 the French were openly at war with Great Britain, and the false trading company and private means of shipping were no longer necessary. Thereafter arms were sent directly from the French government, and also French officers like Lafayette sometimes brought arms with them for their own troops. *(24)*

Other arms purchased in France were not necessarily as good as the standard French army muskets. The profiteers bought their stocks just as cheaply as they could, and consequently they had many obsolete and poorly made arms. Pliarne Penet *et cie* was among the worst offenders. An offshoot of this company operating under the name of James Gruel & Co. bought their guns in Liège in the Austrian Netherlands (modern Belgium), and the Belgian muskets of that period were just as bad as those of the nineteenth century. *(25)*

*Model 1777 French musket.
Fort Ticonderoga.*

French Muskets

The French muskets which the Continental Army obtained are far more difficult to identify than the British types. Whereas there were only two models of British musket in use during the period, there were six French models, each with variations. The differences between models are frequently minor and hard to detect, and there are a great many French muskets in existence which do not conform exactly to any of the standards. Thus the student is often forced to make only an approximate

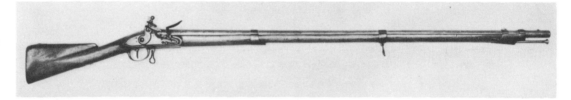

Model 1763 French musket. Author's Collection.

identification. This is usually enough, for the overall characteristics of the major types are easily recognizable and enable the collector to assign a musket to its general period quite easily.

Some very old French firearms may have been sold to the Congress or to the individual states for use by the Continental Line, but the great majority were of recent manufacture. Following their country's disastrous defeat in the French and Indian War, the French had redesigned their infantry muskets, and they had continued to modify and improve them almost constantly from 1763 until 1777. There were official models of 1763, 1766, 1770-71, 1773, 1774, and 1777. Some authorities also include a model of 1768. Each was a little different from the one preceding it, but all had some of the same characteristics. They were, for

instance, all .69-caliber, and all had the barrel fastened to the stock by three iron bands. Both of these characteristics were important design factors, for they permitted a lighter weapon than the .75-caliber Brown Bess, which needed a forestock heavy enough to support the barrel-fastening pins. Also, all the French muskets had flintlocks with reinforced or "throat hole" cocks, as contrasted with the British gooseneck cocks. Again this was an important refinement, for it offered a stronger cock, less apt to snap off at the neck. Finally, all were made at the royal manufactories of Charleville, St. Étienne, and Maubeuge. (26)

The major differences among the various French models can be quickly catalogued. The model 1763 had a flat lockplate, a flat cock, and an angular priming pan. Its barrel was 44 1/2 inches long. The model 1766 was similar but slightly lighter. In 1770 a rounded lockplate, cock, and pan were introduced. In 1773 the arm was lengthened by an inch, but very few muskets of this model were ever made, and probably none found their way to America. The model of 1774 continued the increased length. In 1777 several major changes were made. Most noticeable are the brass priming pan, the cheekpiece carved out of the left side of the stock, and the ribs on the rear tang of the trigger guard. Probably the greatest number of French muskets to reach the Continental Army were of the models 1763 through 1770-71. It is doubtful that any of the model of 1777 were either sold or given to the Americans, since they were still the standard for the French Army and only put into production during the war. (27)

All of these French arms were good ones, and they quickly made their presence felt. As noted above, they were both stronger and lighter than the British models. From 1777 on, they became increasingly easier to obtain, first through Silas Deane's purchases and then, after France entered the war, on a more direct basis. Faced with the availability of these good weapons, American preferences began to change. The British-style muskets were relegated to second place, and French-pattern arms in .69-caliber became the standard. Probably no British-pattern arms were made in America after 1777. The Committee of Safety musket was finished.

Æmerican Rifles

Of all the firearms carried by infantry, however, the rifle was by far the most glamorous and exciting. It was just as glamorous and exciting during the Revolution as it is today. Here was a distinctly American arm, a spectacularly accurate weapon in a day when mediocrity was the best that most military marksmen could expect. It was used by a class of men whose dress and behavior set them apart from other soldiers and whose skill with their chosen firearm was almost legendary. It all started back with those first ten companies of riflemen

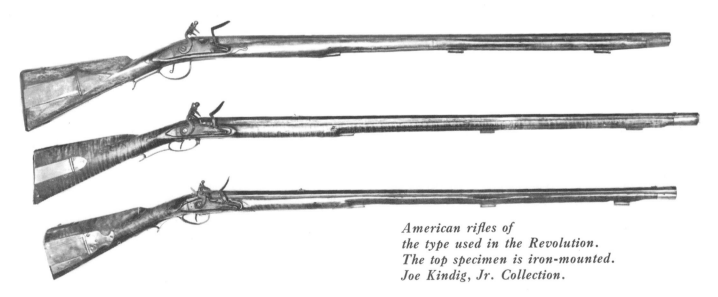

*American rifles of
the type used in the Revolution.
The top specimen is iron-mounted.
Joe Kindig, Jr. Collection.*

who formed the very first unit of the Continental Army. As they made their way north to join the militia and state troops besieging the British in Boston, they created a great impression on the civilians along the route who gathered to wish them well. They dressed in hunting shirts

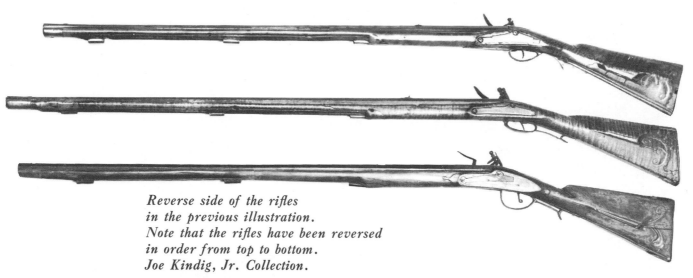

Reverse side of the rifles
in the previous illustration.
Note that the rifles have been reversed
in order from top to bottom.
Joe Kindig, Jr. Collection.

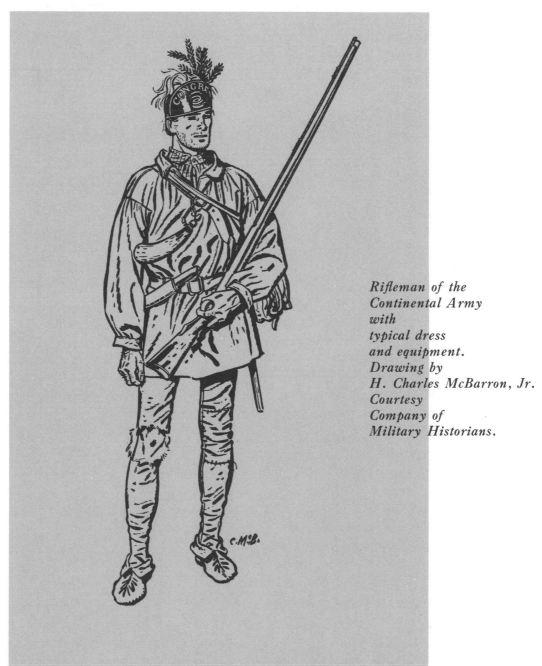

Rifleman of the
Continental Army
with
typical dress
and equipment.
Drawing by
H. Charles McBarron, Jr.
Courtesy
Company of
Military Historians.

of buckskin, with huge scalping knives and tomahawks in their belts. Sometimes they painted their faces like Indians, and they delighted in impressing the city dwellers with their war whoops and their marksmanship. Newspapers ran stories of their competitions as every man in one of the companies reportedly placed shots in a 7-inch target at 250 yards, and a marksman from Virginia was said to have put eight successive shots through a board 5 x 7 inches at 60 yards. Other newspapers copied the stories, and the riflemen's fame spread even to England itself where it created quite a stir. *(28)*

These rifles and the men who used them were highly individual. There were no standard patterns, for these were essentially civilian arms made by a host of different gunsmiths. Many of the

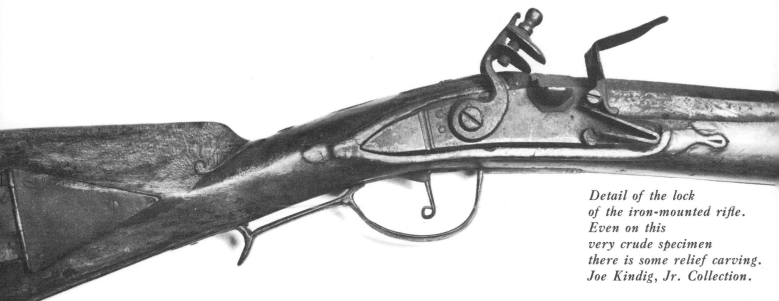

Detail of the lock of the iron-mounted rifle. Even on this very crude specimen there is some relief carving. Joe Kindig, Jr. Collection.

riflemen brought their own weapons with them, but others in the first companies arrived unarmed so that Congress had to purchase rifles for them from gunsmiths in Pennsylvania. Yet there was a certain similarity of design. Calibers averaged .55-.60. Barrels were octagonal and relatively long with a blade front sight and an open V rear sight. Stocks were made of curly maple, and they ran to within a few inches of the muzzle. The stocks of these early rifles lacked the sharp drop that came to characterize later American rifles, and the butts were not so sharply crescentic. Also the butts were quite thick, perhaps three inches through in a typical specimen. Mountings were almost always brass, and most characteristic of all was the hinged patch box cover on the right side of the stock. A few rifles undoubtedly had sliding wooden covers or hinged covers of iron or pewter, but brass was standard. Better rifles had a little relief carving around the lock, barrel tang, and trigger guard mortises and especially around the cheekpiece on the left side of the stock, but there was seldom any other decoration. The multiple metal inlays came on the postwar specimens. The Revolutionary War rifle was simple and efficient.

Because the rifle was so spectacular and glamorous, it has attracted a host of historians. Some of them have written highly glowing accounts of its importance, even calling it "the gun that won the Revolution." Others have tried to discount it as of little importance. Actually the truth lies between these two extremes, and it is not a matter of personal opinion or wishful thinking. There is ample contemporary evidence to show what the rifle could do and what contemporary military men thought of it.

First of all, the rifle's greatest asset was its accuracy even at long range. Many tales have been recounted about this quality, but perhaps the best comments are those of Colonel George Hanger, the trained British marksman, whose comments about the musket were quoted above. Recounting an experience, Colonel Hanger wrote:

> Colonel, now General Tarleton, and myself, were standing a few yards out of a wood, observing the situation of a part of the enemy which we intended to attack. There was a rivulet in the enemy's front, and a mill on it, to which we stood directly with our horses' heads fronting, observing their motions. It was absolutely a plain field between us and the mill; not so much as a single bush on it. Our orderly-bugler stood behind us about three yards, but with his horse's side to our horses' tails. A rifleman passed over the milldam, evidently observing two officers, and laid himself down on his belly; for in such positions, they always lie, to take a good shot at a long distance. He took a deliberate and cool shot at my friend, at me, and at the bugle-horn man. Now observe how well this fellow shot. It was in the month of August, and not a breath of wind was stirring. Colonel Tarleton's horse and mine, I am certain, were not anything like two feet apart; for we were in close consultation, how we should attack with our troops which laid 300 yards in the wood, and could not be perceived by the enemy. A rifle-ball passed between him and me; looking directly to the mill I evidently observed the flash of the powder. I directly said to my friend, "I think we had better move, or we shall have two or three of these gentlemen shortly amusing themselves at our expense." The words were hardly out of my mouth when the bugle-horn man behind me, and directly central, jumped off his horse and said, "Sir, my horse is shot." The horse staggered, fell down, and died.... Now speaking of this rifleman's shooting, nothing could be better....I have passed several times over this ground and ever observed it with the greatest attention; and I can positively assert that the distance he fired from at us was full 400 yards. *(29)*

Colonel Hanger participated in the Burgoyne campaign, and consequently became a prisoner of war after the battle of Saratoga when that whole British army surrendered. This event gave him an even better chance to study the American rifle, as he reported:

I have many times asked the American backwoodsman what was the most their best marksmen could do; they have constantly told me that an expert rifleman, provided he can draw good and true sight...can hit the head of a man at 200 yards. I am certain that provided an American rifleman was to get a perfect aim at 300 yards at me standing still, he most undoubtedly would hit me, unless it was a very windy day.... *(30)*

So much for the rifle's advantages; its disadvantages were serious. It was not equipped with a bayonet, and it was slow to load. The lack of a bayonet left the rifleman helpless in the face of a charge and powerless to charge himself. The technique of loading was briefly this. A charge of powder was poured down the barrel. Then a greased patch was centered over the bore, a bullet placed on this, and both rammed down together with the bullet being wrapped in the patch and thus ensuring a tight fit. It was not normally the practice to use prepared ammunition such as that employed with the muskets, although a device was developed which helped with the patching of the bullet. This device consisted of a board with several holes bored through it. In each hole the user inserted a patched bullet so that when the time came he could place the hole over the bore and push the patched bullet right down the barrel. Still the charge had to be measured separately, and the patched bullet had to be seated accurately, instead of just being thrown in as was the case with the musket.

It will be remembered from the discussion of the musket how much emphasis was placed on rapidity of fire, and consequently how adversely the slowness of the rifle would affect it as a military weapon can well be imagined. The emphasis on the use of the bayonet was not then mentioned, but it should be borne in mind that battles were frequently decided in hand-to-hand combat with the bayonet. Once the opposing troops closed with each other there was no time to reload. The American defeat at Bunker Hill was at least partially attributable to the lack of bayonets, and Samuel Webster, pleading for bayonets after the battle, declared "'tis barbarous to let men be obliged to oppose Bayonets with only gun Barrells...." With this General John Sullivan agreed and added his plea for more bayonets so that the same situation would not be repeated. *(31)*

The popular myth that the Revolution was fought between American troops who shot from behind trees and stone walls and British soldiers who were silly enough to stand in tight formations in the open is completely fallacious. With the exception of Kings Mountain, and of the retreat from Concord and Lexington, no major battle of the war followed this pattern. Even at Concord the American forces charged down the hill toward the British at the Bridge, and at Lexington the minutemen were drawn up in a line across the village green, quite in the open. American troops generally fought in the accepted European fashion, as any tactical study of the battles of the Revolution quickly reveals. The Continental "Regulars" took pride in their firm ranks and their bayonet charges. At Stony Point the muskets were unloaded and American bayonets alone carried the day. Baron von Steuben, the celebrated drillmaster of the Continental Army, never taught "backwoods" warfare, and Washington in the climactic Yorktown campaign exhorted his men to place their principal reliance on the bayonet. *(32)*

Fortunately it is not necessary to depend upon theory for the contemporary military opinion concerning the rifle as a military weapon. There are many written comments by leading officers from both sides. Washington worried about the lack of bayonets and for that reason ordered Morgan's men to carry spears. He also felt there were far too many riflemen in the army. General "Mad" Anthony Wayne said he never wanted to see another rifle, at least without a bayonet, and even then he would prefer a musket. When Maryland proposed to send a rifle company to Philadelphia for the Continental Army, the Secretary of the Board of War replied that they would be delighted to have the men, but--

If muskets were given them instead of rifles the service would be more benefitted, as there is a superabundance of riflemen in the Army. Were it in the power of Congress to supply musketts they would speedily reduce the number of rifles and replace them with the former, as they are more easily kept in order, can be fired oftener and have the advantage of Bayonetts. *(33)*

The British officers also soon appraised the situation and lost their early apprehensions of the rifleman's prowess. Lieutenant Colonel John Simcoe, commander of the famed Queen's Rangers, declared:

The riflemen, however dexterous in the use of their arm, were by no means the most formidable of the rebel troops; their not being armed with bayonets, permitted their opponents to take liberties with them which otherwise would have been highly improper. *(34)*

The *Middlesex Journal* of December 31, 1776 quoted another British officer as remarking:

...about twilight is found the best season for hunting the rebels in the woods, at which time their rifles are of very little use; and they are not found so serviceable in a body as musketry, a rest being requisite at all times, and before they are able to make a second discharge, it frequently happens that they find themselves run through the body by the push of a bayonet, as a rifleman is not entitled to any quarter. *(35)*

Even Colonel Hanger, the great admirer of the rifle's accuracy, wrote:

Riflemen as riflemen only, are a very feeble foe and not to be trusted alone any distance from camp; and at the outposts they must ever be supported by regulars, or they will constantly be beaten in, and compelled to retire. *(36)*

Again, Hanger:

...meeting a corps of rifle-men, namely *riflemen only.* I would treat them the same as my friend Colonel Abercrombie, ...treated Morgan's riflemen. When Morgan's riflemen came down to Pennsylvania from Canada, flushed with success gained over Burgoyne's army, they marched to attack our light infantry, under Colonel Abercrombie. The moment they appeared before him he ordered his troops to charge them with the bayonet; not one man out of four, had time to fire, and those that did had no time given them to load again; the light infantry not only dispersed them instantly but drove them for

43

miles over the country. They never attacked, or even looked at, our light infantry again, without a regular force to support them. *(37)*

What, then, was the usefulness of the American rifle as a military weapon? As has been noted, it had accuracy and range, but it was handicapped by its slowness and lack of a bayonet. Obviously it was useless as an arm for regular infantry, but its assets and the special skills of its users made it a fine weapon for certain troops, such as light infantry, scouts, snipers, and skirmishers supported by regular troops. Morgan himself recognized this, and at the battle of Cowpens when he had command of a force embodying both riflemen and regular infantry, he used them in that manner. He deployed his army in three lines, the first two embodying militia and riflemen and the third line composed of regular infantry of the Continental Line. As the battle developed the first two lines, according to instructions, took as heavy a toll of the advancing British as they could and then retired behind the line of regulars which met the enemy with a volley and the bayonet.

Riflemen were also expert in coping with the Indian allies of the British in the North. They had long been used to dealing with the Indians on their own frontiers, and so took to this task naturally. Washington had this in mind when he sent Morgan's riflemen to join the army opposing Burgoyne on his march south from Canada. In announcing the action he wrote to General Horatio Gates:

> I am forwarding...Colonel Morgan's corps of riflemen, amounting to about 500. These are all chosen men, selected from the Army at large, well acquainted with the use of rifles, and with that mode of fighting which is necessary to make them a good counterpoise to the Indian....*(38)*

The rifle, then, was not, as some have claimed, "the gun that won the American Revolution," but supported by musketry and used in accordance with its special attributes, it was a very useful and deadly weapon.

Carbines and Musketoons

The glamorous rifle and the work-a-day musket were the firearms of the Continental infantry. Horsemen needed other arms altogether. Actually most Continental cavalry leaders considered the sword as the only real weapon of a cavalryman, but they acknowledged the need for some sort of firearm on occasion. In fact, they often recommended two kinds for each trooper—a carbine, or musketoon, and pistols. The musketoon, or carbine, was for longer-range shooting, the pistols for point-blank work. The terms "musketoon" and "carbine" at that time were used interchangeably in most instances, and they referred to any short shoulder arm designed for use by a mounted man.

Very few shoulder arms for cavalry were made by American gunsmiths during the war. In fact, it is even possible that none were. No definite references to their manufacture have been found in contemporary documents, and no surviving specimens are known. The

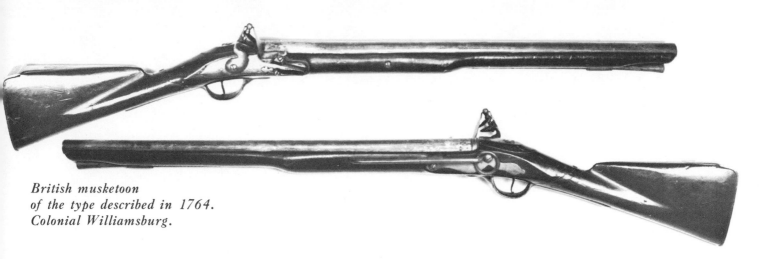

British musketoon
of the type described in 1764.
Colonial Williamsburg.

general source of supply for the Continental horsemen thus came from captured British weapons and purchases or gifts from France. Both are known to have been productive; there is, for instance, the record of the capture of the British store ship *Nancy* in 1775 with 75 carbines aboard, almost enough for a whole troop. There is also the fact that the mounted troops of Pulaski's Legion were issued rifled carbines from stores at Boston in 1778, and these could only have been French. *(39)*

British carbines can readily be recognized because they resemble the contemporary infantry musket in all respects except that they are about .65-caliber and that they have a sliding ring and bar on the left side of the stock instead of the musket's sling swivels. Also they are often shorter. Other details of British carbines varied, and there does not seem to have been a single standard pattern. *(40)*

French carbines and musketoons were more closely standardized, with models of 1763-66 and 1777 plus additional models for hussars and other specialized units. It seems probable, however, that only the model 1763-66 was used by Continental troopers during the war. Like the infantry muskets these musketoons were banded arms,

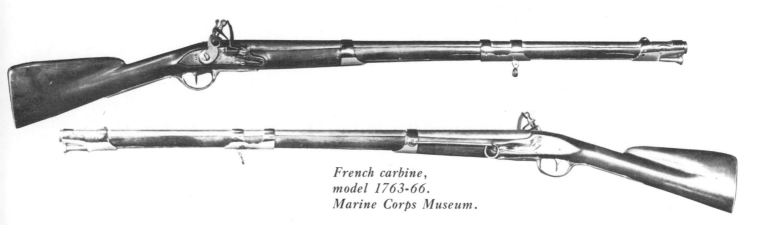

French carbine,
model 1763-66.
Marine Corps Museum.

and in each case the locks resembled those on the musket of the same model. The principal external differences lay in the shorter lengths (45 inches for the model 1763-66 and 46 inches for the model 1777, as compared to 59½ inches for the model 1763 musket), their smaller caliber of about .65, and the fact that the barrel bands were polished brass. There are also differences in the forestocks. The stock of the model '63-66 goes to the very muzzle, and it boasts a double middle band. The stock of the model 1777 stops 14 inches short of the muzzle, and it has no middle band. The big internal difference is that the model '63-66 was rifled with the grooves stopping eight inches short of the muzzle so that they are not noticeable in a casual inspection. The reason for not continuing the grooves to the muzzle was to make loading easier by offering a larger smooth area for the initial insertion of the charge. *(41)*

French musketoon,
model 1777.
Fort Ticonderoga.

These British and French carbines were the sought-after shoulder arms of the Continental cavalryman, but he often had to make do with second-best. Full muskets were sometimes issued despite their clumsiness for use on horseback. There were even suggestions that troopers might do well to carry blunderbusses. Nothing seems to have come of the blunderbuss idea though Washington himself endorsed it. Supposedly the flared muzzles would make the arms easier to load on horseback, and the scattering shot would compensate for a lack of accuracy in shooting from a moving horse. *(42)*

Cavalry Pistols

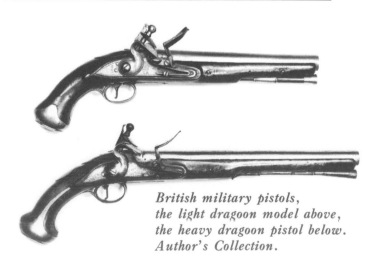

British military pistols,
the light dragoon model above,
the heavy dragoon pistol below.
Author's Collection.

Whether or not a trooper was issued a carbine, musketoon, full musket, or even a blunderbuss, he was certain to have a pair of large pistols in his saddle holsters. The long arms had to be used when dismounted or at least when the horse was stationary, but the pistols could be fired even at a full gallop. It is true a cavalryman had little hope of hitting anything from a moving horse, but accuracy with the cavalry pistol was minimal at best. No one ever fired a pistol at a foe more than a few feet away with any serious hope of hitting him.

Like the infantry muskets the cavalry pistols came from a variety of sources. Some had been left in colonial arsenals. Some were captured from the British. Some were manufactured by American gunsmiths, and, towards the end of the war, some were acquired from France.

The British-pattern pistols dominated the early years of the war, just as British patterns had held sway with the muskets. Once again there were two models, a heavy dragoon pistol and a light dragoon pistol. Of the two the heavy dragoon model was older. Like the long land musket it apparently developed back under George I. It was a handsome graceful weapon with a barrel 12 inches long and a caliber of about .65, the same as the carbine. Polished brass mounts and a full walnut stock added to its dashing appearance.

Like other British firearms the barrel was fastened to the stock by pins, and the locks were smaller versions of the standard British musket patterns. *(43)*

The light dragoon pistol made its appearance in 1759 or 1760. It was a stubbier, more powerful weapon which lacked much of the grace of the longer pistol. Its barrel was only 9 inches long, but it had increased to .69-caliber. The brass mounts also were simplified. The escutcheon plate was eliminated, the long arms of the butt cap were reduced to vestigial lobes, and the number of ramrod thimbles was reduced to one. Neither pistol had sights of any kind. Given the accuracy of the arms, they would have

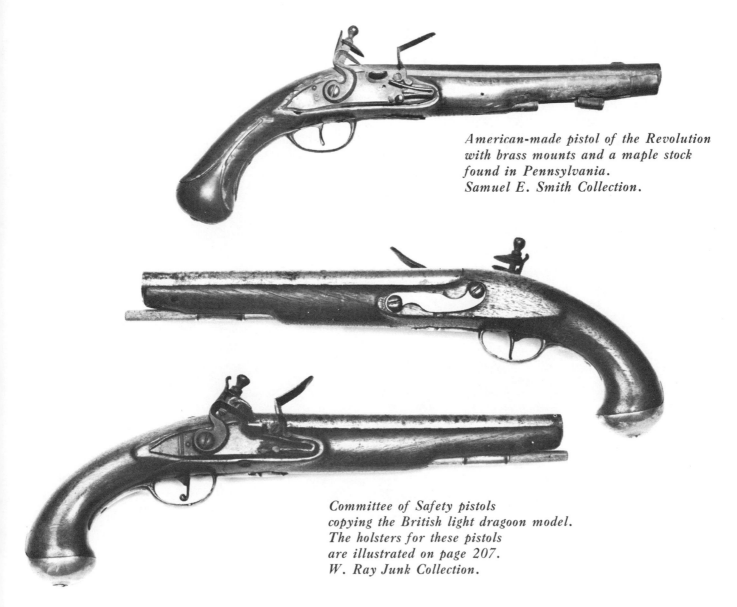

American-made pistol of the Revolution with brass mounts and a maple stock found in Pennsylvania.
Samuel E. Smith Collection.

Committee of Safety pistols copying the British light dragoon model. The holsters for these pistols are illustrated on page 207.
W. Ray Junk Collection.

been superfluous. *(44)*

When American gunsmiths set out to manufacture cavalry or horse pistols, it was usually the British light dragoon pistol that they copied. American products can quickly be recognized, however, even when they are not marked. The workmanship is apt to be cruder. Brass mountings are apt to be thinner than the very substantial hardware on British-made pistols, and of course there is the absence of British proofmarks and other indications of British productions. Sometimes also American pistols were stocked in maple instead of the traditional walnut. Far fewer pistols than muskets were made in America during the Revolution. This is at least partly because there were far fewer horsemen than infantrymen to be armed. Specimens of American martial horse pistols have been identified from Pennsylvania, however, and also a number of pistols and pistol parts survive from James Hunter's famous Rappahannock Forge at Falmouth, Virginia.

As the war wore on, French pistols began to join British and American models just as French muskets had appeared upon the scene. But there was one major differ-

light dragoon model remained preferred to the very end of the war.

Perhaps this was because the French model 1763-66 pistol was a trifle longer, heavier and more complicated to make than the short British weapon. In 1769-1770 the French pistol had been shortened from its previous great length. Its barrel length thereafter was 9 inches, the same as the British, but its straighter butt brought it to an overall length of 15 3/4 inches. Its caliber was the same .69 as the British, which meant that it could use the same ammunition, and this was a welcome feature. Like the British the French pistol also had brass mounts, but here the similarity ended, for the French barrel and stock were held together by a long double band at the muzzle, and the other mounts were equally distinctive. Collectors should beware of similar pistols with iron mounts. They are later. The locks resembled those on contemporary French muskets with their reinforced cocks, but there was one interesting difference. Those pistols made at St. Étienne had convex cocks and rounded lockplates, while those made at Charleville and Maubeuge were flat. There was also another very interesting feature: the

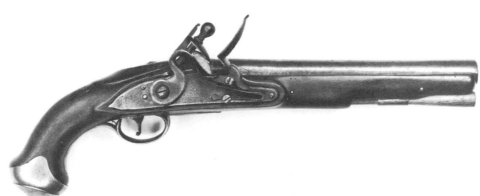

Rappahannock Forge pistol. William M. Locke Collection.

ence between the impact of French muskets and French pistols. Whereas the French musket pattern had quickly supplanted the Brown Bess to become the standard American infantry weapon, the French pistol never became more than an adjunct of the British style. As far as can be determined the British

model date was usually engraved on the barrel tang, and the last two digits of the actual year of manufacture were normally stamped on the left side of the breech just behind the proofmarks. Thus it is possible to date a French pistol far more precisely than any of its contemporaries. *(45)*

The pistol model 1763-66 was manufactured in its shortened version until 1779, but even before that date another shorter cavalry pistol had been adopted in France. This was the model 1777, a very unusual-looking weapon. It is doubtful that many of these later pistols found their way into the hands of Continental troopers; yet the model became sufficiently well known in this country for it to be selected as the pattern for the first official pistol of the new United States in 1799. This despite the fact that the French had by that time long abandoned the model 1777 as too complicated and too fragile. This unusual and colorful pistol had only a 7½-inch barrel of about .67-caliber that tapered evenly from breech to muzzle. Its most characteristic feature, however, was its brass breech housing which held the rear of the barrel, received the ramrod, and served as a mounting for the lock. The priming pan, in fact, was cast integrally with it. Like the earlier model, these pistols too are usually stamped on the left of the breech with the last two digits of their year of manufacture. No other French pistol was ever made in this form, and only the United States copied it elsewhere. (46)

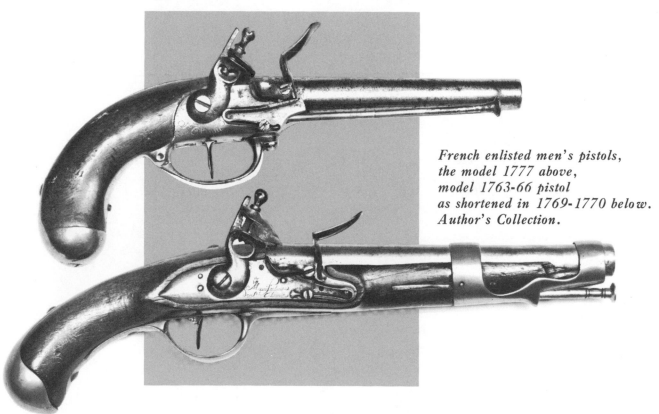

French enlisted men's pistols, the model 1777 above, model 1763-66 pistol as shortened in 1769-1770 below. Author's Collection.

Officers' Pistols

In addition to cavalrymen, mounted officers also carried pistols in their saddle holsters. Foot officers carried spontoons, but men on horseback could not manage such pole arms well, and they needed some weapon in addition to their swords. Thus Washington was willing for them to use pistols. In nine cases out of ten these were English weapons, bought before the war. Often they resembled the enlisted men's pistols with finer workmanship and decorative

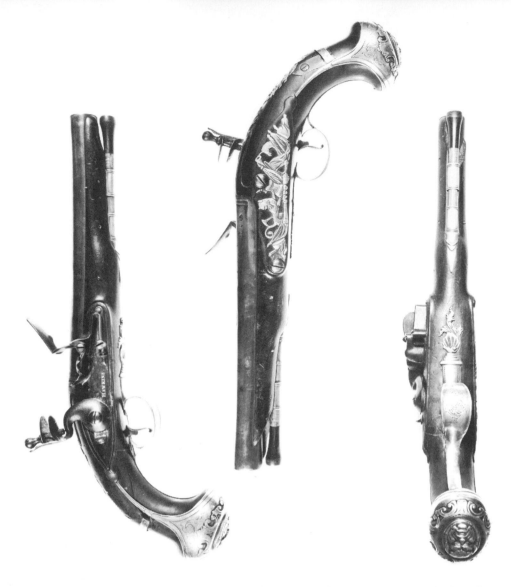

*One of a pair of
silver-mounted pistols
by Hawkins of London
which are believed
to have belonged
to George Washington.
West Point Museum.*

mounts. Silver was a popular metal for the finer pistols, and the decorations often took the form of a mask embossed on the butt cap, an openwork side plate with some relief decoration, and engraved designs on various elements. Brass barrels instead of iron also were popular because of their rust-resisting qualities.

Another and quite different type of pistol which was also popular with American officers during the Revolution was the box lock pattern. In these pistols the lock was mounted in the center of the piece instead of on the side in the more common position. The frizzen and pan were placed on top of the breech of the barrel, and the lock mechanism, including the cock, was mounted in a metal breeching directly behind it. Such pistols had the advantage of offering a more streamlined appearance, and they could be made lighter because no wooden forestock was necessary. Usually the barrels were made to unscrew so that the arms could be loaded at the breech, and this offered several additional advantages. For one thing no ramrod was necessary. Thus another element was eliminated. Also the bullets could be made to fit the bore tighter, and thus these pistols shot much more accurately than those which loaded with loose-fitting balls in the usual manner. Finally, since the piece was loaded by pouring

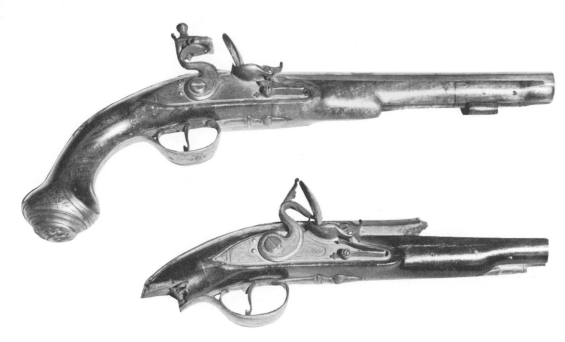

*Pair of British
brass-barrelled pistols
by Wooley
which are believed
to have belonged
to George Washington.
Mount Vernon
Ladies' Association
of the Union.*

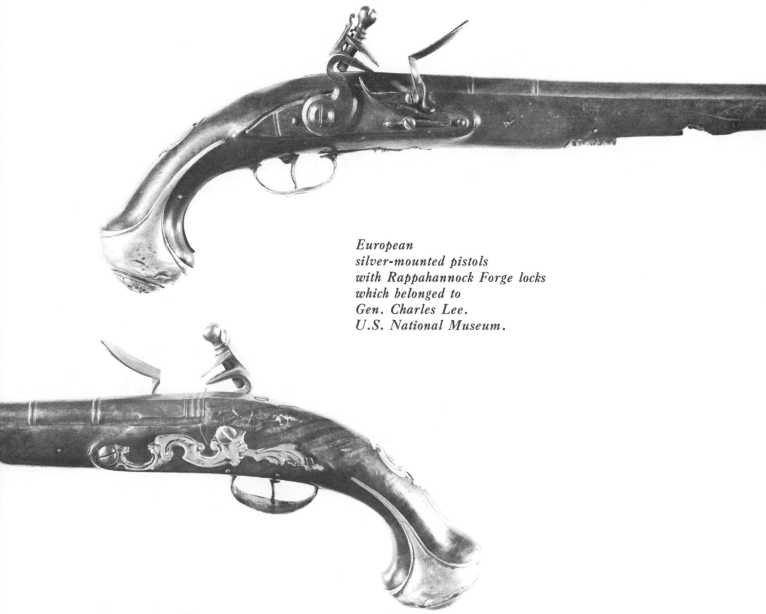

*European
silver-mounted pistols
with Rappahannock Forge locks
which belonged to
Gen. Charles Lee.
U.S. National Museum.*

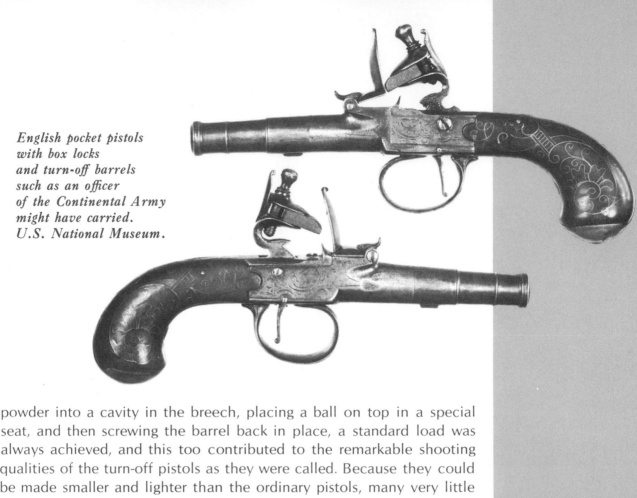

*English pocket pistols
with box locks
and turn-off barrels
such as an officer
of the Continental Army
might have carried.
U.S. National Museum.*

powder into a cavity in the breech, placing a ball on top in a special seat, and then screwing the barrel back in place, a standard load was always achieved, and this too contributed to the remarkable shooting qualities of the turn-off pistols as they were called. Because they could be made smaller and lighter than the ordinary pistols, many very little turn-off pistols were produced for carrying in pockets rather than holsters. These, too, were popular with officers as personal arms, and even some foot officers were happy to thrust one or a pair into the pockets of their uniform coats as a hedge against an emergency.

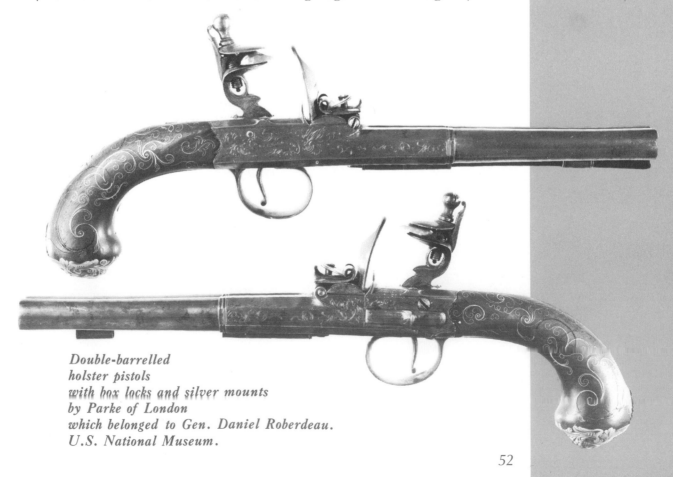

*Double-barrelled
holster pistols
with box locks and silver mounts
by Parke of London
which belonged to Gen. Daniel Roberdeau.
U.S. National Museum.*

There was, however, one pattern of pistol carried by some officers which was strictly American. This was the so-called Kentucky pistol. The name is modern, given the arm because it resembles the contemporary American rifles which are now called Kentucky rifles as an outgrowth of their performance at the Battle of New Orleans in the War of 1812. A popular ballad of the period celebrated the feats of the Kentucky troops with their rifles, and the name Kentucky rifle quickly gained popular acceptance for the standard American long rifle. At the time of the Revolution, however, they were simply called American rifles or long rifles, and the pistols were simply American pistols without any other designation.

These American pistols differed markedly from other contemporary pistols in a number of respects. They were stocked most

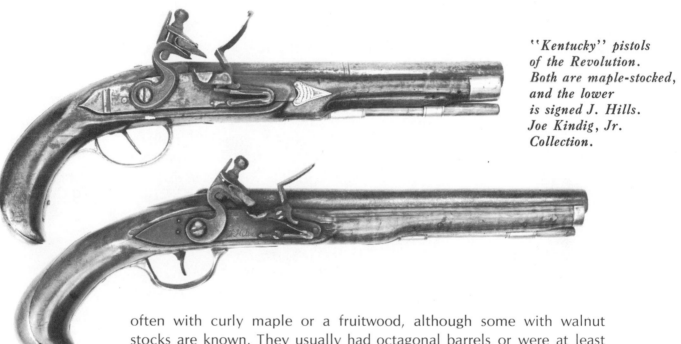

"Kentucky" pistols of the Revolution. Both are maple-stocked, and the lower is signed J. Hills. Joe Kindig, Jr. Collection.

often with curly maple or a fruitwood, although some with walnut stocks are known. They usually had octagonal barrels or were at least octagonal at the breech. They had both front and rear sights in a period when few pistols had either; and they were frequently rifled.

There were also other distinguishing characteristics. The grips were sharply curved, ending in a slender butt with either a close-fitting butt cap or none at all. The mountings were usually brass and resembled those on contemporary American rifles. Frequently there was neither fore-end cap nor ramrod thimble. The barrels were pin-fastened, and the locks were hand-forged, differing only in size from those on the rifles.

Many theories have been advanced concerning whether the "Kentucky" pistol was a civilian or military arm. Probably it was a little of both. However, since almost all known specimens appear to have been made either during the Revolution or War of 1812, it would seem that they were originally made primarily as side arms for American officers in those conflicts.

Wall Guns and Rifles

The pistols, musketoons, rifles, and muskets were widely used firearms of the Revolution, but there was also one very specialized type of firearm that saw important even if infrequent service. This was the wall gun or amusette. It was a huge weapon, shaped like an ordinary musket but so big it could almost be considered heavy ordnance. Mounted on a swivel, it was an ideal weapon for a hastily erected fort or for a small boat. It was lighter than a cannon, but its range and striking power were infinitely greater than those of the usual musket or rifle.

Rappahannock Forge wall rifle. West Point Museum.

As with all other forms of arms during the Revolution, the Continental Line used wall pieces from a variety of sources and in a variety of patterns. Some resembled muskets; some were huge blunderbusses with flared muzzles. There was also one real American innovation of the war, and this was the rifled rampart gun.

These rifled wall pieces were made early in the Revolution and quickly proved effective. On February 4, 1776, Fielding Lewis, Commissioner of the Fredericksburg Manufactory, wrote his brother-in-law, George Washington, as follows:

...I propose making a Rifle next week to carry a quarter of a pound ball. If it answers my expectation, a few of them will keep off ships of war from our narrow Rivers, and be usefull in the beginning of an engagement by land... *(47)*

American iron-mounted swivel gun from the Chesapeake Bay area. Joe Kindig, Jr. Collection.

It is not definitely known that Lewis achieved his goal and produced these rifles. No surviving specimens are known. There are, however, four surviving specimens made at the famed Rappahannock Forge, located directly across the river from Fredericksburg.

These huge rifles all weigh in the neighborhood of fifty pounds and are roughly five feet long. They are full-stocked, have sliding wooden patch boxes and wooden ramrods. The brass mountings are reminiscent of those on the lighter rifles of the period. Three of the surviving specimens have round barrels; the fourth is octagonal. The design of the exterior parts of the locks resembles those on the Fredericksburg muskets so closely that a common origin or at least a common pattern is suggested. *(48)*

General Charles Lee attested to the effectiveness of these weapons when he wrote Washington from Williamsburg on May 10, 1776, "I am likewise furnishing myself with four-ounced rifle-amusettes, which will carry an infernal distance; the two-ounced hit a half sheet of paper 500 yards distance." *(49)*

Belton's Repeating Muskets

Finally, in the great variety of arms for the Continental soldier there was even one type that may never have been made or used at all. This was Joseph Belton's repeating musket of 1777. It all began on April 11 of that year when Belton, who lived in Philadelphia, wrote to Congress: *(50)*

May it Please your Honors,
I would just informe this Honorable Assembly, that I have discovered an improvement, in the use of Small Armes, wherein a common small arm, may be maid to discharge eight balls one after another, in eight, five or three seconds of time, & each one to do execution five & twenty, or thirty yards, and after so discharg'd to be loaded and fir'd with cartrage as [useal?], which I am ready to prove by experimental proof, and can with eaquel ease fix them so as to discharge sixteen or twenty, in sixteen, ten or five seconds of time, which I have kept as yet a secret, thinking that in two or three Months we might have an armey thus equipt, which our enemy should know nothing of, till they should be maid to know it in the field, to their immortal sorrow--

And if you Gentlemen are desirous to enquire into this improvement, your Humble Servant, is ready to wait upon you at any time, or place, or he may be waited on at the Widow Ford's, in Walnut Street,
between second & third Street.

from Your most Obedient
Humble Servant
Joseph Belton

Congress responded promptly and on May 3 it passed a resolution that

...Belton be authorized and appointed to superintend, and direct the making or altering of one hundred muskets, on the construction exhibited by him and called "the new improved gun" which will discharge eight rounds with once loading; and that he receive a reasonable compensation for his trouble, and be allowed all just and necessary expences. *(51)*

Belton's system was actually an old and well-tested one. He used a series of loads piled one on top of the other in the barrel with the bullets pierced through and filled with a fuse composition so that the explosion of the first charge burned through the fuse in the second bullet and set off the second charge, which in 'turn ignited the fuse in the third bullet, and so on down to the eighth and final round. It all worked much like a Roman candle. *(52)*

It is not known whether any of the hundred muskets ordered by Congress in May 1777 were ever completed, but it is doubtful. In June of that year Sir William Howe sailed from New York with a British army, and on September 25 he occupied Philadelphia. Congress fled, and there was no further word of Belton until he turned up in England at the end of the war to attempt to sell his gun to the former enemy. By then the great variety of firearms in Continental hands had done their work. *(53)*

Notes to Chapter 2

1. Friedrich Wilhelm Ludolf Gerhard Augustin, Baron Von Steuben, *Regulations for the Order and Discipline of the Troops of the United States*, eds. of 1779, 1794, and others. Also useful are Humphrey Bland, *A Treatise of Military Discipline*, 4th ed., London, 1740; William Windham, *A Plan of Discipline Composed for the Use of the Militia of the County of Norfolk*, London, 1759; Timothy Pickering, Jr., *An Easy Plan of Discipline for a Militia*, Salem, Mass., 1775; Richard Lambert, 6th Earl of Cavan, *A New System of Military Discipline Founded upon Principle*, Philadelphia, 1776; Col. David Dundas, *Principles of Military Movements Chiefly Applied to Infantry*, London, 1788.

2. *Ibid.*

3. Thomas Simes, *The Military Medley*, London, 1768, p. 23.

4. George Washington, *The Writings of George Washington*, John C. Fitzpatrick, ed., 39 vols., Washington, 1931-1944, II, 113, 180, 181. Frederick Mackenzie, *A British Fusilier in Revolutionary Boston*, Allen French, ed., Cambridge, 1926, pp. 28, 29.

5. Col. George Hanger, *To All Sportsmen and Particularly to Farmers, and Gamekeepers*, London, 1814, p. 205.

6. Howard L. Blackmore, *British Military Firearms, 1650-1850*, London, 1961, pp. 45-66.

7. *Ibid.* General Orders, Valley Forge, December 22, 1777, Washington, *Writings*, X, 190.

8. Worthington C. Ford, ed., *Journals of the Continental Congress, 1774-1789*, 23 vols., Washington, 1904-1909, II, 188, 190, III, 322.

9. Peter Force, compiler, *American Archives*, 4th series, 6 vols., Washington, 1837-1846, III, 1496-1497.

10. *Ibid.*

11. Minutes of the General Assembly, October 1775, Charles J. Hoadly, ed., *The Public Records of the Colony of Connecticut*, 15 vols., Hartford, 1850-1890, XIV, 420; May 1775, *ibid.*, XV, 17, 18.

12. Minutes of the General Assembly, October 1775, Hoadly, *Connecticut Records*, XV, 137; March 22, 1776, *ibid.*, 254, 255; May 1776, *ibid.*, 304, 305; June 1776, *ibid.*, 420, 421.

13. Proceedings of the General Assembly, March 18, 1776, John R. Bartlett, ed., *Records of the Colony of Rhode Island and Providence Plantation*, 10 vols., Providence, 1856-1865, VII, 477, *et passim*.

14. Maj. Jonathan Child to Committee of Safety, July 14, 1776, Nathaniel Bouton and others, eds., *New Hampshire State Papers*, 40 vols., Manchester, N.H., 1867-1941, VIII, 304, 305; Committee in Moultonborough to Jonathan Moulton of Hampton, July 15, 1776, *ibid.*, 305; Committee of Safety to Washington, February 21, 1777, *ibid.*, 496, 497, *et passim*.

15. Proceedings of the Provincial Congress, June 30, 1776, Edmund B. O'Callaghan and others, eds., *Documents Relative to the Colonial History of New York*, 15 vols., Albany, 1853-1887, XV, 13, 14.

16. Minutes of the Council of Safety, February 28, 1776, William H. Egle and others, eds., *Pennsylvania Archives*, 2nd series, 16 vols., Harrisburg, 1890, X, 498; July 3, 1775, *ibid.*, 282; March 6, 1776, *ibid.*, 506.

17. William Whitehead and others, eds., *New Jersey Archives*, 39 vols., Newark, 1880-1946, *passim*.

18. "Journal and Correspondence of the Council of Safety 1775-76," William H. Browne and others, eds., *Archives of Maryland*, Baltimore, 1884—, XI, 75.

19. Charles Beatty to Council, September 20, 1775, Browne, *Archives of Maryland*, XI, 81. Ewing to Council, February 12, 1776, *ibid.*, 155. Journal of the Council of Safety, August 17, 1777, *ibid.*, XVI, 219; July 29, 1777, *ibid.*, X, 320; August 16, 1777, *ibid.*, 335. Council of Safety to Richard Bond, November 15, 1776, *ibid.*, XII, 449; Council of Safety to Col. H. Hollingworth, May 14, 1777, *ibid.*, XVI, 253. Benjamin Rumsey to Council of Safety, March 7, 1776, *ibid.*, XI, 211, 212. Council of Safety to Daniel Bowly, March 14, 1776, *ibid.*, 247. Council of Safety to the Commissioners of the Gunlock Manufactory in Frederick Town, July 30, 1776, *ibid.*, XII, 142.

20. Robert L. Miller, "Fredericksburg Manufactory Muskets," *Military Collector & Historian*, III, no. 3 (September 1951), 63-65.

21. H. R. McIlwaine, ed., *Journals of the Council of the State of Virginia*, 2 vols., Richmond, 1931, I, 177, 178.

22. Journal of the Council of Safety, January 2, 1776, Allen D. Candler, compiler, *The Revolutionary Records of the State of Georgia*, 3 vols., Atlanta, 1908, I, 85, *et passim*. *Journal of the Council of Safety for the Province of South Carolina, 1775* in Collections of the South Carolina Historical Society, II, Charleston, 1858, 199-201, 213, 214, *et passim*. See also Vol. III, 1859. William L. Saunders, ed., *The Colonial Records of North Carolina*, 10 vols., Raleigh, 1886-1890, IX, X, *passim*.

23. Silas Deane to Secret Committee, August 18, 1776, Charles Isham, ed., *Deane Papers*, 5 vols., in Collections of the New-York Historical Society, New York, 1886-1890, I, 195-218. Henri Doniol, *Histoire de la Participation de la France à l'Établissement des États-Unis d'Amerique*, 6 vols., Paris, 1886, I, 133, 377, 482. Robert Morris to Council of Safety, December 23, 1778, Samuel Hazard and others, eds., *Pennsylvania Archives*, 17 vols., Philadelphia, 1852-1892, VII, 125, 126; May 10, 1779, *ibid.*, 386. Heads of an Agreement Made Between the Committee of Congress & Hodges & Bayard & Co., February 2, 1776, *ibid.*, IV, 708. Instructions to Captain Forsythe, January 1776, Browne, *Archives of Maryland*, XI, 98. William Lee to Governor Jefferson, September 24, 1779, William P. Palmer and H. W. Flournoy, eds., *Calendar of Virginia State Papers and other Manuscripts*, 11 vols., Richmond, 1875-1893, I, 328, 331. Henry Laurens to Elisha Sawyers, January 19, 1776, *Journal of Council of Safety of South Carolina*, III, 199-201. Laurens to Capt. Joseph Darrell, January 24, 1776, *ibid.*, 213, 214. Harold L. Peterson, "Silas Deane in France," typescript of Master of Arts thesis, University of Wisconsin, 1946, p. 21.

24. Peterson, "Silas Deane," pp. 21-45.

25. William Lee to Governor Jefferson, September 24, 1779, Palmer and Flournoy, *Calendar of Virginia State Papers*, I, 328-331. Peterson, "Silas Deane," pp. 27, 28.

26. Jean Boudriot, *Armes à Feu Françaises, Modeles Reglementaires, 1717-1836*, 1st and 2nd series, Paris, 1961, 1963, *passim*.

27. *Ibid.*

28. James R. Bright, "The Rifle in Washington's Army," *The American Rifleman*, XCV, No. 8 (August 1947), 8. "Gazette," *Military Collector & Historian*, III, No. 2 (June 1951), 50, 51.

29. Hanger, *To All Sportsmen*, pp. 122-124, 144.

30. *Ibid.*, pp. 207-210.

31. Webster to Committee of Safety, June 21, 1775, Bouton, *New Hampshire State Papers*, VII, 526. Sullivan to Committee, July 19, 1775, *ibid.*, 565.

32. September 27, 1781, *Orderly Book of the Siege of Yorktown from September 26, 1781 to November 2, 1781*, Philadelphia, 1865, p. 5.

33. Richard Peters to the Council of Safety, October 26, 1776, Browne, *Archives of Maryland*, XII, 405. Bright, "Rifle in Washington's Army," p. 10. Washington to Morgan, June 13, 1777, Washington, *Writings*, VIII, 236. Wayne to Peters, February 3, 1778, Anthony Wayne, *Papers*, Revolutionary Series, transcribed by Henry B. Dawson, 1860, from original manuscripts in possession of the Wayne family, 10 bound folios, Morristown National Historical Park, III.

34. John G. Simcoe, *Simcoe's Military Journal*, New York, 1844, p. 237.

35. Frank Moore, *Diary of the American Revolution*, 2 vols., New York, 1860, pp. 349, 350.

36. Hanger, *To All Sportsmen*, pp. 199, 200.

37. *Ibid.*

38. Washington, *Writings*, IX, 78, 102.

39. Inventory of store ship *Nancy* prepared by R. Blight, September 1, 1775, *Papers of George Washington*, Manuscript Division, Library of Congress. Washington, *Writings*, IV, 132, 159. Donald W. Holst and Marko Zlatich, "Dress and Equipment of Pulaski's Independent Legion," *Military Collector & Historian*, XVI, No. 4 (Winter, 1964), 99.

40. Blackmore, *British Military Firearms*, pp. 59, 60, 62, 64.

41. Boudriot, *Armes à Feu*, 2nd series, cahier no. 8.

42. Washington to Board of War, April 4, 1779, Washington, *Writings*, XIV, 331; April 15, 1779, *ibid.*, 390.

43. Blackmore, *British Military Firearms*, pp. 63, 64.

44. *Ibid.*

45. Boudriot, *Armes à Feu*, 2nd series, cahier no. 8.

46. *Ibid.*, 1st series, cahier no. 5.

47. Col. Lewis to Washington, February 4, 1776, *Washington Papers*.

48. Miller, "Fredericksburg Manufactory Muskets," pp. 63-65. The existing specimens of Rappahannock Forge wall guns are located at the following places: one at the United States Military Academy Museum, West Point, N.Y.; one in the museum at the Springfield Armory, Springfield, Mass.; one in the museum at Rock Island Arsenal, Rock Island, Ill.; and one in the Smithsonian Institution, Washington, D.C. Robert L. Miller and Harold L. Peterson, "Rappahannock Forge: Its History and Products," *Military Collector & Historian*, IV, No. 4 (December 1952), 81-85.

49. *Washington Papers*.

50. *Papers of the Continental Congress*, National Archives, I, No. 41, pp. 123, 124.

51. Ford, *Journals of the Continental Congress*, VII, 324.

52. Blackmore, *British Military Firearms*, 249.

53. *Ibid.*

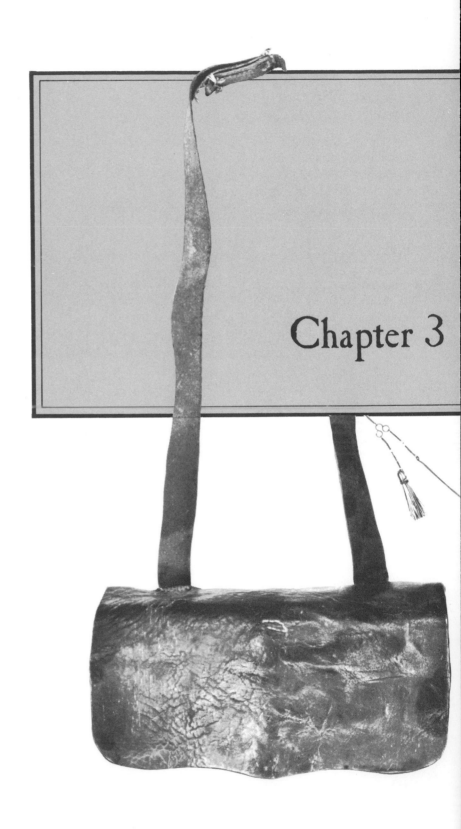

Chapter 3

Bullet, Belt and Box

Being
a survey
of the
ammunition and
accoutrements of
the Continental Army

There was nothing complicated about the ammunition of the American Revolution. The standard load consisted of a simple spherical ball of lead propelled by a load of black powder. The sophisticated bullet shapes of today and the specialized powder types were still far in the future. Revolutionary War bullets differed from one another only in size.

By modern standards, however, this size was huge. The British musket of .75-caliber favored by the Continental Army at the beginning of the war took a ball weighing more than an ounce and measuring about .69 inch in diameter. The smaller .69-caliber French muskets which superseded the British in popularity fired a bullet weighing a trifle less than an ounce and measuring about .63 inch. The difference in diameters between the balls and the bores for which they were intended was known as windage, and it was designed to make the balls load easier and also to leave room for the gummy residue produced by black powder when it is fired. If the balls had fit tightly in a clean barrel, it would have been impossible to ram them home after a few shots had been fired. Rifle balls were designed to fit slightly tighter in order to take the rifling but they were still considerably smaller than musket balls. There was no one standard size for rifle bullets, but most of them measured between .50 and .60 of an inch in diameter.

Big balls like these were decidedly lethal when--and if--they hit, for they had considerable bruising and shattering power. As has been noted, however, the muskets which fired the majority of bullets during the Revolution were low in accuracy. In order to compensate for this and also to fill the air with as many projectiles as possible, it became common practice to load each musket with one regular ball and several smaller buckshot. The number of buckshot varied. One recruit in the "Standing Army" in 1777 mentioned having sixty-four rounds of ammunition with three buckshot each, a number which became standard in the next century. Washington, however, recommended that the men load for their first volley "with one musket ball and four or eight buck Shott, according to the strength of their pieces...." And General Henry Dearborn went still further as he reported in describing an incident during the American assault on Quebec, December 31, 1775.

> I Clapt up my Piece which was Charged with a ball and Ten Buck shott certainly to give him his due, But to my great mortification my Gun did not go off....

The heavy snowstorm during the time the attack was made had apparently wet the priming powder in Dearborn's musket and thus saved his adversary from receiving a very lethal charge. In October 1777, Wash-

Mutilated musket balls excavated from Revolutiona War sites in and around New York City. New-York Historical Societ New York City.

ington made the practice of using buckshot universal by ordering that "Buckshot are to be put into all cartridges which shall hereafter be made." *(1)*

Even this lethality was not enough for some, however. Whether they were more ferocious or just more inventive, such individuals mutilated musket balls by cutting them so that they would fragment or at least flatten out upon impact. A few went even further. In 1776 British General Sir William Howe complained to Washington:

> My Aid de Camp charged with the Delivering of this Letter will present to you a Ball cut and fixed to the Ends of a Nail, taken from a Number of the same Kind, found in the Encampments quitted by your Troops on the 15th Instant. I do not make any comments upon such unwarrantable and malicious Practices, being well assured the Contrivance has not come to your Knowledge.

General Howe was apparently just as ignorant of the fact that the same kind of missile was used by his own men, for several such balls were found in the excavation of a British camp at Inwood, New York, and are now preserved in the New-York Historical Society's museum. *(2)*

Cartridges

As mentioned in the previous chapter, these bullets and the powder charge that propelled them were normally wrapped together in a paper cartridge to speed the loading of muskets, musketoons, and pistols. Timothy Pickering carefully described how this was done at the beginning of the war and supplied a diagram of the operation.

...the best method of making cartridges seems to be that used in the [British] army. It is this.--Take the soft brown paper called whitish brown, or wrapping paper, and cut it into pieces...of these dimensions; the side *ab* measures about six inches, *bc* about five inches and a half, and *cd* about two inches. A piece of wood about six inches long is to be made round so as to fit exactly the size of the ball; this is called a *former*: make

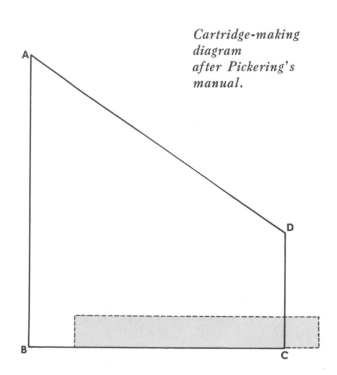

Cartridge-making diagram after Pickering's manual.

one end of it hollow to receive a part of the ball: lay the former upon the straight edge *bc* (as represented by the dotted lines) with its hollow end about an inch from the side *ab*: roll the paper around the former; then with the ball press in the corner of the paper so as to cover the hollow end of the former, and keeping fast the ball, roll on till the paper is all wrapped round the former; having before taken a piece of twine and fastened its two ends to something that will not easily be moved, and so far apart as to leave it slack, you are now to take with the twine a single turn around the paper, below the ball; then running in the end of your fore finger till it touches the ball, pull upon the string that it may girt the paper, and by turning round the former with one hand you will presently form a neck below the ball; which being afterwards tied with a piece of coarse thread will secure the ball from slipping out: then withdrawing the former, the cartridge is ready to be charged with powder; in doing which you must put in the more because part of it is to be taken for priming: having properly filled the cartridge, twist the top, and the work is done. The size of the paper above described will serve for an ounce ball: if your ball be less, the paper may be somewhat smaller. One thing should be remembered, that if the cartridge exactly fits your firelock when the barrel is perfectly clean, it will be too large, and difficult to be rammed down, when it becomes foul by firing; and 'tis dangerous firing when the ball is not rammed well home: for this therefore you are to make allowance. *(3)*

Later in the War as the French arms and ammunition became popular, French-style cartridges also came into use. These generally resembled the British, but they were pasted shut below the ball and along the side seam instead of being tied. *(4)*

The bulk of all cartridges used during the War were probably made at special

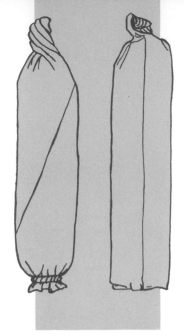

Left:
British cartridge made according to Pickering's description.
Right:
French cartridge.

"laboratories," primarily the one in Philadelphia, and sent from there to the troops in the field. From time to time, however, the soldiers themselves were ordered to make cartridges. Materials were issued, and usually a detail of men was put to work wrapping the charges which were then placed in regimental stores until needed. *(5)*

Properly used, these cartridges greatly speeded the loading of smoothbore weapons, but there is even some evidence that they may also have been used in an attempt to increase the rifle's rate of fire. General Sullivan's expedition against the Indians of central New York State in 1778, for instance, included a number of riflemen, and for that campaign there are orders for cartridges containing balls of .52- to .57- caliber. These would have been too small for any of the standard smoothbores but just right for rifles. As a test of this theory modern students have loaded paper-wrapped cartridges into flintlock rifles of the period and fired them with considerable success. The paper wrapping performed the same function as the normal greased patch, transmitting the spin of the rifling to the ball when it was fired, and at least for a few rounds it also served to keep the powder fouling from becoming a severe problem. There is no evidence that this practice ever became common, but it does seem likely that it was followed at least on some occasions. *(6)*

POCKET PISTOL   **SINGLE BARREL SPORTER**    **RIFLE**   **HORSE PISTOL**

CARBINE    **CARBINE**    **MUSKET**    **MUSKET**

Gun Flints

Flints chipped according to traditional specifications by a modern knapper in England. The illustration is exact size. Drawing by Robert L. Miller. Arthur Woodward Collection. Courtesy Company of Military Historians.

The flints which Continental soldiers used in their gunlocks had achieved their fully developed form by the time the Revolutionary War began. The older spall form had disappeared, and the flat-sided type with bevelled edges was universally in use. As in so many other items, there were two major types of flint in use, the English and the French. The English flint was normally black with straight bevels across point and heel produced by single strokes of the knapping hammer. The French flints were a greasy gray or yellowish color, and the heels were rounded with a gnawed effect produced by many strokes of the hammer. No significant number of flints were ever made in America, and it is interesting to note that the great majority of all flints of all periods found in this country are of the French type. *(7)*

According to tradition there were nine standard sizes of gun flints. These included sizes for the pocket pistol, single-barreled fowling piece, rifle, holster pistol, carbine, musket, long Dane (long Arabian piece), and cannon. Of these the last two were not used at all in the Continental Army, and the sizes most frequently mentioned are musket, holster pistol, and carbine. The Continental soldier normally carried twelve flints for his piece if they were available. *(8)*

Much has been written by modern writers concerning whether the flat or the chamfered side of the flint was usually placed uppermost by the men who originally used the flintlock. Actually, the truth is that there was never universal agreement at the time. Some men favored one position and some another. Often it was the practice to use a flint in one position until it no longer produced a good spark and then turn it over. *(9)*

American cartridge box
with pick and brush
attached to the harness-leather strap.
The leather pouch is soft
and extends below the wooden block
which is nailed in place.
Author's Collection.

Cartridge Boxes and Cannisters

The soldier carried his cartridges and sometimes also his flints in a special pouch called a cartridge box or sometimes a cartouche box. Usually this consisted of a leather pouch enclosing a block of wood with holes bored in it to hold individual cartridges. The number of holes varied but between twenty and thirty was standard. When filled the box might weigh five or six pounds. *(10)*

Three views of
an American cartridge box
with tight-fitting leather cover.
It lacks both the inner flap
and the overhang that Washington advocated.
Robert L. Miller Collection.

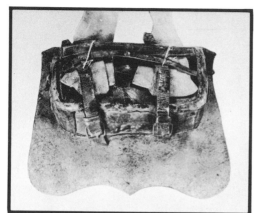

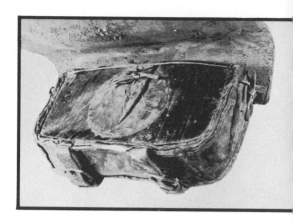

Three views of an American cartridge box based on the old-style British box. Despite the size of the flap the box itself is small. Note the unusual circular purse with drawstring on the front beneath the flap. The shoulder strap is buff leather. George C. Neumann Collection.

Proper cartridge boxes were very important. If an army was to be efficient its cartridge boxes had to be good enough to carry their precious loads safely and to protect them from wet weather and from breakage. Wet or broken cartridges were useless, and a soldier with them lacked the necessary means for firing his weapon. For this reason Washington took especial interest in the cartridge boxes issued to his men, and he continually emphasized the necessity of having good ones. On October 13, 1777, he wrote to the President of Congress:

> With respect to Cartouch boxes, without which it is impossible to act.... I would advise that much care should be used in choosing the Leather. None but the best and thickest is proper for the purpose, and each Box should have a small inner flap for the greater security of the Cartridges against rain and moist weather. The Flaps in general, are too small and do not project sufficiently over the ends or sides of the Boxes. I am convinced of the utility nay necessity of these improvements and that the adoption of them, tho they will incurr an additional expense at first will prove a considerable saving, and of the most beneficial consequences. *(11)*

He went on to point out that cartridge boxes so constructed had recently protected their contents in a severe rain while those with a single flap "of the common construction" had not. *(12)*

Worried about costs and also about the scarcity of good leather, Congress asked his opinion about making the flaps of painted canvas. The General would not hear of it. He pointed out that the paint would soon crack in use and then fail to shed water. He did agree that canvas might be used for the inner flaps "considering the badness and thinness of the leather in general" but again pointed out that "the greatest preservation to the Cartridges, is a small inside flap of pliant leather, which lays close upon the top of them and not only keeps them dry but from being rubbed." *(13)*

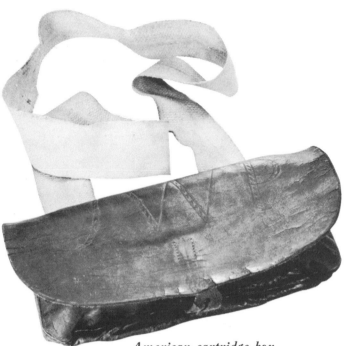

American cartridge box with soft leather pouch enclosing the block and linen shoulder strap. George C. Neumann Collection.

These cartridge boxes were normally worn on a shoulder belt, and according to the informative Timothy Pickering,

The pouch hangs on the right side, but so far behind as not to interfere with the right hand man when the files are close; and at such a height as is most convenient for taking out a cartridge with the right hand. *(14)*

Despite Washington's efforts, however, the cartridge boxes carried by the Continental soldiers frequently failed to come up to standard. Pickering described one of the cheaper substitutes used by both the British and Americans:

...The British have for several years past, furnished their new levies with cartridge boxes made of close wood (as maple or beech) with no other covering than a good leather flap nailed to it at the back near the upper edge, and of sufficient breadth to cover the top & whole front of the box; they are fixed to the body by a waist belt, which passes through two loops that are nailed to the front of the box.... *(15)*

American waist cartridge box with an uncovered wood block. The flap has been slightly raised to show the loops for the belt nailed on the front of the block. George C. Neumann Collection.

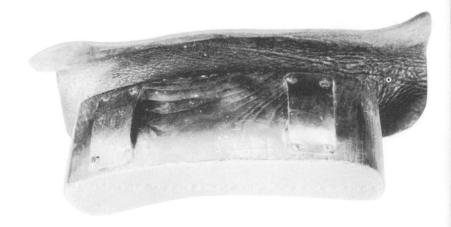

Having the belt loops on the front of the box was extremely uncomfortable, and there is evidence that they were quickly shifted to the back in both the British and American service. There were even worse boxes than these in use, as witnessed by complaints such as these:

Sir, the 300 cartouch boxes, that I informed you I understood were on the road coming from Virginia, are just come in. I have received them and can assure you they are not worthy of the name. Numbers of them are without any straps, others without flaps, and scarce any of them would preserve the cartridges in a moderate shower of Rain-- What straps there are to the boxes are of linen. *(16)*

The arms in general are good but the cartouch boxes bad, many of the old construction and wore out. Some with waist belts, others without any belts at all slung by pieces of rope or other strings—I could therefore...wish that a quantity of British arms and accoutrements not exceeding 600 stands may be sent me. *(17)*

Faced with the shortage of leather and the continuing demand for cartridge boxes, Congress devised a metal cartridge cannister. At first these were designed primarily for carrying extra ammunition, but soon they were pressed into service as substitutes for the standard leather box. References to these cannisters begin to appear in the fall of 1777, by which time they were already in the hands of Continentals on the field. In the spring of 1778 the Board of War set down detailed specifications for their construction:

They are to be six inches and a half deep, or long; three inches and three quarters of an inch broad (this breadth receiving the cartridges lengthways, as they lie in a horizontal position) and two inches and

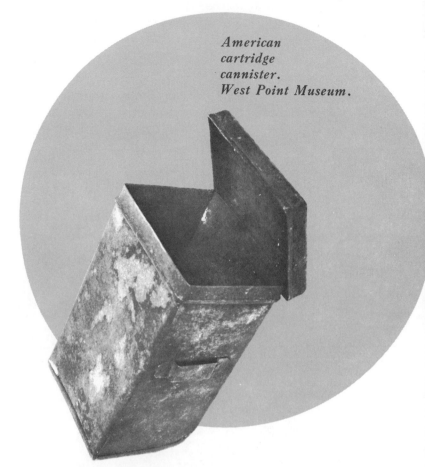

American cartridge cannister. West Point Museum.

seven eighths of an inch thick; (this thickness admitting four cartridges, to lay side by side) a box of these, in the clear, will well contain thirty six cartridges with ounce balls. A wire is to be fixed in all the edges at the top and then each side turned down (outwards) a full half inch and soldered. The cover is to be a full half inch deep, so that when fixed on the cannister the edges shall come close down to the ledge formed by the inclosed wire. This cover at one end turns on a hinge an inch and a quarter long, the wire (fixed as above mentioned) being laid naked, that space, for the purpose; and a piece of tin is run underneath the wire, doubled together, and soldered on the inside of one end of the cover. The soldier carries a cannister by the shoulder belt, as he does a cartridge box: and for this reason the cannister has fixed to it three loops of tin, each half an inch wide, with the edges turned back, to be smooth and strong; one of them is placed underneath the middle of the bottom, and one on each of the narrowest sides, the latter at four inches distant from the bottom to their lower edges. The loops are to be sent down at each end and very well soldered, leaving a space to admit a leathern belt full one inch and a half wide, and nearly an eighth of an inch thick. The cover opens against one part of the belt, which causes it to fall down, after a cartridge is taken out, by w[ch] means the rest are secured from accidental fire. If possible, the cannisters should be japanned, or painted, to preserve them from rust; and all fixed to belts.

The board are of the opinion that these cannisters are preferable to cartridge boxes, as they will infallibly secure the cartridges from rain, and their weight is so trifling as to be no burthen to the Soldier. And seeing leather is so scarce they will be a most excellent substitute for cartridge boxes. *(18)*

Fortunately one specimen of these cannisters survives in the West Point Museum, and it conforms exactly to these specifications.

Cartridge boxes of the regular pattern continued to be made and issued along with

Two views of a deep cartridge box with a metal tray for extra cartridges and flints below. This tray is usually considered a late feature, but the lack of an inner flap and overhang plus the fact that the box holds only seventeen cartridges for a .75-caliber musket indicate that it probably dates from early in the War. George C. Neumann Collection.

the cannisters, however, and late in the War an additional improvement was added to them. This was the inclusion of a tinned iron tray for gun flints which lay under the wooden cartridge block. References to such trays are frequent in the early 1780's, and there are indications that they may first have appeared as early as 1779. *(19)*

Finally there was one other type of cartridge box used at least to some extent during the Revolution. In March of 1778 Congress recommended that mounted troops be equipped with "a cartridge-box to buckle around the waist, with twelve tin pipes for the cartridges." One of these still survives to indicate that some were indeed made. Also Colonel Henry Sherburne carried a similar but dressier version of this type of box with ten tubes. Actually this pattern box had also been in use well before the Revolution as evidenced by the appearance of a similar device in the Copley portrait of George Scott, who died in 1767. *(20)*

Open and closed views of a waist cartridge box with twelve tin pipes as recommended for cavalry in 1778. The flap can be fastened closed with one pewter button at each side. Robert L. Miller Collection.

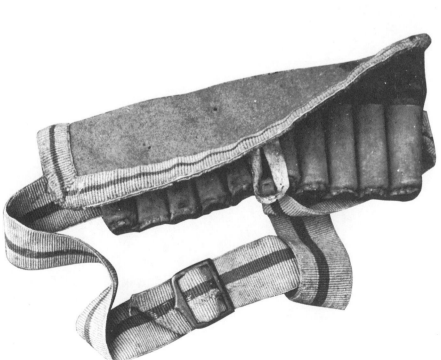

Waist cartridge box with ten tin pipes, each covered in leather, worn by Col. Henry Sherburne of the Continental Army. Newport Historical Society.

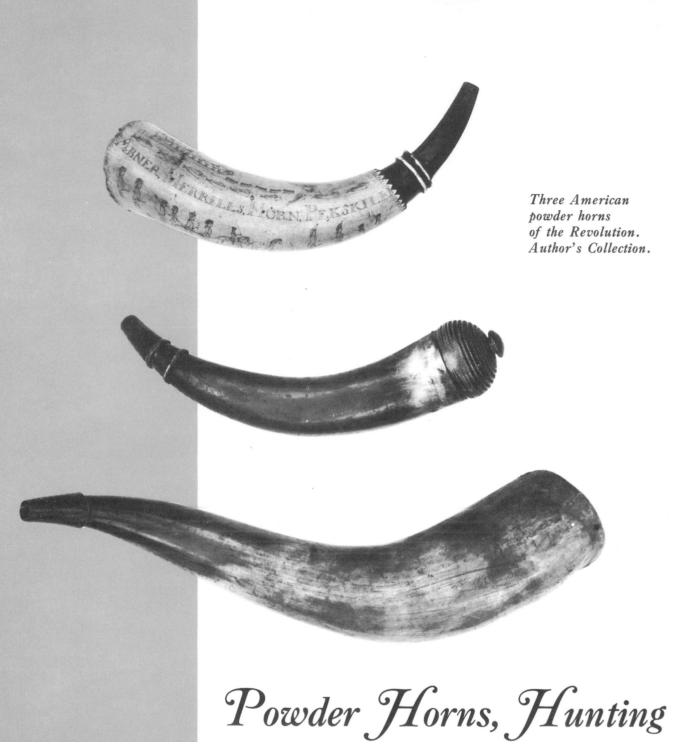

*Three American
powder horns
of the Revolution.
Author's Collection.*

Powder Horns, Hunting Bags, and Bullet Pouches

When neither cartridge boxes nor cannisters could be obtained, Continental infantrymen carried powder horns, hunting bags, and bullet pouches and loaded with loose powder and ball. This was an unfortunate expedient for the man with a musket, but riflemen were so equipped by preference because of their different loading technique calling for patched balls and separate loading. At the beginning of the War the horn and bag were often suspended by separate straps, but before the end of the conflict it was apparently more common to fasten them together on a single shoulder strap. Like the cartridge box these were normally worn on the right side but a little further to the front than was usual with the box. *(21)*

Both powder horns and bullet pouches were easily obtained. The materials were readily available, and the techniques of manufacture were simple. The powder horns were made from the common cattle horns available wherever beeves were slaughtered. The soft inner material was boiled out, and the exterior of the horn was scraped down and smoothed. A hole was cut in the small end and fitted with a stopper, and then a plug was fashioned for the large open end. The horn was softened again in hot water and this plug driven into place and nailed fast. Soldiers frequently carried the manufacture of their horns still further, scraping them down till they became translucent so that the powder level could readily be seen and decorating them with scrimshaw engraving as a pastime during leisure hours in camp.

Hunting bags were made of soft leather, frequently deerhide. Sometimes the hair was left on. The closing flaps were left long, offering extra protection against wet weather to the front of the pouch and helping assure that they would stay closed, since buttons or other fasteners were frequently omitted. Neither horn nor bag required the services of a skilled craftsman, and in fact many riflemen made their own and brought them along when they entered the service. Bullets were sometimes carried loose in the hunting bag, but often they were kept in special smaller pouches of leather with wood or horn throats and stoppers that were in turn placed in the bigger hunting bag.

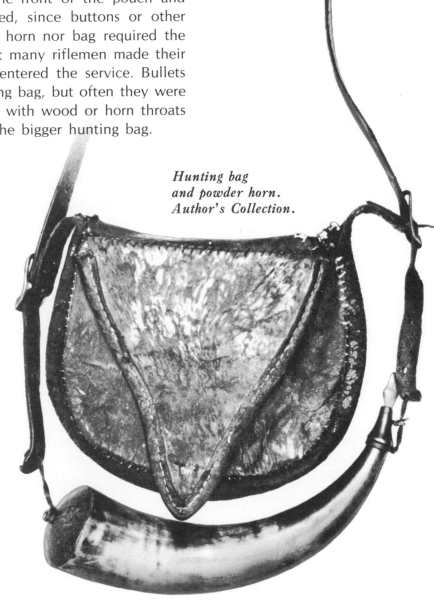

Hunting bag and powder horn. Author's Collection.

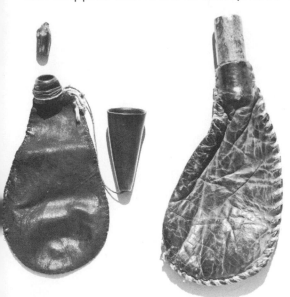

Two leather bullet pouches of the eighteenth century. The specimen at the left has a horn powder measure attached. Both have wooden throats. Crosby Milliman Collection.

71

Small Implements

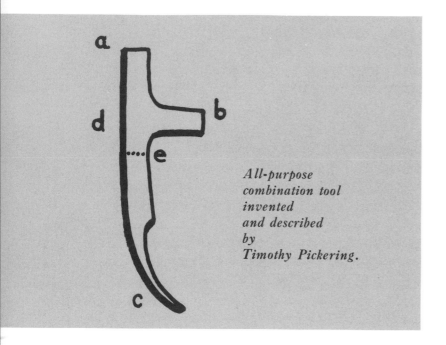

All-purpose combination tool invented and described by Timothy Pickering.

loosened and tightened every time a flint was adjusted or replaced. Lock screws might also become loose and need adjustment. Timothy Pickering devised an ingenious little tool combining a vent pick, screwdriver, and a small hammer, and in describing it he also indicated the form of the common musket screwdriver of the period:

> It is extremely convenient to have something to turn a screw, and break the edge of a bad flint when a better is not at hand to supply its place. The screw-driver used in the army has three blades, each of which is fitted to turn a screw, the blades are united at a common center, and disposed at equal distances so that three lines touching their extremities would form a triangle. But I believe the steel instrument represented [in illustration]...will be much more useful: *a, b,* are screw drivers, *c,* is a picker, and serves instead of a priming wire to clear the touch-hole, and at *d* the back is near a quarter of an inch thick, and serves for a hammer, the whole length of it from *a* to *c* is four inches, and from *d* to *b* is about an inch and a quarter. As the tapered end will seldom be used, a leathern case may inclose it up to *e;* which will render the instrument fitter to be carried in the pouch, and more easy to use as a screw-driver. *(23)*

In addition to the cartridge boxes, horns, pouches, and other accoutrements used for carrying his ammunition, the Continental soldier also needed a number of smaller implements to maintain his weapons in good operating condition. Among these were a vent pick to keep the touchhole of his firearm open and a little brush to clean out the priming pan. The pick was normally a simple piece of stiff wire with a loop at one end. The brush was a plain bristle or straw affair looped and tied at the base end. Both were usually attached to brass chains and fastened to the front of the cartridge box strap so that they hung down from the middle of the chest. Each was necessary, since the black powder fired in the weapons could plug a touchhole and foul a pan quickly. *(22)*

Another useful tool was a screwdriver. The top jaw of the flint vise on the cock operated on a screw, and it had to be

There is no evidence that Pickering's tool was ever made or issued in quantity, but the standard screwdriver he described certainly was.

Still other small items of equipment were concerned primarily with protecting the guns from the weather or from mechanical damage. These included tampions or plugs of wood to stop the muzzles of muskets and smaller plugs to close touchholes and thus keep the powder charge dry. Leather covers for the gunlocks were also recommended. These covers usually wrapped around the entire gun at the breech and laced or buckled on the left side. They were, thus, as effective as any device could be in protecting the locks of soldiers who had to be outside in inclement weather. For those arms which were stored in special tents, or bells of arms as they were called, leather covers for the frizzen only had been recommended by General Wolfe as early as 1750, and they undoubtedly also saw some use in the Revolution. In this case, however, the covers were intended as safety devices to prevent accidental discharge rather than as measures to keep the arms dry. Finally, there were wooden drivers designed to be clamped in the jaws of the flint vise to prevent wear and damage in practice dry firings. *(24)*

Another very useful little implement was the worm or scourer. This corkscrew-like device was normally threaded to attach to the small end of the ramrod. With it the soldier withdrew the wad holding the bullets in his piece and so removed a charge that might have become damp and unfirable. He could also use it to engage a bit of rag for cleaning purposes. The usual worm consisted of two prongs pointed at the ends and making two and a half turns. In a few instances the end of the ramrod itself was pointed and twisted slightly so that it could serve as a worm.

Bullet Molds and Ladles

Finally there was the bullet mold. Most bullets were cast at the special ammunition laboratories and forwarded to the troops, but some molds definitely accompanied troops in the field. Most of these were brass or iron gang molds casting numerous bullets. Maryland, for instance, specified brass molds that would cast twelve bullets on one side and as many buckshot as

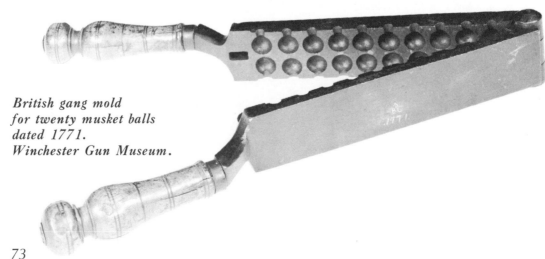

British gang mold for twenty musket balls dated 1771. Winchester Gun Museum.

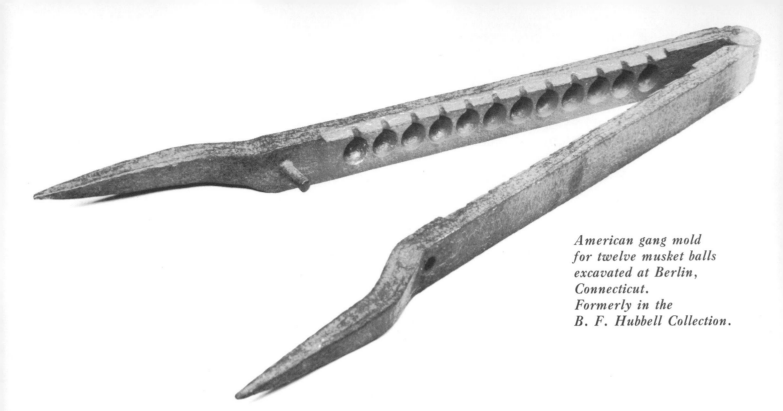

American gang mold for twelve musket balls excavated at Berlin, Connecticut. Formerly in the B. F. Hubbell Collection.

possible on the other. A ratio of one mold to every eighty muskets was called for. Virginia required that its molds cast sixteen bullets and established a ratio of one mold to every forty muskets. These molds were long and rectangular. They were made in two halves or leaves with half of each bullet cavity in each leaf. There was a pivot hinge at one end and short shanks for the attachment of wooden handles at the other. In order to use one, the molder first heated the mold over a fire. Then, as an assistant held the mold by the wooden handles and pressed the two leaves tightly together, he poured melted lead into a trough cut along the top edge of the mold. From this trough the lead ran through a series of little holes into the bullet cavities. When this lead had cooled sufficiently to set, the mold was turned over and the process repeated to fill the cavities on the other side. When both sides had hardened, the mold was opened and the castings knocked out of their cavities. If the pour was successful, there would be a series of balls each sprouting a stem or sprue of lead which had hardened in the holes leading down from the pouring trough. It only required a jackknife to trim off these sprues,

and the bullets were ready for loading into cartridges. *(25)*

Some Continental soldiers also carried their own personal molds with them. This was especially true of riflemen whose weapons were not standardized by calibers. Rifle bullet molds looked somewhat like a pair of pliers with plain iron handles and the pivot in the middle between the handles and the end holding the casting cavity. Some even boasted a little sprue cutter between the handles at the pivot. Rifle bullet molds were the commonest of the personal molds, but there were also some other types in the field, especially at the very beginning as the Army organized around Boston. These were usually brass and were actually smaller versions of the big gang molds. Normally they were provided with three or four cavities for balls of different sizes so that the same mold could be used for several different guns, say a musket, a fowling piece, and two sizes of pistol. Frequently there were two musket sizes, one for the British caliber and one for the French size. Sometimes also there were a series of holes for buckshot as well. *(26)*

The Continental who carried a personal bullet mold needed to have a ladle

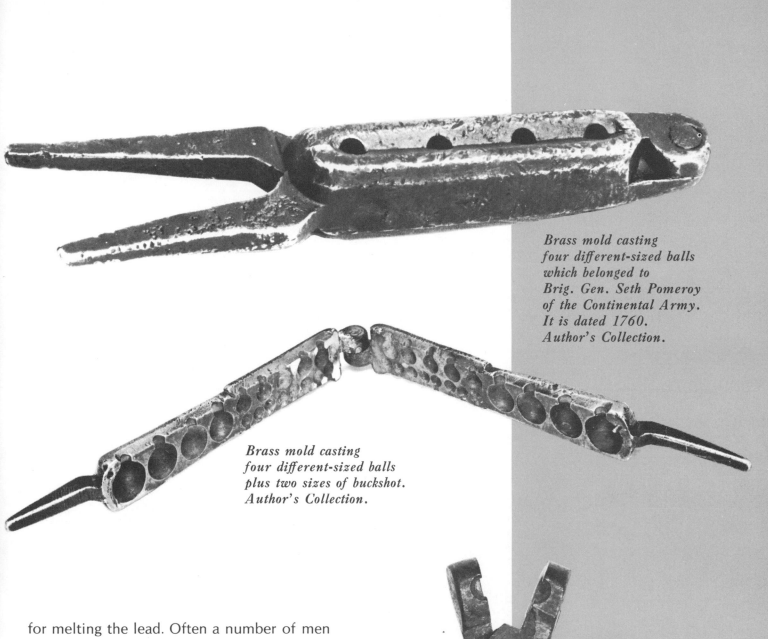

*Brass mold casting
four different-sized balls
which belonged to
Brig. Gen. Seth Pomeroy
of the Continental Army.
It is dated 1760.
Author's Collection.*

*Brass mold casting
four different-sized balls
plus two sizes of buckshot.
Author's Collection.*

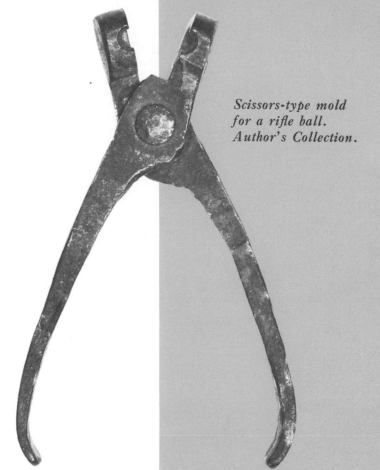

*Scissors-type mold
for a rifle ball.
Author's Collection.*

for melting the lead. Often a number of men shared the same ladle; undoubtedly ladles were often carried on wagons as part of the regimental stores. These ladles were simple iron affairs, round on the bottom and with a pouring spout on one side. Normally they were forged with a handle from one piece of iron. Still they were heavy for their size, and so the soldiers much preferred to draw their ammunition directly from regimental stores and dispense with both mold and ladle. After all, a five- or six-pound cartridge box plus the other necessary accessories for the care of his firearm already represented a considerable weight to devote to ammunition and accoutrements even if they were indispensable to his success.

Suspensory Equipment

Finally, the Continental soldier also had need of various accoutrements for carrying his weapons. These included gun slings, carbine belts, sword and bayonet belts. The first of these, the gun sling, was a simple affair when compared with its more complex modern counterpart. Usually it was made of buff leather, although occasionally cloth, especially linen, was used. One end was passed up through the lower swivel on the musket, doubled back, and tied with a thong. The other end was passed up through the upper swivel, doubled back to the outside, and fastened with a buckle or slide to permit adjustment. (27)

There were two principal means for carrying the carbine or musketoon. One was by belt and swivel; the other by boot and strap. The first of these was a broad buff leather belt with a buckle and sliding snap on a swivel. It was normally worn over the left shoulder, and the buckle might be either in front or in back. The snap gravitated

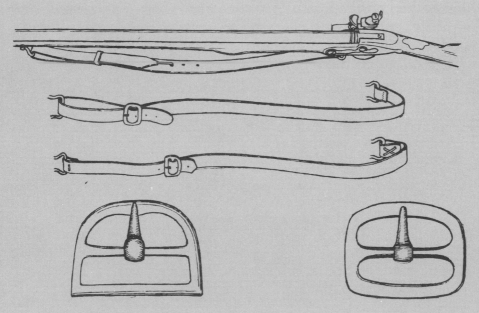

Three methods of attaching a gun sling derived from contemporary British prints and paintings. The two brass buckles are based on existing specimens. Drawing by Donald W. Holst and Peter Copeland.

to the lowest spot of the strap on the right side, and it hooked to the ring on the swivel bar on the carbine. When the soldier was dismounted the carbine thus hung, muzzle down, on the right side. When the soldier was mounted the carbine was often turned muzzle up, and the butt was inserted in a carbine boot that hung from the saddle just in front of the rider's leg. The boot and strap arrangement will be described in the chapter on horse equipment along with holsters and other bits of equipment that were attached to the horse rather than to the soldier. (28)

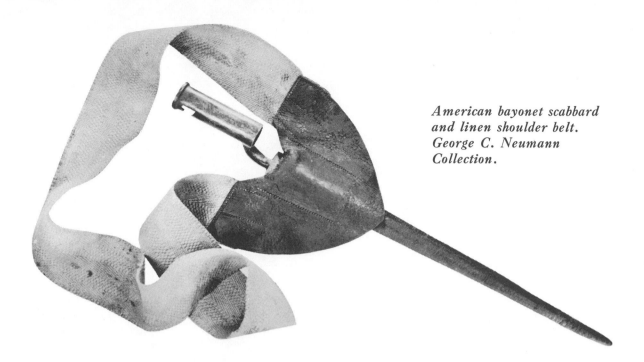

American bayonet scabbard and linen shoulder belt. George C. Neumann Collection.

The belts on which soldiers carried their bayonets and swords were of two types: waist belts and shoulder belts. During the period of the colonial wars the waist belt had been by far more popular, but shortly after the French and Indian War the switch to shoulder belts began in earnest, and by the time of the Revolution they were definitely the preferred standard. Still, some waist belts continued in use, especially during the early years of the war. This waist belt consisted of a heavy band for the waist with a frog on the left side. This frog was normally designed to hold only the bayonet. Non-commissioned officers, however, might have a double frog designed to carry both the bayonet and a sword. Such double frogs were actually the older standard type when most soldiers were required to carry both weapons. By the time of the Revolution, however, only the bayonet was required for Continental privates. (29)

Like the waist belts, shoulder belts were made with both single and double frogs. Normally the belt itself was a broad band of buff leather, perhaps two and a half inches wide. Sometimes it had a buckle; sometimes it was a solid loop. Because of shortages, however, American belts were sometimes made of harness leather or even linen instead of the preferred and more durable buff leather. The frogs assumed a variety of forms. The commonest was the simple sleeve through which the bayonet scabbard could be slipped and buttoned in place with a stud and slit. Sometimes, however, the scabbard itself was sewed fast to the belt. Again double frogs were used by non-commissioned officers to carry their swords as well as their bayonets, and there is one reference indicating that some Maryland soldiers were issued double frogs for carrying tomahawks as well as bayonets. Since none of these tomahawk frogs is known to survive, the design is a matter of speculation, but there must have been a scabbard or some other method of covering the blade. Otherwise it would have been a hazard

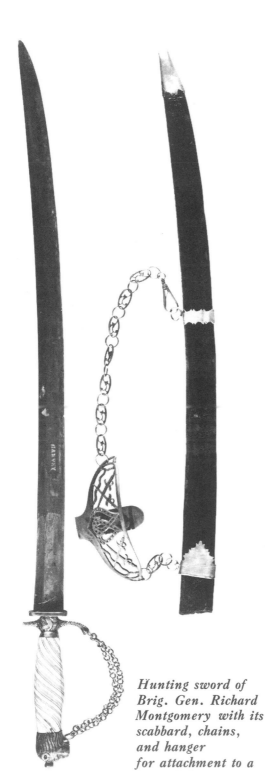

*Hunting sword of
Brig. Gen. Richard
Montgomery with its
scabbard, chains,
and hanger
for attachment to a
waist belt.
U.S. National Museum.*

*Accoutrements of the American
Revolution drawn by H. Charles
McBarron, Jr.*

1. *The British old-pattern cartridge box of the 1740's and 1750's. Despite its large size it held only 9-18 rounds.*

2. *British-pattern cartridge box in use from the mid-1750's through the Revolution.*

3. *Conventional type of cartridge box of the War with inner flap and holding 24 cartridges in 3 rows.*

4. *Cheap provisional cartridge box made of a block of wood with flap nailed fast and worn on a waist belt.*

5. *Interior arrangement of late cartridge box with tin for extra rounds and flints.*

6. *Early arrangement of powder horn and hunting bag suspended from separate belts.*

7. *Later version of the horn and bag attached to the same belt.*

8. *Cartridge cannister as described by the Board of War in 1778. A surviving specimen (plate 3-10) shows some differences with a rounded corner and alternate hinge arrangement.*

9. *Cartridge pouch with tin pipes as recommended for cavalry.*

10. *Sword and bayonet frogs attached to waist belt.*

11. *Reconstruction of the double frog for tomahawk and bayonet on a shoulder belt as described in the Maryland Archives.*

12. *Bayonet frog on a waist belt as shown in the Schaak portrait of General Wolfe.*

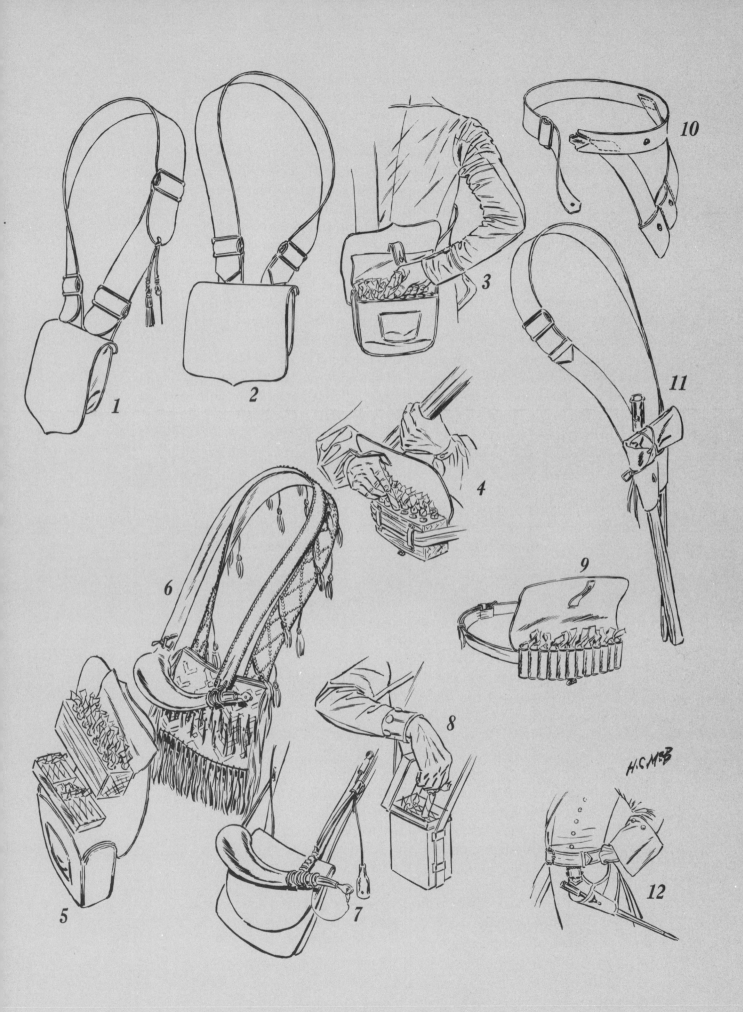

79

to the left hand as it swung in walking. Bare-bladed tomahawks were normally carried thrust through a waist belt at the soldier's back with the head to the right side since this was the most convenient and yet safe position. *(30)*

Despite substitutions of materials, bayonet belts and scabbards of all types were in short supply, and it was not unusual for an American soldier to be without one. At one point, in fact, Washington issued a standing order to his troops to adopt the practice of keeping the bayonet fixed to the musket at all times except when the piece was being cleaned. This would, he felt, enable the soldier to retain his bayonet safely even if he lacked the usual suspensory equipment. *(31)*

The belts on which officers wore their swords followed the same evolution as those of the men. At first it was the practice to wear a waist belt, sometimes under and sometimes over the waistcoat. Such belts were made of cloth or buff leather as a rule. About 1768 British officers began to carry their swords on a shoulder belt of buff leather with a buckle in the center of the chest, worn under the coat. Gradually, however, the practice developed of wearing this belt outside the coat, and the buckle was changed to an oval or sometimes rectangular plate, gilt or silver depending upon the buttons of the regiment. By 1776 this was standard in the British Army, and that year it was also adopted for French officers. *(32)*

American officers of the Revolution used both the waist belt and the shoulder belt. Contemporary portraits and paintings show both, thus substantiating the existence of a situation that would be expected because of the shortages that forever plagued the American troops. Both black and white shoulder belts were worn.

When the sword was carried on a shoulder belt, it was almost always attached by a frog. When it was worn on the waist belt it could also be attached by a frog, but two other methods were also used. One of these was an arrangement of two straps suspended from the belt which snapped to rings on the scabbard. The other was a hook or hanger, a metal frame which hooked over the belt and from which two chains with snaps provided the means of attachment for the scabbard.

Mounted troops were sometimes equipped with waist belts, sometimes with shoulder belts. The shoulder belt, however, seems to have been more common.

For its cartridge boxes, gunslings, belts, and scabbards, the Continental Army turned to a variety of sources. British stores supplied both goods and patterns. French supplies purchased and donated became increasingly important during the later years of the war. But there were strictly American patterns and expedients also. The cartridge cannister was one. The double frog for bayonet and tomahawk was another, and of course the hunting bag for riflemen was completely native. Beyond these were American adaptations of European designs forced by shortages of materials and skilled craftsmen. They offer the student a fascinating study in eclecticism and improvisation.

Notes to Chapter 3

1. Samuel Blakeslee, "Narrative of Colonel Samuel Blakeslee," *Buffalo Historical Society Publications,* VIII (1905), 428. General Orders, Headquarters, New York, June 29, 1776, Washington, *Writings,* V, 198; General Orders, Perkiomy, October 6, 1777, *ibid.,* IX, 313. Henry Dearborn, *Revolutionary War Journals of Henry Dearborn, 1775-1783,* ed. by Lloyd A. Brown and Howard H. Peckham, Chicago, 1939, p. 69.

2. Howe to Washington, September 21, 1776, Washington, *Writings,* VI, 74 n. William L. Calver and Reginald P. Bolton, *History Written with Pick and Shovel,* New York, 1950, pp. 75, 76.

3. Pickering, *Easy Plan,* Part I, pp. 2, 3 and Plate I.

4. "Instructions sur les Cartouches dont les Troupes Dolvent se Servir," J. Margerand, *Armement et Equipement de l'Infanterie Française des XVe au XXe Siècle,* Paris, n.d., p. 69.

5. General Orders, camp near Potsgrove, September 23, 1777, Washington, *Writings,* IX, 251; also October 5, 1777, *ibid.,* 311; October 16, 1777, *ibid.,* 379.

6. Ezekiel Cheever to Gen. Sullivan, July 31, 1778, John Sullivan, *Letters and Papers of Maj. Gen. John Sullivan,* ed. by Otis G. Hammond, 2 vols., Concord, N.H., 1931, II, 160.

7. Robert Donkin, *Military Collections and Remarks,* New York, 1777, p. 189. Arthur Woodward, "Some Notes on Gun Flints," *Military Collector & Historian,* III, No. 2 (June 1951), 29-36. T. M. Hamilton, "Gunflint," in Harold L. Peterson, ed., *Encyclopedia of Firearms,* New York and London, 1964, pp. 145, 146.

8. Woodward, "Gun Flints," pp. 32-36. July 18, 1775, Ford, *Journals of the Continental Congress,* II, 188.

9. Woodward, "Gun Flints," p. 32. Donkin, *Military Collections,* p. 189.

10. Resolution, March 19, 1778, Hazard, *Pennsylvania Archives,* VI, 375. Samuel Chase to Daniel of St. Thomas Jennifer, February 9, 1776, Browne, *Archives of Maryland,* XI, 150, 151. July 18, 1775, Ford, *Journals of the Continental Congress,* II, 188. General Orders, Headquarters, Perkiomy, October 8, 1777, Washington, *Writings,* IX, 341. Pickering, *Easy Plan,* Part I, pp. 1,2.

11. Washington, *Writings,* IX, 366.

12. *Ibid.*

13. Washington to Board of War, October 22, 1777, Washington, *Writings,* IX, 415; November 3, 1777, *ibid.,* 497.

14. Pickering, *Easy Plan,* Part I, pp. 1, 2.

15. Pickering to Gov. Jefferson, July 3, 1780, Palmer and Flournoy, *Calendar of Virginia State Papers,* I, 364, 365.

16. Edward Stevens to General Gates, July 21, 1780, *ibid.,* 365.

17. Col. Christian Febiger to Col. Davies, December 3, 1781, *ibid.,* II, 636.

18. Gen. Horatio Gates to Thomas Johnson, March 28, 1778, "Journal and Correspondence of the Council of Maryland, 1777-78," Browne, *Archives of Maryland,* XVI, 558, 559. For references to the issuance of cannisters in the field, see General Orders, Headquarters, Perkiomy, October 8, 1777, Washington, *Writings,* IX, 341; General Orders, Headquarters, Towamensing, October 13, 1777, *ibid.,* 363, 364; Washington to Gen. Knox, May 27, 1779, *ibid.,* XV, 158. Resolution, March 19, 1778, Hazard, *Pennsylvania Archives,* VI, 375.

19. Commissary of Stores, Memorandum Book for 1782, Record Group 93, Vol. 21470, National Archives, 9, 11, 13, 15, 17, 18, 20, 21.

20. George Clinton, *Public Papers of George Clinton,* ed. by Hugh Hastings, 8 vols., New York, 1899-1904, II, 829, 830.

21. General Orders, Headquarters, Towamensing, October 13, 1777, Washington, *Writings,* IX, 363, 364; Washington to Gen. Greene, April 5, 1779, *ibid.,* XIV, 338, 339.

22. August 30, 1775, "Journal and Correspondence of the Council of Safety, 1775-76," Browne, *Archives of Maryland,* XI, 75. July 18, 1775, Ford, *Journals of the Continental Congress,* II, 188. Broadside order, 1779, Ralph H. Gabriel and others, eds., *The Pageant of America,* 15 vols., New Haven, 1925-1929, VI 187.

23. Pickering, *Easy Plan,* Part I, pp. 1, 2 and Plate I.

24. "Extracts from the Orders of the Late General Wolfe," Pickering, *Easy Plan,* p. 162. Col. Wayne to the officers of his regiment, December 11, 1776, *Wayne Papers,* II, Revolutionary Series.

25. August 30, 1775, "Journal and Correspondence of the Council of Safety, 1775-76," Browne, *Archives of Maryland,* XI, 75. September 28, 1776, H. R. McIlwaine, *Journals of the Council of Virginia,* I, 177, 178.

26. Calver and Bolton, *Pick and Shovel,* pp. 74-77.

27. Peterson, *Arms and Armor,* pp. 244, 247.

28. *Ibid.,* pp. 247, 248.

29. *Ibid.,* pp. 248, 249.

30. Samuel Chase to Daniel of St. Thomas Jennifer, February 9, 1776, Browne, *Archives of Maryland,* XI, 150, 151.

31. General Orders, Headquarters, Peekskill, August 2, 1780, Washington, *Writings,* XIX, 304.

32. Maurice Bottet, *L'Arme Blanche de Guerre Française au XVIIIe Siècle,* Paris, 1910, p. 60. Charles M. Lefferts, *Uniforms of the American, British, French, and German Armies in the War of the American Revolution, 1775-1783,* New York, 1926, pp. 193, 194. Calver and Bolton, *Pick and Shovel,* pp. 156-166, 176-180.

Chapter
4

Keen
of
Edge

In the Continental Army, edged weapons were weapons indeed. Swords and spontoons might indicate rank and station, but these were secondary functions. Their principal purpose was fighting. Hand-to-hand combat was frequent, and such encounters were more often decided with cold steel than with firepower. Bayonets were the

and Sharp of Point

Being
a survey
of the
edged
weapons

commonest of the edged weapons, and an effort was made to provide one for every regular infantry private and also for some artillerymen. Non-commissioned officers normally carried bayonets and usually a short saber as well. Mounted officers and all cavalrymen wore swords while those officers who performed on foot went doubly armed with both sword and spontoon. And there were other cutting arms, too—tomahawks and knives for riflemen and some infantry, long spears for defending or assaulting fortifications, folding spears for riflemen, and even sharp-pointed caltrops designed to be strewn in front of defensive positions to cripple attackers. (1)

Bayonets

Of all the edged weapons, the bayonet was probably the most important as well as the most common. In a close encounter a soldier had no time to reload his muzzle-loading musket, and a fixed bayonet was a necessity. With it the musket was still an efficient weapon. Without a bayonet it was useful only as a club. The Battle of Bunker Hill emphasized the difference. Few of the American defenders had bayonets, and when they ran out of ammunition they could only club their muskets and strike out at the charging British troops with butt or barrel. The result was a rout. Crying "'tis barbarous to let men be obliged to oppose Bayonets with only gun Barrels....," Samuel Webster promptly sent a plea to the New Hampshire Committee of Safety for 500-1,000 bayonets for the troops from that colony, and other military men also noted the lesson well. (2)

Washington, for one, became a great believer in the bayonet. He made every effort to assure an adequate supply of that weapon for his troops, and at one point even directed that the soldiers keep their bayonets fixed at all times because of a scarcity of scabbards. Finally, in the climactic campaign of Yorktown, he exhorted the men to place their principal reliance on the bayonet. (3)

As the war progressed the Continental soldier learned the art of bayonet fighting well. In the beginning it was a new weapon, and the Americans were no match for the trained British veterans in close combat. Few colonies had even required bayonets for their militia in the years before the Revolution, most permitting either a sword or hatchet in its stead, and there were few experienced officers who could teach the proper techniques of thrust and parry. British soldiers were said to pray for rain to dampen gunpowder so that they could get at the Continentals with their bayonets without suffering any punishing volleys. Once close, they felt confident of winning easily. Even sad experiences, however, brought greater American familiarity with the weapon, and then came Baron von Steuben. His training and discipline contributed significantly to the growing efficiency of the Continental Army in bayonet combat. By 1779 well-trained Americans could take Stony Point with unloaded muskets, relying solely on cold steel and defeating the veteran British garrison with their own weapons. This was the turning point. Thereafter Americans could confidently meet bayonet with bayonet. (4)

The bayonets that Continental soldiers used followed both British and French patterns. As with most other weapons, the British designs predominated at first and then gave way to French styles later in the War. Both types were socket bayonets with

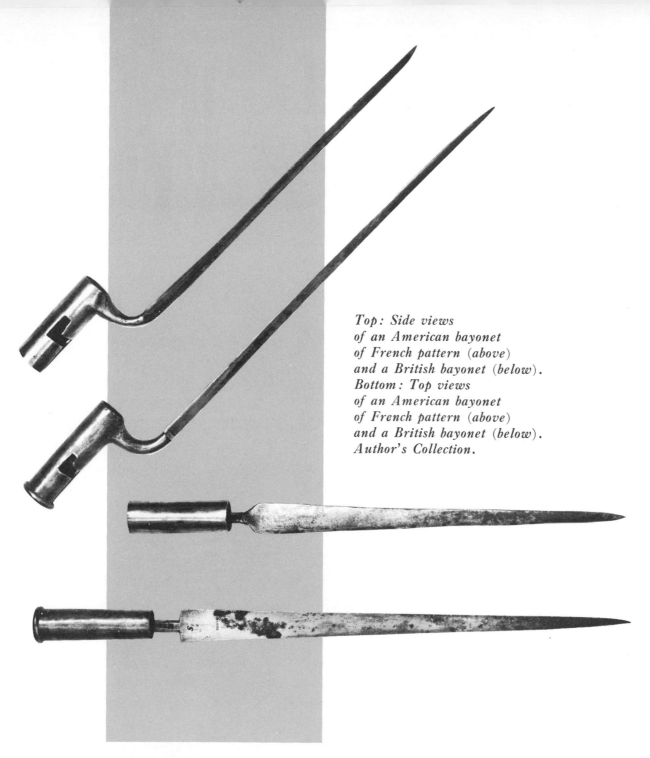

Top: Side views of an American bayonet of French pattern (above) and a British bayonet (below). Bottom: Top views of an American bayonet of French pattern (above) and a British bayonet (below). Author's Collection.

a sleeve that fitted around the muzzle of the musket and an elbow to offset the blade so that it would not interfere with loading and firing. The blades themselves were triangular in cross section and designed primarily for thrusting rather than cutting. The British bayonets were the longer of the two types, usually with 16- or 17-inch blades, flat on the top and grooved on the two lower sides. The base of the blade was cut square, and the elbow angled sharply up to the sleeve. This sleeve was some four inches long with a heavy ring around its base and a locking slot with two right-angled turns on the right side to engage a stud on the top of the musket barrel and hold the bayonet in place. The bayonets made under contract to the American Committees of Safety at the beginning of the Revolution all followed this pattern, but there were some differences in the blade lengths specified by the individual colonies. Massachusetts and Virginia, for

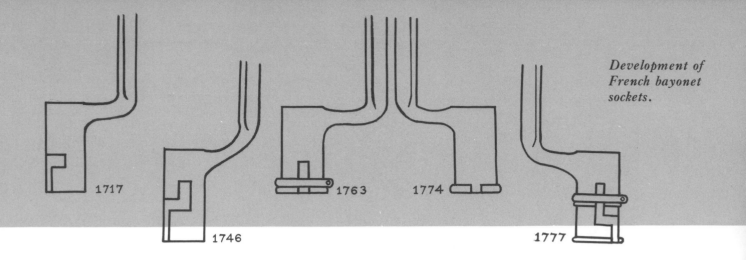

Development of French bayonet sockets.

1717

1746

1763

1774

1777

instance, required 18-inch blades, Maryland ordered 17 inches, and Connecticut, a short 14 inches. (5)

In requiring 14-inch blades for its bayonets, Connecticut was coming close to the French model which averaged that length for its blades. But there were many other differences that set the French-pattern bayonet apart from the British. For one thing the blade was not cut square at the base. Instead it was made with sloping shoulders that blended into the elbow. The socket also was much shorter than the British, and there were a variety of systems for locking it in place on the muzzle of the musket. The model of 1763, for instance, had a straight slot and a locking ring held in place by a collar at the base of the socket. In 1766 the locking ring was replaced by a flat spring, but it returned again in 1768. In 1774 both the turning ring and the slot were omitted. Instead a spring retainer on the gun barrel slipped over the collar and held the bayonet. Finally in 1777 the locking ring returned but this time with a slot boasting two right-angled turns similar to those on the British bayonets except that it was on the left side of the socket instead of the right because the bayonet stud of the model 1777 musket was mounted on the bottom of the barrel. When bayonets of the French pattern were made in America, they usually omitted both the collar and the locking ring and relied simply on a slot with two turns, much as the French themselves had done back in 1746. (6)

Infantry Swords

Next to the bayonet, the most widely used edged weapon was the sword, which appeared in a bewildering variety of shapes and sizes. There were short sabers, long sabers, broadswords, small swords, and hunting swords, and the variations in design and decoration within each category were almost limitless. Nevertheless, there was at least a general pattern of use and design that held true in the majority of cases.

Non-commissioned officers of infantry and artillery normally carried short sabers or cutting swords. This was the most efficient type of sword for their duties. Long swords would have been cumbersome for a man who performed his duties on foot, and they would have been unwieldy in close combat for men fighting in ranks. The most common forms of sword for Continental sergeants again were

British models left over from colonial days or captured in battle or French swords obtained with other weapons from that country. Among the British swords there were two principal patterns that were so popular they have been given informal "model" designations by modern collectors. The first of these has been called the "model" 1742 because it is so clearly delineated in the *Representation of the Cloathing of His Majesty's Household, and of all the Forces upon the Establishments of Great Britain and Ireland,* which was compiled for the Duke of Cumberland in that year. Actually, this sword was probably in use much earlier. A typical specimen has a slightly curved single-edged blade with a single fuller. The hilt is of cast brass and consists of grips moulded in a spiral pattern, a large globular or urn-shaped pommel with a capstan rivet, a simple knuckle-bow which expands to form a heart-shaped counterguard, and a downturned quillon that terminates above the blade in a slightly bulbous finial. The principal variations of this type include straight blades, wooden grips wrapped with wire, and grips with the crests of the regiments cast upon them.

The second general pattern is often called the "model" of 1751 because it appears in a series of paintings of British grenadiers that were made by David Morier at that time. This pattern differs from the previous only in that it has one or two branches connecting the knuckle-bow and counterguard on the obverse side, thus forming a half-basket guard. It is also subject to the same variations in the construction of the grips and blade. The scabbards for both of these patterns were of black or brown leather with brass tips and a brass stud for attachment to a frog on the obverse side near the throat. Almost all British infantry swords found in America with histories of use here are of one or the other of these two patterns.

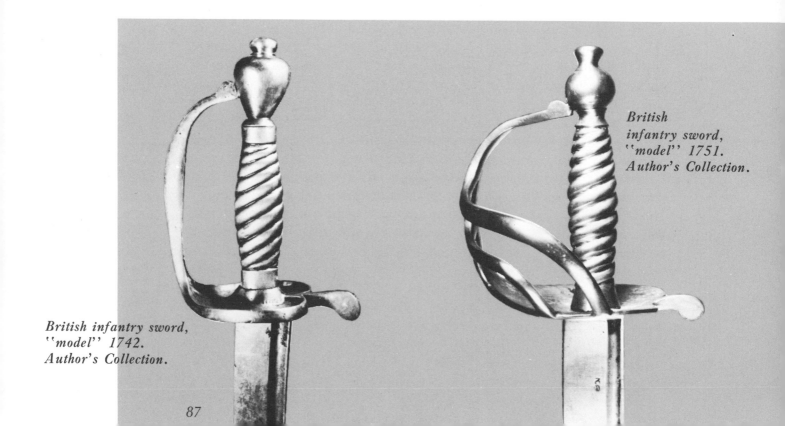

British infantry sword, "model" 1742. Author's Collection.

British infantry sword, "model" 1751. Author's Collection.

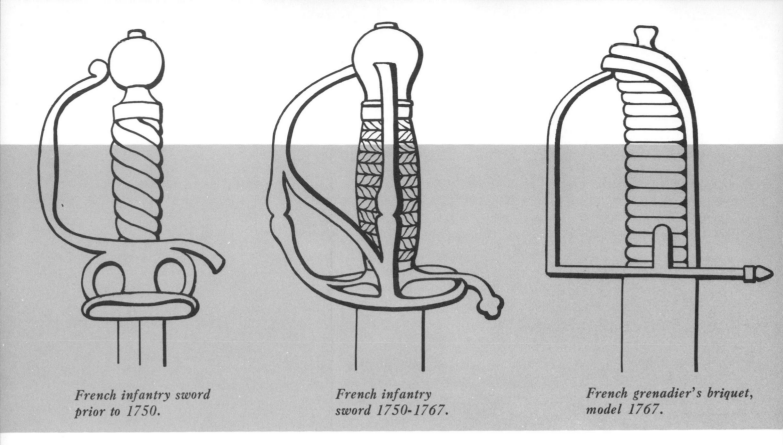

French infantry sword prior to 1750.

French infantry sword 1750-1767.

French grenadier's briquet, model 1767.

The French infantry swords used by the Continental Army seem primarily to have been of the grenadier briquet pattern specified in 1767. Like the British swords these too had short slightly curved blades and cast brass hilts. According to the specifications the blades were to be 22.8 inches long. The hilts had helmet or bird's-head pommels, and single knuckle-bows and quillons. The grips were ribbed. In general the earlier examples of this briquet are found with the hilt made in two pieces: one comprising the grips and pommel, the other the knuckle-bow and quillon. Sometimes, however, hilts cast in a single piece are found, and sometimes wooden grips are encountered. The scabbard was of black leather with a brass throat and tip. There was a ball finial on the tip, and the throat had a staple and strap for attachment to a frog. *(7)*

There were also some American-made swords, and these might follow almost any design. One particular model, however, has turned up in sufficient quantity and over a sufficiently wide area of the eastern seaboard to indicate that it must have had some popularity. Swords of this pattern, apparently all made in the same shop, have barrel-shaped grips covered in leather without any ribbing or wrappings. The pommel is a simple cap made by flattening out the round iron knuckle-bow. At its other end this knuckle-bow is screwed fast to a round, slightly dished counterguard. Blades vary, depending apparently on what could be obtained. All known specimens have foreign-made blades, but some are straight and double-edged while others are slightly curved. None are pretty or well finished, but they handle well and must have made efficient weapons.

American infantry sword of the Revolution. Author's Collection.

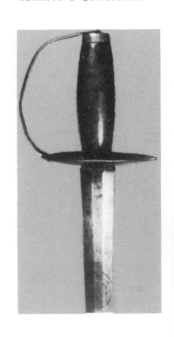

Cavalry Sabers and Broadswords

Undoubtedly the most important swords carried by enlisted men, however, were those of the cavalry. Troopers frequently carried other weapons also, it is true, but neither the musket nor the musketoon, the carbine nor the pistol seriously challenged the supremacy of the sword. Firearms might serve their purpose when the cavalryman was on picket duty or when he was dismounted; but once he was ahorse and in formation he had no use for them. William Washington, gallant commander of the Third Continental Cavalry, called the sword the "most destructive and almost the only necessary weapon a Dragoon carries," and Henry Lee, the famous "Light Horse Harry" of the Revolution, expressed himself forcefully on the subject:

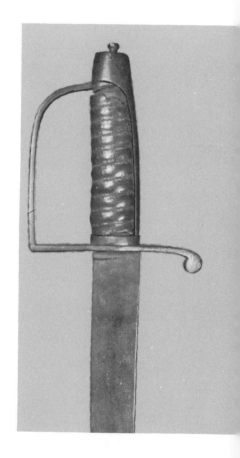

American stirrup-hilted saber. Harry D. Berry, Jr. Collection.

...the fire of cavalry is at best innocent, especially in quick action.... The strength and activity of the horse, the precision and celerity of evolution, the adroitness of the rider, boot-top to boot-top, and the keen edge of the sabre, with fitness of ground and skill in the leader, constitute their vast power so often decisive in the day of battle. *(8)*

Perhaps the best summary of the contemporary attitude, however, was made by Epaphras Hoyt, a cavalry captain from Massachusetts who became famous after the Revolution for his military treatises:

It is generally agreed by experienced officers, that fire arms are seldom of any great utility to cavalry in an engagement, while they are drawn up in regiments, squadrons, or other considerable bodies: Indeed there is little hope of success from any who begin their attack with the fire of carbines or pistols; numerous examples could be cited from military history to show their inefficiency. It is by the right use of the sword they are to expect victory: This is indisputably the most formidable and essentially useful weapon of cavalry: Nothing decides an engagement sooner than charging briskly with this weapon in hand. By this mode of attack, a body of cavalry will generally rout one that receives it with pistols ready to fire. *(9)*

These swords were of two principal types, the saber and the broadsword, with the saber predominant. Both were big weapons. The sabers normally had slightly curved blades as much as 35 or 36 inches long. Most of those made in this country had flat-sided blades, but some imported blades had three narrow grooves or fullers on each side. The commonest hilt had an iron flat-cap pommel and backstrap, wooden grips, and an iron stirrup guard. This was generally similar to the British light cavalry saber of the period, and James Hunter is known to have made 1,000 of them at his Rappahannock Forge in 1781, copying a captured specimen sent him by William Washington. Epaphras Hoyt's own saber, now in Memorial Hall, Deerfield, Massachusetts, is also of this pattern. But there were other hilt types as well. Some had huge domed or cylindro-conoidal pommels, and in some the iron guard widened and divided as it turned across the blade. (10)

When broadswords were used by the Continental dragoons, they were usually of the Scottish pattern, with straight single- or double-edged blades and iron basket hilts. Captain Nicholas Ruxton Moore of the Fourth Continental Dragoons is known to have carried such a sword, and it is probable that many other cavalrymen did also. After all, it had been the standard pattern for British dragoons for many years.

There were also some German broadswords in use, however, for an order of January 1, 1778 from General Washington directed the officer commanding at Albany to issue the Brunswick dragoon swords captured at the Battle of Bennington to Colonel Sheldon's Second

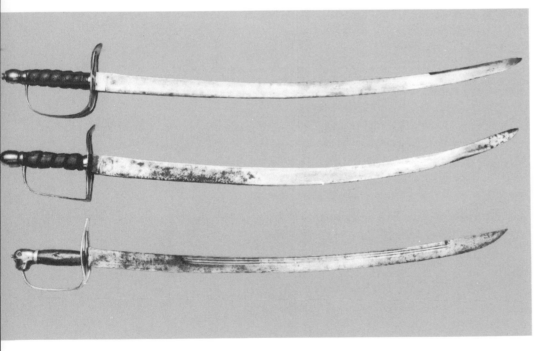

American horsemen's sabers.
Top: officer's saber
by James Potter
of New York City
which belonged to
Maj. Benjamin Tallmadge
of the Second Continental Dragoons.
Center: enlisted man's saber
by Potter.
Bottom: brass-mounted saber
with lion's-head pommel.
Mrs. H. Blakiston Wilkins,
Hermann W. Williams, Jr.,
and Author's Collections.

Continental Dragoons along with the rest of the horse equipment captured in that campaign. These German swords were long heavy weapons with straight double-edged blades and brass basket hilts, heavier even than the Scottish broadswords and not nearly so manageable as the saber. (11)

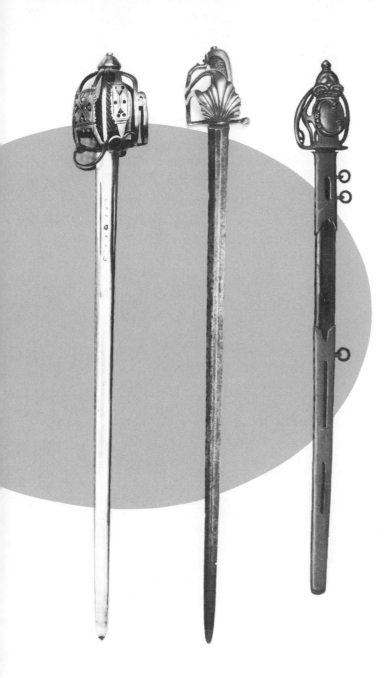

Left: basket-hilted broadsword
carried by
Capt. Nicholas Ruxton Moore
of the Fourth Continental Dragoons.
Maryland Historical Society.

Center: French broadsword
carried by
Sgt. Elijah Churchill
of the Second Continental Dragoons.
New Windsor Cantonment.

Right: Brunswick dragoon
officer's sword
captured at Bennington.
State House, Boston.

Brunswick dragoon
believed to have been drawn by
a participant in the Burgoyne campaign.
The basket-hilted broadswords
of this regiment
were issued to the
Second Continental Dragoons.
New York Public Library.

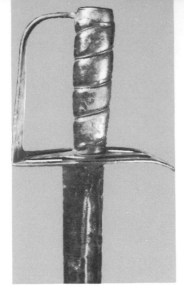

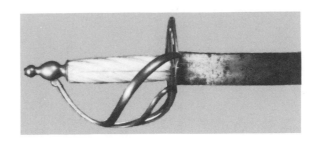

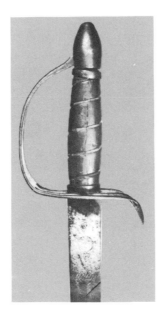

*A variety of
American saber hilts.
Hermann W. Williams, Jr.,
and Author's Collections.*

Officers' Swords

The greatest variety of swords, however, were found among the weapons carried by officers. Some were purely civilian swords, some semi-military types, and others strictly military weapons. These were the products of local smiths, importations from Europe, family heirlooms, and captured arms.

Among them, perhaps the most popular single pattern for both mounted and foot officers was the small sword. It had long been a popular military weapon in all European armies, and it had also been the standard civilian sword for many years, so that it was available to many who were not

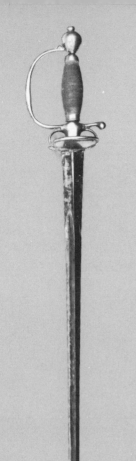

able to obtain a strictly military piece. These weapons had straight slender blades, usually triangular in cross section though some flat double-edged blades are also encountered. By the time of the Revolution, most of these blades tapered evenly from hilt to point, but a few of the earlier colichemarde types were still in use. The colichemarde was characterized by a blade that was broad and stout near the hilt, then narrowed suddenly and tapered gradually on to the point. It had been an especially popular type of blade for military purposes early in the eighteenth century. The guard consisted of both a knuckle-bow and a double-shell, elliptical, or even boat-shaped counterguard. Between the knuckle-bow and the counterguard were a pair of loops called the *pas-d'âne*. In the beginning these had been big loops designed

The commonest form of small sword worn by junior officers of the Continental Army. The hilt is silver-plated brass. Author's Collection.

English silver-mounted small sword with colichemarde blade, c. 1760-1770, used by George Washington. According to tradition he favored this sword for state occasions. Mount Vernon Ladies' Association of the Union.

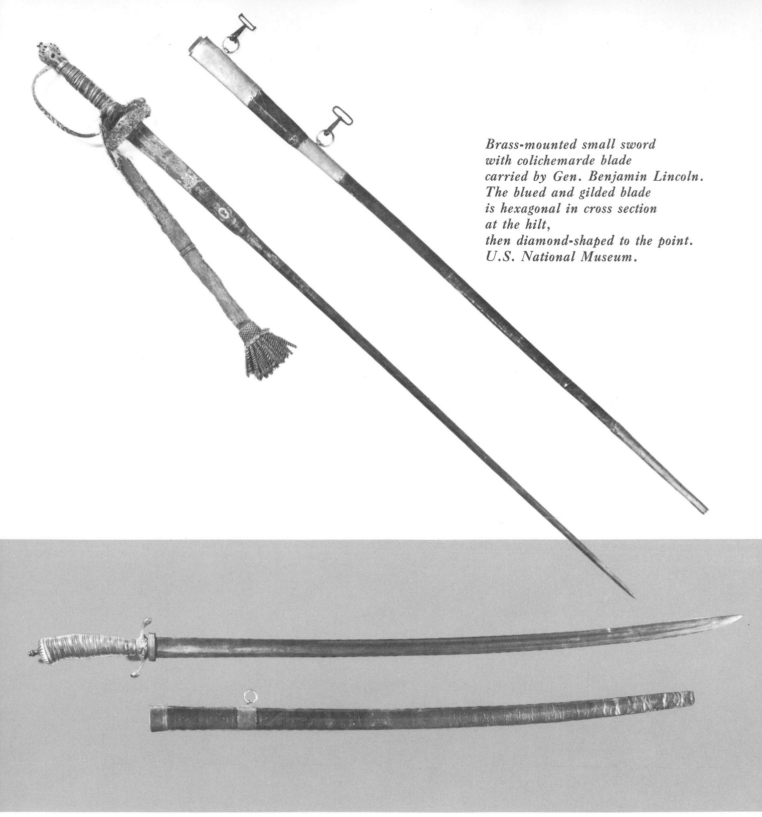

Brass-mounted small sword
with colichemarde blade
carried by Gen. Benjamin Lincoln.
The blued and gilded blade
is hexagonal in cross section
at the hilt,
then diamond-shaped to the point.
U.S. National Museum.

Silver-mounted hunting sword
by John Bailey
worn by George Washington
during the Revolution.
U.S. National Museum.

to protect the thumb and forefinger, but by the 1770's they had become quite small, often really only half-circles or less. The pommel was usually ovoid, and the grips were wrapped with wire. The metal parts of the hilt might be made of silver in the more elegant specimens or possibly cut steel. Brass hilts are also encountered and sometimes they are silver-plated. There was one pattern of small sword which seems to have been especially popular with foot officers of the Continental Army to judge by surviving examples with histories. It had a plain silver-plated hilt, an ample *pas-d'âne,* double-shell counterguard, and a blued blade that was deeply grooved and tapered almost evenly with just a slight flare near the hilt. Despite its simplicity and inexpensive appearance, it was a well-balanced and highly efficient weapon, well calculated to appeal to a man of small means who nevertheless wanted a good sword. *(12)*

Another form of sword which was popular among American officers was the hunting sword. This sword had been designed originally for the chase as its name implies, and it had little to recommend it for combat, as it was short and without an efficient guard. For these reasons it seems principally to have been worn by high-ranking officers who had little expectation of personal conflict. George Washington had one, for instance, and was painted wearing it in the portrait at the battle of Princeton by Charles Willson Peale. General Artemas Ward also owned one, as did Israel Putnam, Henry Dearborn, and others. Yet surviving examples

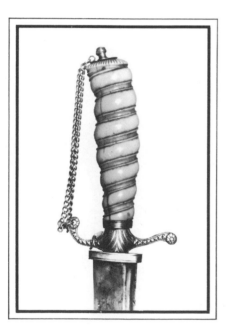

Silver-mounted hunting swords. The one at the right belonged to Gen. Artemas Ward. The one below was made by C. Chouso. John K. Lattimer, Massachusetts Historical Society, and Author's Collections.

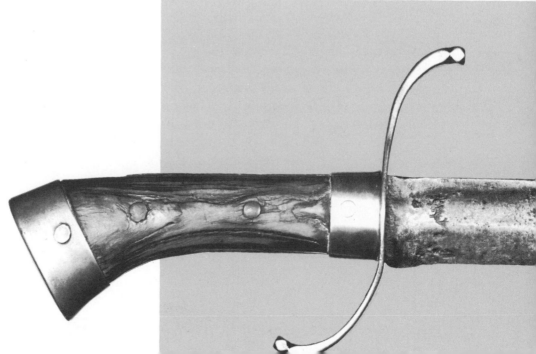

95

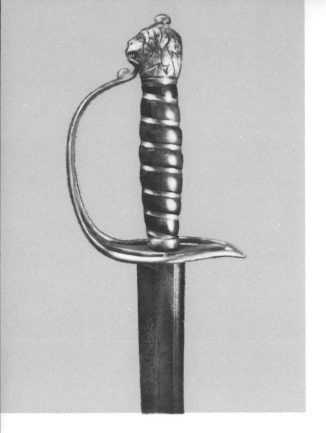

often exactly the same as those of the hunting swords. The hilts, however, had a more substantial guard. Usually this took the form of a knuckle-bow with one or more branches forming an open-work counterguard. Sometimes both branches were on the obverse side, but most often there was one on either side with connecting crossbars. The grips were frequently wood covered with fish skin instead of the horn and ivory found on the hunting swords, and iron mounts are encountered as well as brass and silver.

The most efficient military sword, however, was probably the heavy saber, and next to the small sword it was the most widely used type. Both mounted and foot

Officer's short saber
with lion's-head pommel.
Author's Collection.

American officer
wearing a short saber
on a shoulder belt.
From a drawing believed
to have been made
by a participant in the
Burgoyne expedition.
New York Public Library.

carried by colonels, captains, and ensigns are also known. *(13)*

These hunting swords were short, cut-and-thrust weapons. The blade was normally slightly curved and usually less than two feet long. The grips were horn, bone, or ivory, frequently carved and sometimes colored. The guard consisted of simple straight or S-curved quillons. The pommel was sometimes a flat cap and sometimes in the form of an animal's or bird's head. Frequently it was connected to the quillon by a chain. Brass and silver were the most popular metals for the mountings.

Closely akin to the hunting sword was a form of light saber carried by some officers. The blades of these weapons were officers carried such swords. Indeed, they were almost mandatory for the mounted officer who expected to become personally involved in a hand-to-hand conflict, for none of the other types were practical for actual use on horseback.

The individual variations among sabers in this category are infinite; yet they all have certain features in common which make the type readily recognizable. The broad blade is normally slightly curved and about thirty inches long. It is sometimes flat, but more often there are three narrow fullers, with the one nearest the back shorter than the other two. The grips are most often of plain wood, sometimes smooth, sometimes carved in a spiral pattern. Bone and ivory grips are occasionally found, however. The standard metal for mounts is brass. The pommels are of many designs, lion's head,

dog's head, ball, urn, ovoid, baluster, and some unclassifiable shapes. The guards are sometimes cast but more frequently cut from a heavy sheet of brass. The simple separated guard with a knuckle-bow and one branch on either side is most common, but there are several variations of the half-basket on existing specimens. Much depended upon the ingenuity and ability of the individual smith. The scabbards, few of which survive, are almost always of leather with brass throat and tip and a stud for attachment to a frog.

It should be noted also that many officers carried sabers that cannot be distinguished from those used by enlisted men. This was particularly true of cavalry officers who customarily equipped themselves for the field from the same supply of sabers as their men.

Sergeants' Halberds

After the bayonet and sword in importance came a series of pole arms, some serving primarily as weapons, some as both weapon and symbol of rank, and, at the beginning, some, such as the sergeant's halberd, serving only as rank designation. These halberds were a combination of axe and spear mounted on a long pole with a total length of seven or eight feet. There was a spear point at the top with an axe blade below and a pointed beak opposite the axe. Originally the halberd had been a weapon, but by the time of the Revolution it had

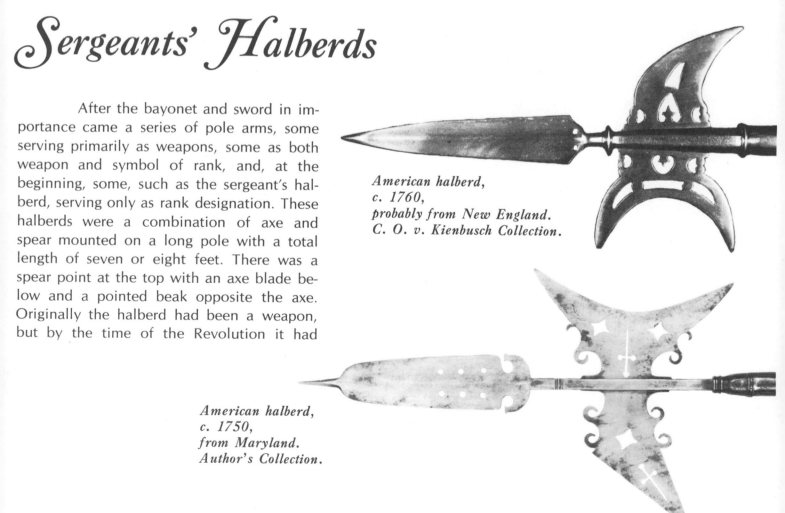

American halberd,
c. 1760,
probably from New England.
C. O. v. Kienbusch Collection.

American halberd,
c. 1750,
from Maryland.
Author's Collection.

American halberd,
c. 1750-1760,
probably from New York
or Pennsylvania.
West Point Museum.

American halberd,
c. 1750-1760,
probably from New York
or Pennsylvania.
West Point Museum.

degenerated to an ornament, often a very attractive one. The spear point was forged nicely and frequently pierced with a series of circular holes, but it was almost never tempered or sharpened. The axe blade and beak were normally cut from a sheet of metal without any cutting edge whatsoever, and these, too, were often pierced decoratively while the borders were sometimes ornamented with scrollwork. Such halberds can in fact be fine examples of folk art. Other halberds were simpler and sturdier, but still not efficient weapons. Ever since the founding of the first British colonies sergeants had carried halberds in the various colonial militias, although the British Army itself had started to abandon them here during the French and Indian War. Undoubtedly some of the sergeants who joined the newly formed Continental Army outside Boston brought their halberds with them, but they soon abandoned them as useless for battle, and took instead the regulation sword and fusil with bayonet. *(14)*

Officers' Spontoons

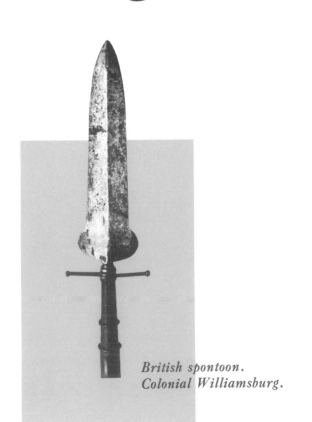

British spontoon.
Colonial Williamsburg.

The officer's spontoon, however, was an entirely different matter. It was both a badge of rank and an efficient weapon. Sometimes called a half-pike, it was a simple spear about 6-6½ feet long. There were a number of different patterns of spontoon. In the beginning a few were decorative specimens with piercings and scrollwork similar to the halberds, but these soon disappeared. Many followed the British pattern which featured a simple point with a bulbous base and a crossbar or toggle below, a short socket, and long straps to attach it to its haft. Others omitted the crossbar and presented only a simple leaf-shaped point with socket and straps. Since the function of these straps was to prevent the haft being broken or cut by a sword as well as attaching the head, most spontoons designed as weapons retained them. In 1778 an attempt was made to standardize spontoons, and a general council of brigade commanders recommended that:

> ...the Quartermaster General be directed to cause spontoons or pikes made for the officers, the staff six feet long and one inch and one quarter diameter in the largest part, and that the iron part to be one foot long.

This recommendation was approved by Washington who ordered it put into effect immediately. (15)

Unlike the British, the Americans did not abandon their spontoons during the Revolution. Some military men, such as Timothy Pickering, advocated their abandonment at the outbreak of the war, but Washington was a firm believer in the use of pole arms, as were Wayne and many others. Thus, throughout the war one finds frequent general orders to the effect that all platoon officers who did not have spontoons were to apply to the quartermaster immediately, and that no such officer or any other officer who was performing his duties on foot was to appear with his men without being so armed. Apparently there was no shortage of these weapons since all orders assumed that the quartermaster could supply them. (16)

In stating his reasons for arming his officers with spontoons, Washington wrote:

> As the proper arming of officers would add considerable strength to the Army, and the officers themselves derive great confidence from being armed in the time of action, the General orders every one of them to provide himself with a half pike or spear as soon as possible—fire-arms, when made use of, withdrawing their attention too much from their men, and to be without either, has a very awkward and unofficer-like appearance. (17)

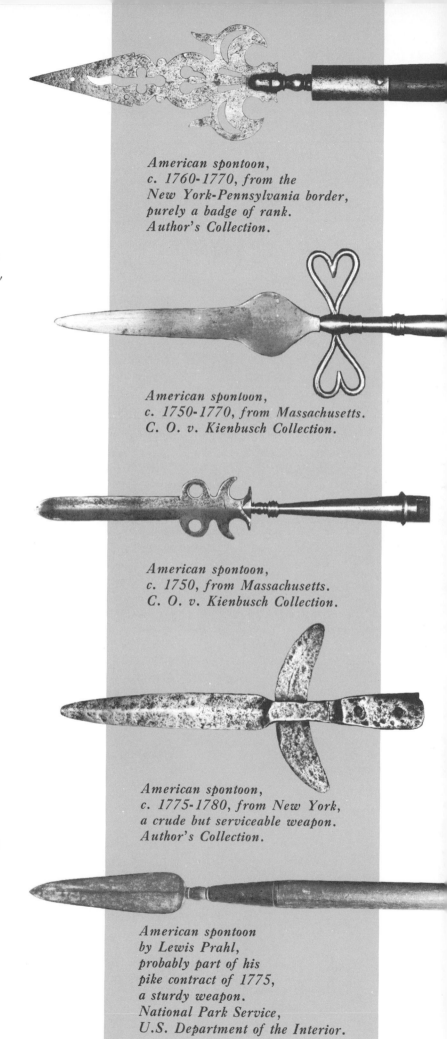

*American spontoon,
c. 1760-1770, from the
New York-Pennsylvania border,
purely a badge of rank.
Author's Collection.*

*American spontoon,
c. 1750-1770, from Massachusetts.
C. O. v. Kienbusch Collection.*

*American spontoon,
c. 1750, from Massachusetts.
C. O. v. Kienbusch Collection.*

*American spontoon,
c. 1775-1780, from New York,
a crude but serviceable weapon.
Author's Collection.*

*American spontoon
by Lewis Prahl,
probably part of his
pike contract of 1775,
a sturdy weapon.
National Park Service,
U.S. Department of the Interior.*

Wayne emphasized the fact that they were to be used in action when he wrote Washington stating that his officers had no means of defense in close fighting and asking for fifty spontoons as soon as possible so that the officers could practice with them before the impending attack on Stony Point. The arms were sent promptly, and in that famous assault, Wayne himself, who commanded his men on foot, carried a spontoon. (18)

Other instances of the use of spontoons in combat also survive. At the Battle of Cowpens in 1781, for instance, Captain Ewing was ordered to charge the enemy in order to capture some British cannon, but as "Light Horse Harry" Lee recalled:

Captain Anderson, hearing the order, also pushed for the same object and both being emulous for the prize kept pace until near the first piece, when Anderson, by putting the end of his spontoon forward into the ground, made a long leap which brought him upon the gun and gave him the honor of the prize. (19)

A little later, on October 14, 1781,

Captain Stephen Olney of the Second Rhode Island Regiment participated in the night assault on British Redoubt Number 10 during the siege of Yorktown. One of the first men to mount the walls of the dirt fort, he reported:

...I had not less than six or eight bayonets pushed at me; I parried as well as I could with my espontoon, but they broke off the blade part, and their bayonets slid along the handle of my espontoon and scaled my fingers: one bayonet pierced my thigh, and another stabbed me in the abdomen just about the hip bone. One fellow fired at me and I thought his ball took effect in my arm; by the light of his gun, I made a thrust with the remains of my espontoon, in order to injure the sight of his eyes; but as it happened, I only made a hard stroke in his forehead. (20)

It was a gallant encounter, and though Olney's abdominal wound was judged mortal, he managed to recover and live on as the hero of what was undoubtedly the last use of the spontoon in combat during the Revolutionary War.

Spears, Pikes, and Lances

Spears were also used by enlisted men in the Continental Army, especially during the early months of the War. Muskets were scarce, and bayonets were even scarcer. Pikes, on the other hand, could be made quickly and cheaply, and so they were issued to the various regiments around Boston to relieve the weapon shortage. Repeated mention of them in orders and directives aimed at their proper care and twice weekly greasing indicate that they remained important weapons throughout the entire siege, and that they were still in use at the Battle of White Plains, October 28, 1776. (21)

These infantry pikes were much longer than the spontoons or half-pikes of the officers. A general order of July 23, 1775 issued by Washington at Cambridge gives some indication of their construction:

The people employed to make spears, are desired by the General to make four dozen of them immediately, thirteen feet in length, and the wood part a good deal more substantial than those already made, particularly in the New Hampshire Lines, are ridiculously short and

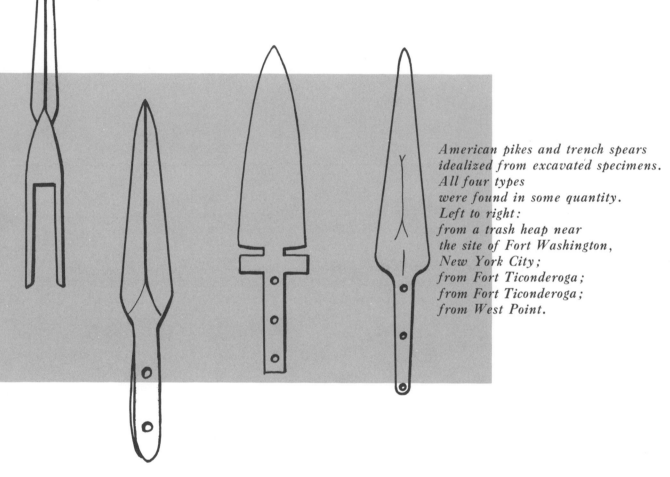

American pikes and trench spears idealized from excavated specimens. All four types were found in some quantity. Left to right: from a trash heap near the site of Fort Washington, New York City; from Fort Ticonderoga; from Fort Ticonderoga; from West Point.

light, and can answer no sort of purpose, no more are therefore to be made on the same model. (22)

Another general order at Cambridge on December 15, 1775, indicates how the spears were to be used:

Every colonel will appoint thirty men that are bold, active and resolute, to use the spears in defense of the lines instead of guns; to form in the center of the rear of the regiments and to stand ready to push the enemy off the breastworks. (23)

Spears also were used in attacking fortifications. Thus it was that a council of war held by American officers before the walls of Quebec in 1775 reported that: "A majority...was for Storming the Garrison of Quebec as soon as the men are well equip'd with good arms, Spears, hatchets,...&c." The attack was delayed until Captain Hanchet and his six smiths could make those spears which they considered so necessary. (24)

A special and unusually interesting type of spear was that devised in 1777 for Morgan's Riflemen. The lack of a bayonet, which was one of the principal drawbacks of the rifle as a military weapon, worried Washington considerably, and he turned to the spear as an auxiliary weapon. On June 13, 1777, he wrote Morgan:

I have sent for Spears, which I expect shortly to receive and deliver you, as a defence against Horse; till you are furnished with these, take care not to be caught in such Situation as to give them any advantage over you. (25)

American pike
or trench spear head,
one of a small number
found in central New York State.
Author's Collection.

By June 20 the spears had arrived, but although they had a folding joint in the haft, they were not exactly what Washington desired, and so he wrote the Board of War:

The Spears have come to hand, and are very handy and will be useful to the Rifle Men. But they would be more conveniently carried, if they had a sling fixed to them, they should also have a spike in the but end to fix them in the ground and they would then serve as a rest for the Rifle. The Iron plates which fix the spear head to the shaft should be at least eighteen inches long to prevent the Shaft from being cut through, with a stroke of a Horseman's Sword. Those only, intended for the Rifle Men, should be fixed with Slings and Spikes in the end, those for the Light Horse need neither. There will be 500 wanted for the Rifle Men as quick as possible. (26)

The Board of War referred the letter to Colonel Benjamin Flower, who was in charge of the manufactory at Philadelphia. Flower prepared a sketch and returned it to the Board with the following comment:

Below is a drawing of a Rifleman's Pike intended to be seven feet long and the manner of slinging it agreeable to your request, which if you approve of, I will give directions and have the five hundred made as soon as possible....The Letters and explanations show the different parts of the Pike

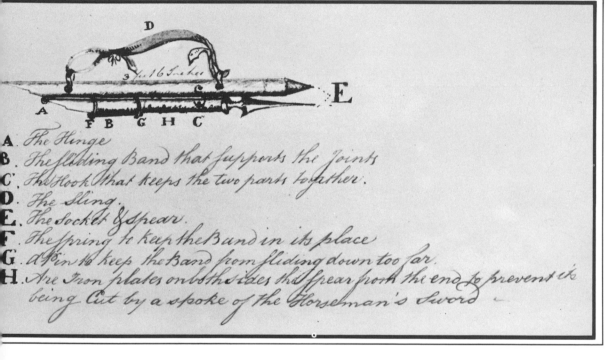

Col. Flower's original drawing of the pikes to be made for Morgan's riflemen, 1777. Library of Congress.

Viz.--
A. The Hinge
B. The Sliding Band that Supports the Joints
C. The Hook that keeps the two parts together
D. The Sling
E. The Socket & Spear
F. The Spring to keep the Band in its place
G. A Pin to keep the Band from Sliding down too far
H. Are Iron plates on both sides the Spear from the end to prevent its being Cut by a stroke of the Horseman's Sword. *(27)*

The sketch met with approval all along the line, and Washington asked that they be sent forward as quickly as possible. Unfortunately there is no evidence to indicate whether Morgan's men carried these spears at Saratoga a few months later. *(28)*

As was noted above in Washington's letter about the riflemen's spears, he also contemplated arming the light horse with a similar weapon, without sling and ground iron. It is not clear just what light horse Washington had in mind on June 20, but in December he did approve a "corps of lancemen" for Count Pulaski which eventually evolved into the lancers of Pulaski's Independent Legion who actually saw action in the South in 1779 and 1780. Nothing is known about the appearance of these lances except that they were decorated with foxtails in place of the usual pennants. *(29)*

Hatchets and Tomahawks

One other weapon that was technically a pole arm was the tomahawk or hatchet. Throughout the colonial period American militia had favored the tomahawk as a side arm, and it had become especially popular after 1700 when the militia laws of almost all colonies had directed that each soldier provide himself with either a bayonet, a sword, or a hatchet. Since hatchets were cheaper and easier to obtain than swords and more useful around the house than either swords or bayonets, there was a natural tendency for the militiaman who had to provide his own weapons to select the hatchet as his cutting weapon. Many of the soldiers who joined the Continental Army around Boston undoubtedly brought their tomahawks with them, but as the War progressed they were generally abandoned for regular infantry and replaced by bayonets. Riflemen, however, retained the tomahawk as a standard weapon throughout the conflict, and so did some of the light infantry, including those in Pulaski's Legion. *(30)*

Most of these military tomahawks were simple belt axes of the period. The predominant pattern resembled the standard European half-axe. It had a relatively long blade that flared slightly on the side towards the haft so that the edge might be almost twice as wide as the base of the blade. The

Simple poll-less belt axes of the commonest form for tomahawks. William O. Sweet Collection.

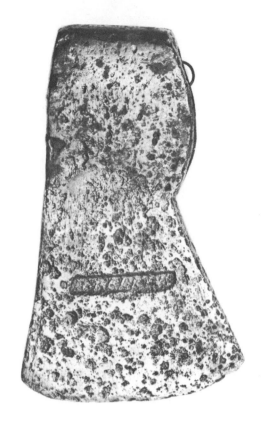

*Tomahawk heads copied from
the Anglo-American felling axe
of the period.
Author's Collection.*

eye or hole was either oval or teardrop-shaped, and there was no thickened poll above the eye, the piece of iron that formed the eye remaining the same thickness on all sides of the hole. The second commonest form of hatchet was a miniature version of the American felling axe of the period, complete with a thickened flat poll opposite the blade and usually with short pointed or rounded ears projecting back along the haft. For both types the handle would have been a straight piece of wood with generally the same cross section as the shape of the eye. *(31)*

Other forms of tomahawk were undoubtedly used also. Two hatchets with hammer polls are known that are marked "US" in large letters typical of the Revolutionary War period, and they may well have been issue items either as weapons for riflemen or tools for regular infantry or artillery. The spiked tomahawk which was popular with colonial troops before the War may also have been used, especially at the beginning, and perhaps even the pipe tomahawk as well. Pipe tomahawks are known to have been carried by white men, and one fine example survives with inlaid patriotic mottoes of the War period. Dated 1777, it is in the Museum of the American Indian. It is safe to assume, however, that pipe tomahawks would never have been issue weapons. They could only have found their way into service among the arms that individual riflemen brought with them when they enlisted. *(32)*

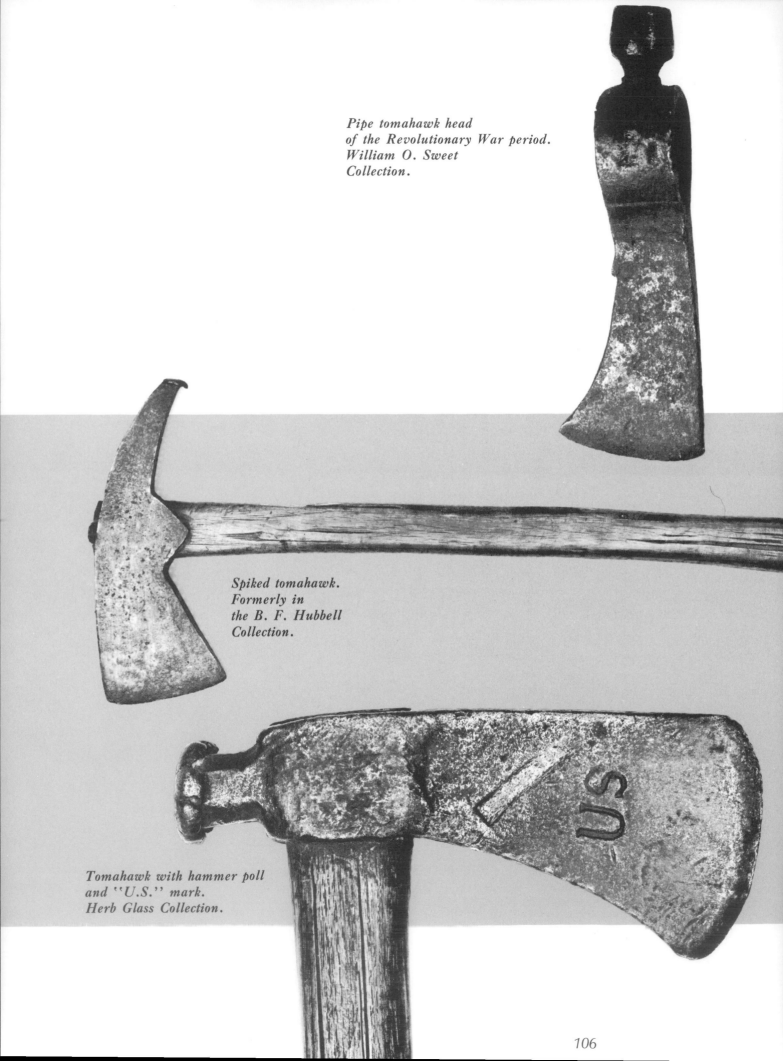

*Pipe tomahawk head
of the Revolutionary War period.
William O. Sweet
Collection.*

*Spiked tomahawk.
Formerly in
the B. F. Hubbell
Collection.*

*Tomahawk with hammer poll
and "U.S." mark.
Herb Glass Collection.*

Knives and Daggers

Along with their tomahawks most riflemen also carried knives. They used them for cutting the cloth patches that they wrapped around their rifle balls when loading; they used them for general woods work; and on occasion they undoubtedly used them for fighting though there are no specific references to this. For the most part riflemen's knives were large single-bladed weapons worn in a sheath on the belt or occasionally on the strap of the hunting bag. They were apt to be rough affairs with blades hand-forged or made from ground-down files. Handles might be wood or antler, but they were usually simple with little shaping and no metal trim. Hand-made knives from the frontier changed very little over the years, and so it is impossible to distinguish between a rifleman's knife of the Revolution and one made perhaps fifty years later for the same general purposes. Luckily, however, one definitely identifiable knifeblade from the Revolution has survived. Found in the parapet of an earthwork thrown up near Fort Ticonderoga in 1777, it could only have been lost at the time, and so it offers at least one reliable guide to the belt knife of the war. It is single-edged and slightly curved with a narrow tang that originally passed through a wooden handle. From hilt to point it is 9 1/2 inches long and 1 1/8 inches wide at the base, a good workable size for whittling, eating, or fighting.

There was also one other form of sheath knife that saw some use in the Continental Army. This was the dagger. Never an official arm or even a popular one, it was nevertheless carried by those few officers who favored a small arm of last resort. One such knife fancier was Captain William Walton of the First North Carolina Regiment, and fortunately his dagger is still preserved in the Smithsonian Institution. It is a relatively plain weapon, undoubtedly of Ameri-

Blade from a rifleman's knife excavated near Fort Ticonderoga. Author's Collection.

107

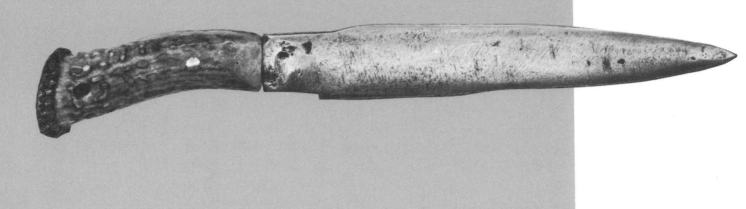

can manufacture. The 6½-inch double-edged blade may have been salvaged from a sword, and the wooden grips and gilded brass mounts also seem to suggest the sword hilt though they were undoubtedly made especially for the purpose. The leather scabbard looks homemade. Since Captain Walton was captured at Charleston in 1780 and undoubtedly lost all his weapons at that time or when he escaped, he probably obtained the surviving dagger when he rejoined his command. If so, it means that daggers were carried all through the war and that they were more than the whim of civilians suddenly become soldiers. A few other daggers of the period but without definite provenience also survive in other collections to indicate that Captain Walton was not unique in carrying such a knife and that specimens of the type range all the way from crudely forged pieces with iron guards and pewter mounts to fine silver-hilted examples with ivory grips. Some are true weapons while others appear more like glorified letter openers. There was apparently a wide choice for any Continental officer who felt inclined to augment his personal arms in such a manner.

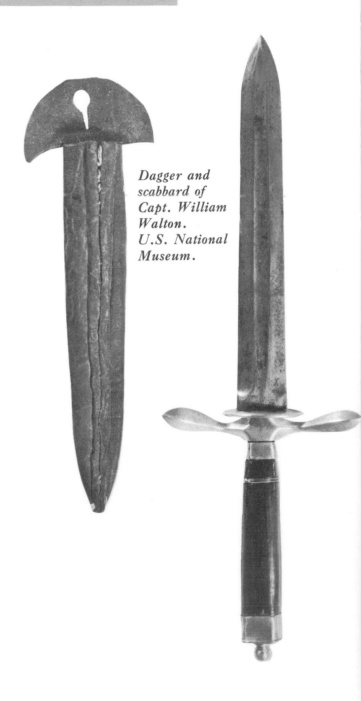

Dagger and scabbard of Capt. William Walton. U.S. National Museum.

Caltrops

Finally in the edged weapon category came the caltrop, though this might also be considered as a piece of engineering equipment. Whatever its classification it was an ingenious and wicked little device that had appeared in warfare at least as early as the Bronze Age. Caltrops were used to defend forts in colonial America, and the British at least employed them in the Revolution. The chances are the Continental Army used them, too. Captain George Smith's military dictionary of 1779 describes the caltrop as "a piece of iron having 4 points, all disposed in a triangular form; so that three of them always rest upon the ground, and the 4th stands upwards in a perpendicular direction. Each point is 3 or 4 inches long. They are scattered over the ground and passages where the enemy is expected to march, especially cavalry, in order to embarrass their progress." *(33)*

James Thacher, however, encountered a slightly different form of the weapon when the Continental Army entered Boston in 1776, and he noted in his journal:

Caltrops.
The large specimen
is forged;
the smaller one
is cut from
a sheet and bent.
Author's Collection.

I accompanied several gentlemen to view the British fortification on Roxbury neck, where I observed a prodigious number of little military engines called caltrops, or crow-feet, scattered over ground in the vicinity of the works to impede the march of our troops in case of an attack. The implement consists of an iron ball armed with four sharp points about one inch in length, so formed that which way soever it may fall one point still lies upwards to pierce the feet of horses or men.... *(34)*

Whether the points were one or four inches long, they were well calculated to disrupt an attack. They were also simple to make, and the combination was enough to recommend them to any defensive commander of the period. Along with the bayonet they remain the only edged weapons used by the Continental Army that are still actively used by major armies today.

Notes to Chapter 4

1. Von Steuben, *Regulations,* 5.

2. Rev. Samuel Webster to the Committee of Safety at Exeter, June 21, 1775, Bouton, *New Hampshire State Papers,* VII, 526. General Sullivan to the Committee of Safety, *ibid.,* 565.

3. *Orderly Book of the Siege of Yorktown,* 5. General Orders, Valley Forge, January 18, 1778, Washington, *Writings,* X, 315. General Orders, Peekskill, August 2, 1780, *ibid.,* XIX, 304.

4. Mark M. Boatner, III, *Encyclopedia of the American Revolution,* New York, 1966, pp. 64, 65, *et passim.*

5. Force, *American Archives,* III, 1496,1497. Minutes of the General Assembly, April 1775, Hoadley, *Connecticut Records,* XIV, 420; May 1775, *ibid.,* XV, 17, 18. "Journal and Correspondence of the Council of Safety, 1775-76," Browne, *Archives of Maryland,* XI, 75. September 28, 1776, McIlwaine, *Journals of the Council of the State of Virginia,* I, 177, 178.

6. Margerand, *Armement,* pp. 48, 49. Bottet, *L'Arme Blanche,* pp. 67, 68. Boudriot, *Armes a Feu, passim.*

7. Margerand, *Armement,* pp. 53-56. Bottet, *L'Arme Blanche,* pp. 28-30.

8. Major Richard Call to Jefferson, March 29, 1781, Palmer and Flournoy, *Calendar of Virginia State Papers,* I, 605. Henry Lee, *Memoirs of the War in the Southern Department,* New York, 1869, p. 91 n.

9. Epaphras Hoyt, *A Treatise on the Military Art,* Brattleborough, 1798, pp. 101, 133.

10. James Hunter to Col. O. Towles, November 22, 1781, Palmer and Flournoy, *Calendar of Virginia State Papers,* II, 618.

11. Washington to the Officer Commanding at Albany, New York, January 1, 1778, Washington, *Writings,* X, 246.

12. An excellent discussion of the evolution of the small sword is given in J. D. Aylward, *The Smallsword in England,* London, 1945.

13. Harold L. Peterson, *American Silver Mounted Swords, 1700-1815,* Washington, 1955, *passim.* This scarce booklet has also been reprinted as a supplement to Peterson, *The American Sword, 1775-1945,* rev. ed., Philadelphia, 1965.

14. Harold L. Peterson, *Arms and Armor in Colonial America, 1526-1783,* Harrisburg, 1956, pp. 279-286.

15. *Ibid.,* pp. 287-289. General Orders, Valley Forge, January 18, 1778, Washington, *Writings,* X, 314.

16. Pickering, *Easy Plan,* Part I, p. 4. General Orders, Valley Forge, December 22, 1777, Washington, *Writings,* X, 190; January 17, 1778, *ibid.,* 311; January 18, 1778, *ibid.,* 314; March 23, 1778, *ibid.,* XI, 133. General Orders, Moore's House, October 12, 1779, *ibid.,* XVI, 458. General Orders, Morristown, April 4, 1780, *ibid.,* XVIII, 215. Von Steuben, *Regulations,* 5.

17. General Orders, Valley Forge, December 22, 1777, Washington, *Writings,* X, 190.

18. Wayne to Washington, July 10, 1779, *Wayne Papers,* V. General Claiborne to Wayne, July 11, 1779, *ibid.* Wayne to Major Posey, August 28, 1779, *ibid.*

19. George F. Scheer and Hugh F. Rankin, *Rebel and Redcoats,* New York, 1957, p. 432, quoting Henry Lee, *The Campaign of 1781 in the Carolinas,* Philadelphia, 1824, pp. 97, 98.

20. Catherine Williams, *Biography of Revolutionary Heroes,* Providence, 1839, p. 277.

21. General Orders, Cambridge, July 14, 1775, Washington, *Writings,* III, 338; February 29, 1776, *ibid.,* IV, 362. General Orders, New York, May 17, 1776, *ibid.,* V, 51; June 6, 1776, *ibid.,* 99; June 7, 1776, *ibid.,* 105; June 8, 1776, *ibid.,* 106; August 12, 1776, *ibid.,* 421; August 14, 1776, *ibid.,* 436. March 20,

1776, Ford, *Journals of the Continental Congress,* IV, 215; March 21, 1776, *ibid.,* 224. Wright, *Notes on the Continental Army,* p. 12.

22. Washington, *Writings,* III, 357.

23. Wright, *Notes on the Continental Army,* p. 12.

24. Dearborn, *Journal,* p. 64. Matthias Ogden, *Journals of Major Matthias Ogden,* Morristown, N. J., 1928, p. 13. Capt. Simeon Thayer, "Journal," in Kenneth Roberts, compiler, *March to Quebec,* New York, 1940, p. 264. Return J. Meigs, "Journal," *ibid.,* p. 187.

25. Washington, *Writings,* VIII, 236.

26. June 20, 1777, Washington, *Writings,* VIII, 272. Washington to Maj. Gen. Thomas Mifflin, June 10, 1777, *ibid.,* 222.

27. Benjamin Flower, Commissary General of Military Stores, to Richard Peters, Secretary of War Office, June 23, 1777, *Washington Papers,* XLIX, 112.

28. Washington to Board of War, July 7, 1777, Washington, *Writings,* VIII, 367.

29. Washington to Pulaski, December 31, 1777, *ibid.,* X, 235. Holst and Zlatich, "Dress and Equipment of Pulaski's Legion," pp. 97-103. Epaphras Hoyt, *Rules and Regulations for Drill, Sabre Exercise, Equitation, Formation and Field Movements of Cavalry,* Greenfield, Mass., 1813, xvi.

30. Harold L. Peterson, *American Indian Tomahawks,,* New York, 1965, pp. 40-42, Holst and Zlatich, "Dress and Equipment of Pulaski's Legion," p. 101.

31. Peterson, *Tomahawks,* pp. 42, 89.

32. *Ibid.,* pp. 42, 100, 139.

33. Smith, *An Universal Military Dictionary,* unpaged, London, 1779. Peterson, *Arms and Armor,* p. 303.

34. James Thacher, *Military Journal of the American Revolution,* Hartford, 1862, p. 42.

Being a

In the eighteenth century the practice of artillery was both an art and a science. Gunners memorized tables giving angles of elevation and ranges for various sizes of guns, howitzers, and mortars as well as other tables that told how long they could expect it to take for

Great Guns
and
Mighty Mortars

survey of the artillery

a projectile to reach its target at these angles and ranges. This was a matter of mathematical science. But every time he fired his piece, the gunner also had to estimate his range by eye, make allowance for wind drift and air resistance, and estimate the probable effect upon

Chapter 5

his target at various points of impact. No mathematical tables could help him here. This was an art. It could be mastered only by a feeling for the business and weeks or months of practice.

In addition to these techniques, the artillerist had many other important fields of study. Firing a piece was a team effort often requiring fourteen or more men. The drill had to be practiced until it was second nature, and efficiency was greatly increased if each man knew the duties of every other person on the team. It was a necessity for the officers and non-commissioned officers to know this, and every matross with any ambition made it his business, too. Officers and gunners also studied the theory of artillery employment. For each size of gun and for each type of target they could recite the proper type of ammunition and aiming point whether in a field encounter or a siege, whether attacking or defending. Furthermore, an artillery officer was supposed to know the theories and techniques of designing and constructing the pieces with which he fought so that he could supervise their production if necessary.

Continental artillerymen looked upon themselves as a class apart. Only the engineers equalled them in specialized training and knowledge. And there was a big difference here, for among the engineers it was only the officers who were trained, while in the artillery many of the enlisted men needed specialized skills and knowledge to perform their tasks. Under the able direction of Henry Knox the artillery got its technical training, and the men learned their jobs thoroughly. Although the Continental artillery was organized into four regular regiments, it did not serve in such units. Instead it was split up and associated with the infantry, usually with four guns to each brigade, while the remaining men and guns formed a reserve and siege unit for the Army. Morale and spirit were high throughout the war, and proficiency improved rapidly in the early months until the British acknowledged wryly after the Battle of Monmouth that "no Artillery could be better served" than that of the Continental Line. In every artillerist's eye that reluctant accolade reinforced their position as the elite of the army. (1)

Types of Artillery Pieces in the Continental Army

When one considers the number of different artillery pieces used during the War this achievement becomes staggering. Simplified systems of artillery had just begun in Europe and the idea had hardly reached America. Besides there was the matter of expediency. The American artillery had to use whatever pieces it could obtain whether American-made, purchased from France, or captured from the British or Hessians. Some of the pieces were relatively new, but others were as much as eighty years old and represented antiquated theories of design. Some were brass or bronze; some were cast iron. Some were based upon the British and American system of inch and pound measurements. Others were manufactured on the French inch and French pound. The latter were a fraction larger and heavier than the American so that, for instance, a French 8-pounder approximately equalled an American or British 9-pounder. At that point there was some interchangeability, but above and below it French pieces either had to be segregated from the others or else rebored to a new size.

There were, in all, at least the following pieces of artillery in general service during the War: 1-, 3-, 4-, 6-, 9-, 12-, and 24-pounder guns; 4½-, 5½-, 8-, 10-, 13-, and 16-inch mortars; 5½- and 8-inch howitzers, all of brass. In addition there were 1-, 2-, 3-, 4-, 6-, 9-, 12-, 18-, 24-, and 32-pounder guns; 13-inch mortars; 18-pounder carronades, and 3½-inch howitzers of iron. Judged by the standards of later years this is a staggering array of different pieces, each one requiring its own ammunition and its own special handling. Normally the brass 3-, 4-, and 6-pounder guns and sometimes the howitzers were attached to the infantry brigades. The 12- and 24-pounders were held out as weapons for defending a fixed position. The siege artillery, used for attacking a fortified enemy position, included the iron 18-, 24-, and 32-pounder guns, the iron 13-inch mortar, and the brass 5½-, 8-, and 10-inch mortars. *(2)*

Some idea of the complexity of an American artillery train can be obtained from Henry Knox's estimates of the needs for the campaign in 1778:

Brigade artillery, seventeen brigades, with four guns each, sixty-eight pieces to be 3, 4, or 6-pounders; with the park, two 24-pounders, four 12-pounders, four 8-inch howitzers, eight 5½-inch howitzers, ten 3 or 4-pounders, ten 6-pounders; for the *reserve*, to be kept at a proper distance from camp, thirty 3, 4, and 6-pounders, two 12-pounders, one 24-pounder; all the foregoing brigade, park, and reserve guns and howitzers *to be of brass.* In addition, twelve 18-pounders, twelve 12-pounders, battering pieces, on travelling carriages, together with two 5½-inch and twelve 8, 9, and 10-inch mortars; the battering pieces and mortars to be of *cast-iron. (3)*

Guns

Each of these types of cannon had a specific purpose. Guns were relatively long pieces, weighing from 150 to more than 200 times the weight of their projectile. All of them were smooth bores. Practical rifled cannon had not yet developed. Since they were intended primarily for firing solid shot, guns were given designations based upon the weight of the spherical iron balls they threw. Thus a 3-pounder gun fired a 3-pound ball; a 6-pounder threw a ball weighing 6 pounds, and so on. These guns were designed to fire with a flat trajectory and a high velocity. Depending upon size, guns developed muzzle velocities of 900 to 1,300 feet per second and commanded maximum ranges from about 1,200 to well over 2,000 yards. They were seldom fired at such ranges, however. The lateral deflection caused by the drift of a spherical ball fired from a smooth bore was so great that it would have been impossible to hit any but the largest target at such distances. Effective ranges, where a gunner could be reasonably sure of coming close to his objective, ran well under 1,000 yards for solid shot and less for other types of projectiles. Another factor that curtailed ranges was the method of aiming. Indirect aiming had not yet been developed. A gunner had to be able to see his target to lay his gun and to judge the effect of his shot so that he could compensate for any error in the pointing or elevation. This could best be done under 500 yards against another army in the field. Sieges which offered big targets in the form of fortifications or houses permitted greater distances. (4)

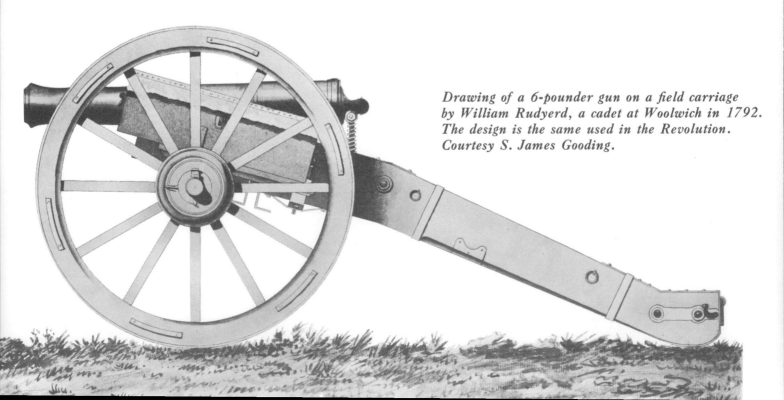

Drawing of a 6-pounder gun on a field carriage by William Rudyerd, a cadet at Woolwich in 1792. The design is the same used in the Revolution. Courtesy S. James Gooding.

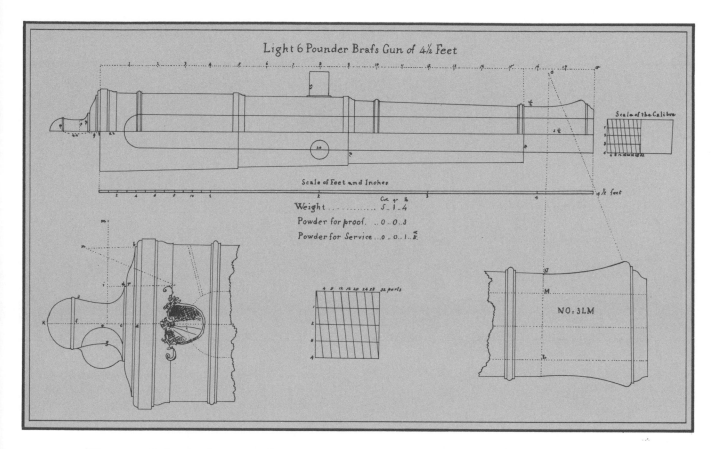

Light 6 Pounder Brafs Gun of 4½ Feet

Scale of Feet and Inches

Weight . . . . 5 . . 1 . . 4

Powder for proof . . 0 . . 0 . . 3

Powder for Service . . . 0 . . 0 . . 1 . . ½

Diagram of 6-pounder gun tube
by William Rudyerd.
Courtesy S. James Gooding.

Howitzers

Howitzers were much shorter and lighter than guns. Often their bores were only three calibers long, and there was usually a narrowed chamber at the base of the bore to hold the powder charge. These pieces were designed for firing shell, grapeshot and other anti-personnel projectiles. With their short barrels and special carriages, howitzers could be fired either horizontally like a gun for short-range work or at a higher elevation to lob shells over a fort wall or similar obstruction. Because they were not designed to fire solid shot, howitzers were designated according to the diameter of their bore as 5½-inch, 8-inch, etc. (5)

*Section of an 8-inch howitzer
on its carriage
by William Rudyerd.
Courtesy S. James Gooding.*

Mortars

Mortars were the shortest pieces of all. They were made to fire shell only at high elevations. Some were even fixed on their beds at an angle of 45°-70° so that the range could be controlled only by the amount of powder. Mortars were the principal weapon for hurling projectiles inside an enemy fort. Like howitzers, they were chambered for the powder charge, and they were also designated according to the diameters of their bores. (6)

Mortar on bed. National Park Service, U.S. Department of the Interior.

Decoration and Markings

No matter whether they were guns, howitzers, or mortars, the artillery pieces of the Revolutionary War were not the streamlined simple tubes of a later day. Both brass and iron specimens boasted decorative moldings at the breech and at each of the major sections of the barrel as well as at the muzzle, which flared out from the chase in a graceful muzzle swell. Almost all bronze pieces bore decorative handles called dolphins on top of the barrel. These were used in lifting the pieces on and off their carriages or beds. Sometimes they were actually sculptured to resemble dolphins. At other times they bore leaf designs or the representation of some real or imaginary creature. And there were other marks and decorations as well. Most of the

English howitzer mounted on its carriage. West Point Museum.

French pieces that fell into Continental hands were of the so-called Système Vallière. These pieces were characterized by sculptured cascabel knobs with a different design for each caliber—a lion's head for 4-pounders, an ape's head for 8-pounders, and a rooster for 12's. In addition there were also relief decorations including military trophies, the lillies of France, and a motto such as *"Ultimo Ratio Regum"* (Ultimate Argument of Kings). Usually the name of the piece itself appeared on the chase just behind the muzzle swell. In most instances the name of the founder and the date and place of manufacture were cast or chiseled on the breech ring. *(7)*

British pieces were almost as decorative. Usually the monogram of the king appeared near the breech. The monogram of the master general of the ordnance under whom the piece was cast might also appear on the chase, and the broad arrow denoting government ownership was almost always chiseled on the top of the tube. On brass pieces the name of the founder and the place and date of manufacture sometimes appeared on the breech ring as it did on French pieces. And on each piece its actual weight was usually inscribed either on the breech ring, on the breech itself or just above the cascabel knob. For British pieces this weight was always given in hundredweights as a series of three figures separated by a dash or a dot as, for instance, 17-3-1. In this series the first number represents the hundredweights, the second the quarters of hundredweights, and the last the remaining pounds. Since the British hundredweight actually weighed 112 pounds, the weight would be translated as follows: 17 x 112 plus 3 x 28 plus 1, or 1,989 pounds. *(8)*

American-made artillery pieces varied tremendously. Some of them were simple and crude with only rudimentary moldings and no marks whatsoever. Others were fine examples of the molder's art with raised designs of liberty caps, sunbursts, and other patriotic motifs as well as the name of the founder and the date of manufacture.

Carriages and Beds

For use, guns and howitzers were mounted on wheeled carriages. Mortars were usually mounted on beds. The standard field or travelling carriage had two wheels for mobility. The tube itself was mounted between two planks which formed a trail. One end of this trail rested on the ground; the other was supported by the axle of the wheels. Three cross braces called transoms held the sidepieces in proper relation to each other and supported the mechanism for elevating or depressing the tube. This mechanism might be either an elevating screw for the usual field piece or a wedge

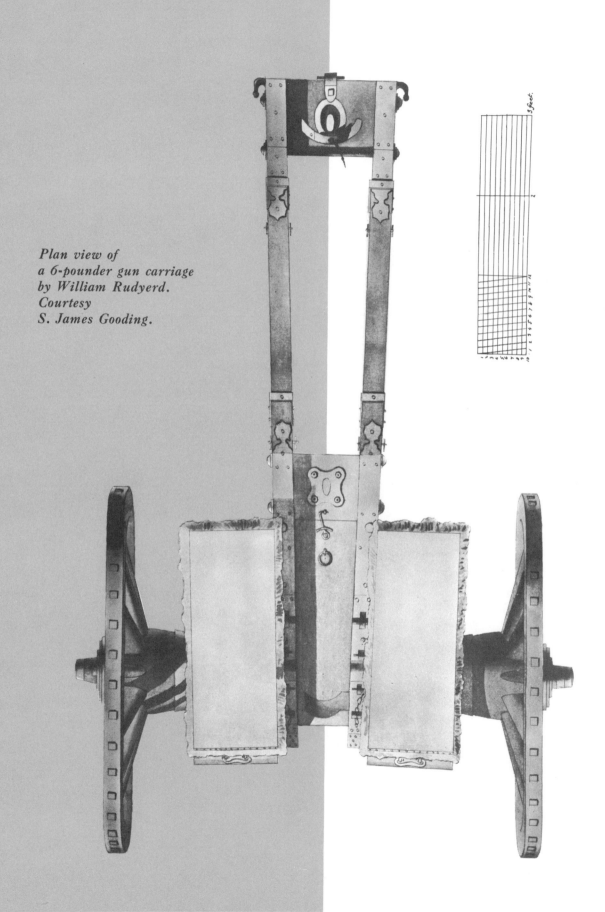

Plan view of
a 6-pounder gun carriage
by William Rudyerd.
Courtesy
S. James Gooding.

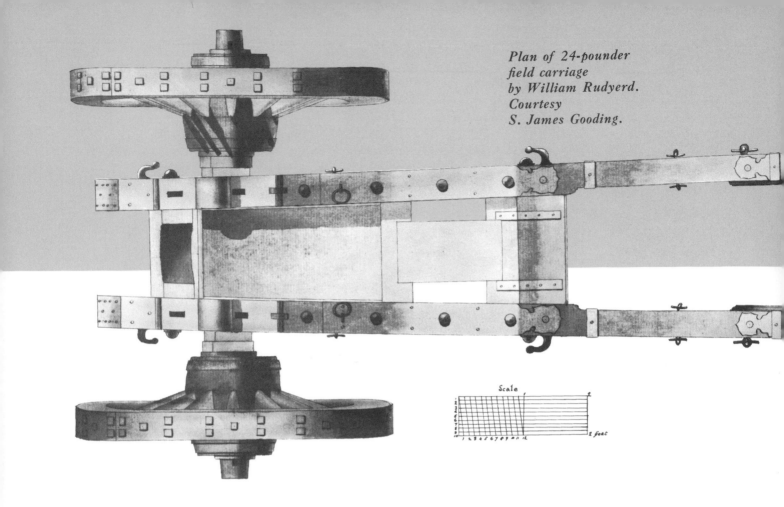

Plan of 24-pounder
field carriage
by William Rudyerd.
Courtesy
S. James Gooding.

Scale

2 feet

for the heavier cannon. Americans, however, sometimes used wedges on lighter pieces because the heavy metal elevating screws were hard to obtain. The rear or trail transom was pierced with an iron-lined hole which hooked over a pintle on a two-wheeled cart called a limber when it was desired to move the cannon from one place to another. In effect, coupling the carriage with the limber created a four-wheeled wagon ready to drive.

Almost all of the cannon carriages used by the Continental artillery during the Revolution were of the British pattern or as close a copy of it as American artificers could produce. Some very few French carriages of the Vallière system were imported, but usually just the tubes were shipped. Carriages, after all, could be made here without a great deal of difficulty, and the precious cargo space was reserved for items more difficult to produce in America. France had adopted the fine new Gribeauval system

of artillery just before the outbreak of the war, but it seems certain that no Gribeauval barrels or carriages ever fell into the hands of American artillerists. It is probable that American gunners saw them in the French artillery train at Yorktown, but British designs remained standard for Americans throughout the war and the years thereafter. It was not until 1809 that the Gribeauval system was adopted for American service. (9)

The reasons for the popularity of the British artillery designs were similar to those for the ascendancy of British musket patterns in the early years of the war. They were the familiar patterns, learned through more than 200 years as British colonies. But there was one other factor as well. In 1757 John Muller, a professor of fortification and artillery at the Royal Military Academy, Woolwich, had published a book entitled *A Treatise on Artillery*. Revised and enlarged a few years later as *A Treatise of Artillery*, it became a highly influential volume,

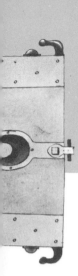

especially in America. Knox and other American artillery officers studied it carefully. It was the only manual on artillery design and construction available to American artificers and ordnance officers during the war, and indeed a pirated edition was actually published in Philadelphia in 1779 and dedicated to "George Washington, General Henry Knox and Officers of the Continental Artillery"! Thus it became the standard handbook for carriage construction, and Muller, who had experienced difficulty in getting some of his ideas and refinements accepted in England, found himself much more successful in America. (10)

These British-style field or travelling carriages were called bracket trail carriages. The two long sidepieces spread out slightly from the front to the rear, and the wheels on all were 51 inches in diameter. Field guns, whose bore was relatively small in proportion to their size, boasted two side boxes to carry a supply of ammunition immediately available. These boxes rested on a platform fastened to the trails and supported by the axle. They were made in two major pieces, the lower platform including a tray to hold

Galloper carriage.
National Park Service,
U.S. Department
of the Interior.

the cannon balls, and an upper detatchable box holding the bagged charges of powder. Extra ammunition and the ammunition for the bigger guns, the howitzers and mortars were hauled in separate wagons. The limbers consisted only of a pair of wheels, usually slightly smaller than the wheels on the carriage itself, an axle with a pintle on which to hook the trail transom, and a pair of shafts for harnessing the team of horses required to pull the piece. In the British system this team was hitched in tandem, that is, single-file with one horse in the shafts and the others directly in front of it. Despite the inefficiency of this arrangement it worked reasonably well on the lighter pieces. (11)

There was also one other type of carriage for the light field pieces. Called a galloper carriage, it was sometimes used for the 1 1/2-, 2-, and 3-pounders. Instead of the usual trail it boasted a pair of shafts so that a single horse could be hitched directly to it. Colloquially this carriage was sometimes called a grasshopper to distinguish it from the light guns with limbers which were called butterflies. These terms, however, were used confusingly, and some officers at the time objected to them because of it. (12)

Howitzer carriages were similar to gun carriages except that they had shorter trails. The short trails permitted greater elevations of the muzzle for lobbing shells over obstructions. (13)

Mortars were normally mounted on beds without wheels. In their simplest forms these beds were great blocks of wood hollowed out to receive the breech of the mortar and permit it to pivot on its trunnions. Elevation was controlled by means of a wedge driven beneath the tube from the front. In

Garrison carriage
with iron wheels
drawn by William Rudyerd.
Courtesy S. James Gooding.

*Rear view of port
waist gun of the Philadelphia
with a swivel gun
on the starboard gunwale
in the foreground.
U.S. National Museum.*

*Waist gun of the Philadelphia
on original ship's carriage.
U.S. National Museum.*

*Bow gun of the Philadelphia
with sliding track carriage.
U.S. National Museum.*

some instances, however, mortars were mounted on a stock trail carriage and fired like howitzers, but this only happened when necessity required it. *(14)*

Finally there were two other types of artillery carriages which seem to have been used at least to a small extent by the Continental Army. One was the garrison carriage, a substantial vehicle with solid sides and four small wheels or trucks. These carriages could not be moved around rapidly as could the field or travelling carriages with their big wheels. They were used primarily to defend permanent fortifications. Since the Continental Army held Fort Ticonderoga, West Point, and one or two other similar though smaller installations during the war, it is probable that a good number of these garrison carriages were used. British recommendations called for iron wheels for these mounts, and Continental specimens followed this suggestion at least in some instances even though solid wooden wheels were much easier to make than cast iron ones. *(15)*

When wooden trucks were used the garrison carriage became identical with the naval carriage. Strange as it may seem, the Continental Army actually employed such naval carriages—on board ship! When a small American fleet was built in 1776 to slow down the British advance on Lake Champlain, it was manned by soldiers of the Continental Army and commanded by General Benedict Arnold. The gun boats in this fleet mounted cannon on naval carriages. Fortunately one of the vessels, the *Philadelphia,* has been recovered to show both guns and their carriages in their original position. There are two waist guns mounted on traditional naval carriages and one bow gun on which the trucks have been removed in favor of a sliding track. Interestingly two of the guns are of Swedish manufacture. All three of these surviving guns are iron. *(16)*

Carriages and beds of all types were made of wood with iron mountings. Oak was the preferred material for the principal mem-

bers, but there is evidence that other woods, including walnut and chestnut, were used on occasion. Elm and beech were recommended for the wheels, but hickory also sometimes appeared. In emergencies almost any hard and tough wood was pressed into service. *(17)*

Both wood and iron needed paint for preservation. The iron barrels of the pieces themselves were always painted black, and the mountings of the carriages were also painted black as a general rule. On some occasions, however, the mountings seem to have had only a coat of a red lead. Probably this was caused by a shortage of paint. The wooden parts of the carriages, on the other hand, seem to have been painted a variety of colors. At the beginning of the war there is evidence that the Americans painted their carriages the same light lead gray color that the British Army favored. On November 30, 1776, for instance, General Philip Schuyler requisitioned sufficient materials "to paint 250 carriages of a lead colour...." The Charles Willson Peale portrait of Washington at Princeton shows him leaning against a gray gun carriage, and the painting of the Battle of Princeton by William Mercer, done shortly after the event and accurate in all verifiable details, shows a similar gray carriage. At the same time, however, the Mercer painting also illustrates a red brown carriage. This may have been intended to indicate an imported Vallière System carriage since these were customarily painted red in France or it might have been an American carriage, for there is documentary evidence that American carriages were sometimes painted that color, too. By 1780 there are references to painting carriages blue, perhaps under the influence of the French, who had changed to that color when they adopted the Gribeauval System. Before the end of the war blue seems to have become standard for American carriages, and it remained so through the War of 1812. *(18)*

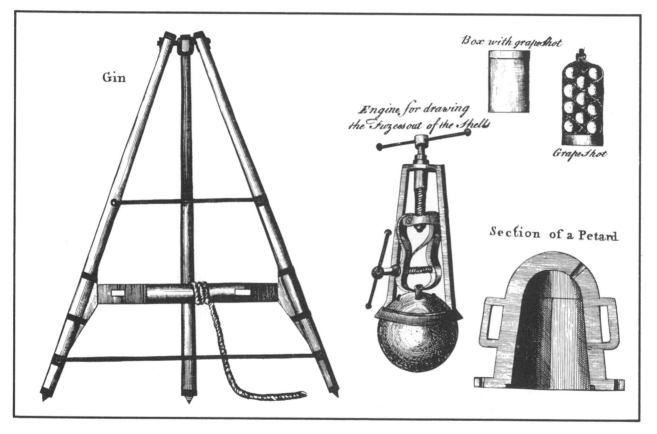

Gin

Box with grapeshot

Engine for drawing
the Fuzes out of the Shells

GrapeShot

Section of a Petard

*Plate from John Muller's
Treatise of Artillery,
showing among other
things a petard
and both canister
and grapeshot.*

Two types of artillery pieces of the Revolution served without
carriages. These were the petard and the swivel gun. The petard was
a short heavy piece like a mortar used for blowing down doors or
gates of fortifications. Usually it was shaped like a frustrum of a cone
with the smaller end rounded off. As a general rule there were two
handles for carrying, and around the larger end there was a lip pierced
with holes for attaching a heavy plank. To use a petard it was loaded
full of powder, and the plank was screwed on. A detail of men then

dashed up and fastened it to a door or gateway by means of hooks on the plank, and set it off. This was a highly dangerous operation, and it had almost been abandoned by the time of the Revolution. Nevertheless the American forces that invaded Canada took some petards with them, and they were duly listed in the captured stores after the disastrous siege of Quebec which ended in May 1776. Two more were listed in American hands at Fort Ticonderoga the next year. *(19)*

Swivel Guns

English swivel gun,
a ¾-pounder,
from the Philadelphia.
U.S. National Museum.

The swivel gun was usually a 1- or possibly a 2-pounder, similar in all respects to the pieces used for mounting on grasshopper carriages. In the instances when it was used as a swivel, however, it was equipped with an iron yoke similar to a huge oarlock. The trunnions fitted into loops on the upper extremities of the yoke, and the pintle was fitted into a socket in the gunwale of a boat or in a stout post set in the ground. Such swivels were used on the boats of the Army's fleet on Lake Champlain, and they were also mounted in many a field fort. Since they offered longer range than any of the small arms and yet were light enough to carry easily they were a popular form of artillery, and they served their purpose well.

*Swivel gun with socket
and pointing pole.
National Park Service,
U.S. Department of the Interior.*

Service of the Piece

Two men could load and fire a swivel gun. Loading was little different from a musket, and all it took to fire was one man to aim and hold the piece in position and another to apply the fire to the vent. Loading and firing a larger piece, whether siege, field or garrison, however, was a more complicated process. Guns and howitzers required crews of men ranging in number from eight or nine for garrison pieces or those too heavy to be moved by drag ropes to fourteen or fifteen for the popular field 6-pounders. With one of the 6-pounders the first six men manned the drag ropes. When prepared for action they stood three on either side of the carriage opposite the wheels. Number 7 stood at the right of the muzzle with the sponge and rammer to push home the charge and to sponge out the barrel between shots. Number 8 stood at the left of the muzzle and actually placed the ammunition in the barrel. Number 9 stood to the right of the breech and served the vent, covering the hole with his thumb in a protective covering while Number 7 sponged and rammed. This prevented smoldering pieces of cartridge cloth or paper from being forced up into the vent, and it also created a suction as the rammer was withdrawn that helped put out any sparks that might have survived the sponging. Such sparks were always a worry, for they might set off a charge as it was being rammed home with dire consequences to Number 7 and possibly to other members of the crew. Number 9 probably also primed the vent before firing. Number 10, on the opposite side of the breech, held the lighted portfire and fired the piece upon command by reaching over the wheel and touching the flaming compound to the primer in the vent. Number 11 manned a lever called a handspike that fitted into a socket in the trail transom. With it he pointed the gun as directed by the officer in charge. Number 12 stood clear of the trail transom on the right side and held the water bucket, the linstock with its lighted wick or match for igniting portfires, and a spare portfire in a holder ready to supply Number 10 upon demand. Number 13 was a runner who carried ammunition from Number 14's supply to Number 8, who placed the load in the gun. Number 15 also presided over a supply of ammunition, and at the same time he held the limber horse. The civilian driver who did not count in the crew had meantime unhitched the lead horse and led him around to the rear. (20)

This was the ideal crew. In action the functions were often carried on with fewer men as casualties depleted the number available. Mortars which did not have to be dragged and which had no limber could be fired with a much smaller crew although all of the other services of sponging, loading, pointing and firing had to be carried out in the same general manner. With pieces such as mortars and howitzers firing explosive shells, the men handling ammunition had the additional task of setting the fuses properly before they handed the projectile to the runner. All in all, the firing of a muzzle-loading artillery piece was a complicated procedure requiring careful teamwork, a sense of rhythm and weeks of practice. In the best crews every man practiced each position until he could function in any spot an emergency might require. At such times officers pitched in, and so occasionally did artillerists' wives, including Margaret Corbin and Molly Pitcher, both of whom are reported to have served the Number 7 and Number 13 positions, two of the most demanding positions in the crew.

Artillery Equipment

The equipment with which these crews worked has been touched on briefly in describing their tasks. First of all there was the rammer used by Number 7. This was a staff slightly longer than the bore of the gun. One end was enlarged so that it almost fit the bore. This was the end he used for seating the charge. On smaller guns the other end usually bore a sponge either with bristles or covered in lamb's wool that the user dipped in a bucket of water before swabbing the bore. Sometimes there was an extra rammer with a corkscrew-like device on the opposite end. This was called a worm or a wad hook. It was used both for pulling out the wad which held a charge in place if it was desired to unload a piece without firing and for removing the residue of cartridge fragments that sometimes built up in a piece during firing. For bigger guns the rammers, sponges and worms were made as separate implements. There was also one other hafted implement carried but seldom employed. This was the powder ladle. It consisted of a pole with a copper ladle to hold one measured charge of powder. It was not used when loading with cartridges, and loose powder was only employed in emergencies when cartridges could not be obtained. At the other end of the piece, Number 9 protected his thumb from the hot metal of the gun breech with a padded leather cover called a thumb stall or finger stall. Usually it had laces so that it could be tied in place. Other bits of equipment included sharp picks that could be run down through the vent after the charge was in place to puncture the cartridge cloth and expose the powder inside. Sometimes a powder horn was used to pour a priming charge down the vent and leave a small mound on top to be ignited by the portfire. Other times a primer made of a tube of paper or the quill of a feather filled with a quick-burning compound was used.

The portfire used by Number 10 was also a tube of quick-burning composition, usually powder mixed with alcohol. He held it in a stick with a socket in one end called a portfire holder. Since portfires burned rapidly and with a hot flame they had a relatively short life. Number 12 kept a spare one ready in a holder and when the one in use showed signs of burning out, he lit a new one from the slow match smoldering in his linstock. This linstock or lint stock was a short staff with a forked end. Both ends of the fork bore clamps to hold the burning ends of the match, a loosely twisted hemp

rope that had been soaked in a solution of saltpeter or sugar of lead.

Number 11 used heavy wooden levers called handspikes for shifting the trail of the carriage to the right or left. There were two types of these levers. One was straight. The other, called a crooked handspike, was slightly curved at the tip. Each had a shaped forward end which fitted the rings on the trail transom and thus gave the man who manipulated it a purchase on the trail of the carriage.

In addition to these tools, there were also large haversacks sometimes called cartouches for holding and carrying ammunition, and there was an interesting little implement for extreme situations. This was a soft iron wire just small enough in diameter to pass through the hole of the vent, and it was used for spiking a cannon that had to be abandoned to the enemy. At such times, an artillerist took one of these spikes and inserted it in the vent of the piece until the

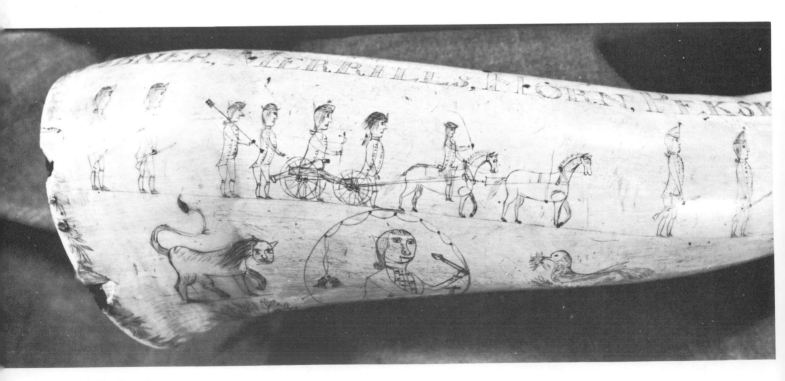

A limbered gun
with the horses in tandem hitch
as shown on a
Revolutionary War powder horn.
Author's Collection.

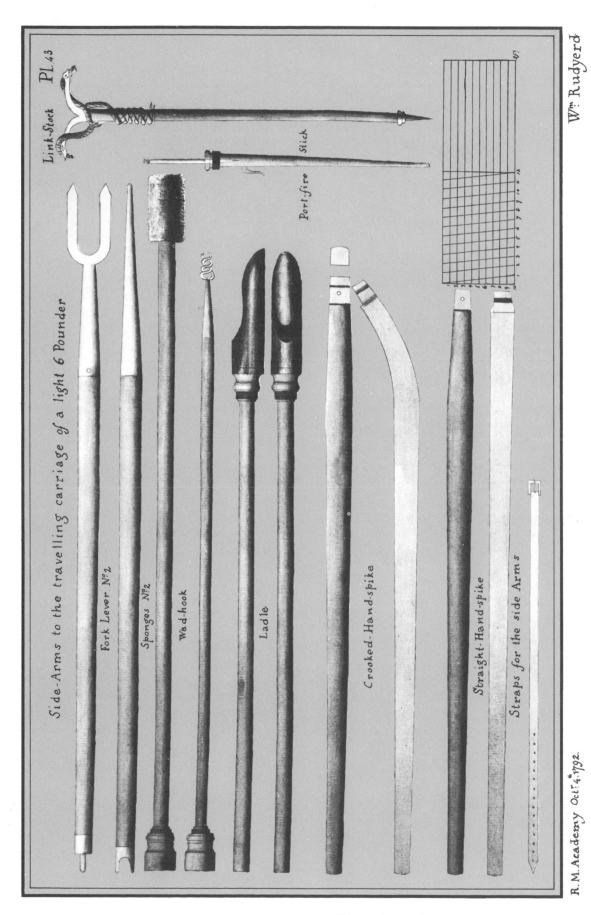

Gunner's implements
as drawn by William Rudyerd.
Courtesy S. James Gooding.

lower end rested on the bottom of the bore. Then he proceeded to hit it with a hammer until the lower end bent over and clinched so that it could not be pulled out again. Sometimes these spikes had one end split in the hopes that they would spread out like a cotter pin. A well-spiked gun was utterly useless to its captors until a trained artificer bored out the spike. Even then it was sometimes necessary to rebush the vent before the piece could be returned to service.

Artillery Instruments

Artillery officers also occasionally had tools or instruments to help them perform their tasks. The most common of these was the quadrant, an L-shaped bar with an arc across the angle where the arms joined. This arc was laid off in degrees and minutes. To use the quadrant the officer laid the long arm of the instrument on the bottom of the bore with the short arm pointing down. A string with a weight of lead at its free end was pivoted in the angle of the two arms, and its position as it crossed the arc gave the angle at which the piece was elevated. A second tool was a set of gunner's calipers. This handy instrument could be used as outside calipers for measuring solid shot, and it gave the actual weight of the projectile as well as its diameter. By reversing the arms, the same instrument could be used for measuring the inside of a gun bore, and here again it gave both the diameter and the weight of the solid shot which that gun would throw. With both arms in a straight line it offered a foot rule, while another scale

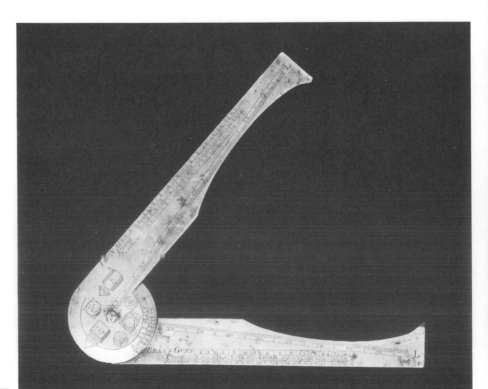

Gunner's calipers, mid-eighteenth century. Author's Collection.

served as a protractor when the arms were moved. In addition, tables of proof and service charges, specific gravities of various materials, and other useful information were engraved on the sides. With the quadrant and the calipers an artillery officer was well equipped with the instruments of his day, but instruments of all kinds were scarce. Many had to function without even these, let alone such esoteric baubles as gunner's levels for determining the line of sight when the wheels of a carriage were on uneven ground. After all, this was something that any experienced gunner should be able to judge by eye and confirm with a test shot or two. *(21)*

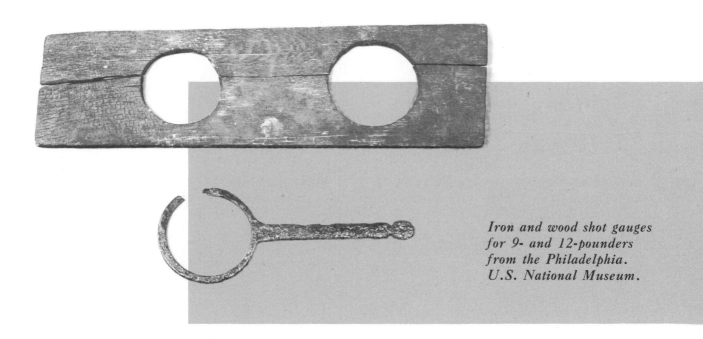

Iron and wood shot gauges for 9- and 12-pounders from the Philadelphia. U.S. National Museum.

Artillery Ammunition

Such shots, as mentioned before, might be solid spheres of iron, explosive shells, anti-personnel projectiles that scattered shot or even incendiaries. The solid shot was fired from guns and used for battering purposes, for counter-battery fire in the hope of smashing an enemy cannon and carriage, or for anti-personnel purposes when the enemy was in mass formations at a considerable distance. There were also double-ended or crossbar shot which looked somewhat like exercise dumbbells. These were sometimes used against troops but more often against ships, where they were especially designed to cut rigging as they whirled through the air. Such shot were almost never used by field guns, but they were sometimes kept in stores at such forts as Ticonderoga where there might be ships as targets.

Shells were specifically anti-personnel. They consisted of a hollow iron sphere filled with a charge of powder. A tapered wooden fuse pierced and filled with a quick-burning compound was driven into a hole in the shell just prior to firing. The flash of the powder charge in the piece firing the shell lit this fuse, which then burned through and set off the charge inside the shell. By regulating the length of the fuse the gunner could control at least in a rough manner the length of time before the shell would burst. Airbursts over the heads of enemy troops were theoretically possible though it was difficult to control the fuses that precisely. The favorite trick of gunners firing shell at enemy troops formed in line of battle was the ricochet shot. In employing this they tried to cause a shell to land, bounce, and roll along as near the line of troops as possible. As it rolled along, its fuse burned and eventually it would explode. This was especially useful against green troops. It was difficult for them to watch shells rolling past the front of their line, knowing that they might explode any moment with deadly effects. Often they broke and ran. Veterans learned to stand fast no matter what, but then the shells could be made to bounce into the lines, destroying men with their battering force as well as with the flying fragments when they exploded. Mortars, of course, threw bigger shells into enemy fortifications where they exploded, hurling fragments at the men who were protected from direct shots by the fort walls. (22)

For direct anti-personnel work at short ranges, the standard projectile was grapeshot. A stand of grape consisted of a wooden disc called a sabot with a vertical spindle inserted in it. Around this spindle were clustered a number of small iron balls held in place by a covering of canvas or burlap quilted with cord. When this projectile was fired the wrapping came apart and the shot scattered much like the buckshot fired by a musket. It was deadly at close quarters but useless at long range because the small shot scattered too widely and also tended to lose momentum quickly. Another anti-

personnel scatter projectile called case or cannister shot was also known. In this round the shot were packed in a tinned iron cylinder or can fastened on a wooden base. It also disintegrated upon firing and scattered its contents like a modern shotgun shell. It was a more efficient package than grape, but it was also more difficult to manufacture. It had been known since at least the seventeenth century, and by the time of the American Civil War it had supplanted grape for field guns, but it was apparently little used during the Revolution. (23)

The principal incendiary projectile of the Revolution was the carcass. This was either a spherical ball or one shaped somewhat like the modern football. It consisted of a framework of iron rods and was filled with pitch, sulphur, saltpeter, gunpowder, bits of iron, glass, tallow, and other odds and ends. The outside was covered with a pitch-soaked cloth. The propelling charge set the carcass afire, and it burned with a hot, almost inextinguishable flame. Carcasses were thrown by mortars, and the usual targets were enemy buildings or ships. (24)

Another form of incendiary that was occasionally used was the hot shot. This was a standard solid shot heated red-hot in a furnace and fired from a gun. It was a tricky form of shooting. Special tools were required for handling the hot shot, and a wad of turf had to be inserted between the shot and the powder charge to keep the red-hot iron from setting the gun off prematurely. When they struck a wooden or canvas target, however, these shot were usually very effective in starting fires, and they were particularly useful against ships. At Yorktown, for instance, several vessels of the British fleet were set afire and sunk by just such hot shot from the allied batteries. (25)

The powder charges which propelled all of these projectiles were normally packaged in cartridges. Such cartridges were actually bags of cloth or paper filled with the proper amount of propellant and sewed or tied shut. Flannel was the preferred material for cartridge bags, but parchment was considered satisfactory, and in an emergency any stout paper or readily combustible cloth could be pressed into service. For most of the bigger guns and all the mortars and howitzers, the powder charge and the projectile were usually loaded separately. For the smaller guns, however, artillerists often employed fixed ammunition with the shot and the propellant fastened together. Grapeshot and case or cannister shot were normally made with a wooden base or sabot. For fixed ammunition this sabot was grooved to receive a stout cord that held the powder bag in place. When they desired to fix round shot, artificers fastened it to a similar sabot with straps of tinned iron that crossed over the ball and were nailed fast at both ends. Fixed ammunition was more complicated to manufacture, but it cut loading time almost in half, and artillerists were happy to have it on hand. To them a few seconds' loading time could sometimes mean the difference between success and failure, between breaking an enemy charge and being overrun by it. (26)

Actually, however, this difference between success and failure depended upon many things. The type of ammunition was only important if the gun crew was well trained, if each man knew his job well and could perform it swiftly and courageously in the face of danger, and if his officers had mastered both the art and the science of eighteenth-century artillery.

Notes to Chapter 5

1. General Orders, June 29, 1778, Headquarters, Freehold, Washington, *Writings*, XII, 131. William E. Birkhimer, *Historical Sketch of the Organization, Administration, Matériel and Tactics of the Artillery, United States Army*, Washington, 1884, *passim*.

2. Birkhimer, *Artillery*, p. 275.

3. *Ibid.*

4. John Muller, *A Treatise of Artillery*, London, 1768, *passim*. The most useful edition of Muller for the scholar is a 1965 reprint by the Museum Restoration Service, Ottawa, Ontario, Canada, which adds contemporary pictures to supplement those in the original. Jac Weller, "The Artillery of the American Revolution," Part I, *Military Collector & Historian*, VIII, No. 3 (Fall 1956), 61-65.

5. *Ibid.*

6. *Ibid.*

7. Louis Napoleon and Col. Favé, *Etudes sur la Passé et l'Avenir de l'Artillerie*, 6 vols., Paris, 1846-1871, IV, 67-91. George L. Clark, *Silas Deane*, New York, 1913, pp. 80-100.

8. S. James Gooding, *An Introduction to British Artillery in North America*, "Historical Arms Series" No. 4, Ottawa, 1965, *passim*.

9. Birkhimer, *Artillery*, pp. 223-229. General Orders, Valley Forge, December 21, 1777, Washington, *Writings*, X, 181.

10. *Ibid.*

11. Muller, *Treatise*, pp. 94-138. Smith, *Military Dictionary*.

12. Muller, *Treatise*, pp. 115, 116. Smith, *Military Dictionary*. Maj. Gen. James Pattison, *Official Letters of Maj. Gen. James Pattison* in Collections of the New-York Historical Society, New York, 1876, p. 115.

13. Muller, *Treatise*, pp. 119-125. Smith, *Military Dictionary*.

14. *Ibid.* "Diary of the Pennsylvania Line, May 26, 1781-April 25, 1782," John B. Linn and William H. Egle, eds., *Pennsylvania in the War of the Revolution*, 2 vols., Harrisburg, 1880, II, 693, 694.

15. Muller, *Treatise*, pp. 94-99. Smith, *Military Dictionary*.

16. *Ibid.*

17. Muller, *Treatise*, pp. 107, 108.

18. Calculation for Ordnance Stores for the Northern Department, November 30, 1776, manuscript in the Fort Ticonderoga Museum library. Account of painting work done in the Ordnance Yard at Philadelphia, January 1780, Record Group 93, item 21128, National Archives.

19. Muller, *Treatise*, pp. 145-147. Smith, *Military Dictionary*. "A Journal of Carleton's and Burgoyne's Campaigns," *Bulletin of the Fort Ticonderoga Museum*, XI, No. 5 (December 1964), 236; No. 6 (September 1965), 320.

20. Manuscript notebook of an artillery cadet at Woolwich, c. 1790, in the Smithsonian Institution. Washington to Maj. Gen. Philip Schuyler, July 24, 1777, Washington, *Writings*, VIII, 457, 458.

21. John Robertson, *A Treatise of such Mathematical Instruments as are usually put into a Portable Case... with an Appendix containing the Description and Use of the Gunners Callipers...*, 3rd ed., London, 1775, pp. 148-205.

22. Smith, *Military Dictionary*. Muller, *Treatise*, pp. 161-163.

23. Smith, *Military Dictionary*. "A Military, Historical and Explanatory Dictionary," in Thomas Simes, *The Military Guide for Young Officers*, 2nd ed., London, 1776. Muller, *Treatise*, p. 161.

24. Smith, *Military Dictionary*. Muller, *Treatise*, p. 206.

25. Henry P. Johnston, *The Yorktown Campaign and the Surrender of Cornwallis*, New York, 1881, p. 140.

26. Manuscript notebook of an artillery cadet at Woolwich, c. 1790, in Smithsonian Institution. Smith, *Military Dictionary*. Muller, *Treatise*, pp. 201, 202.

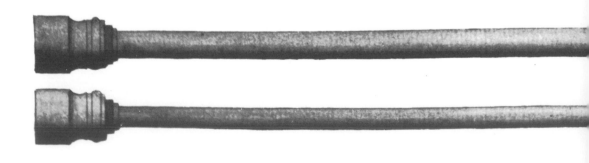

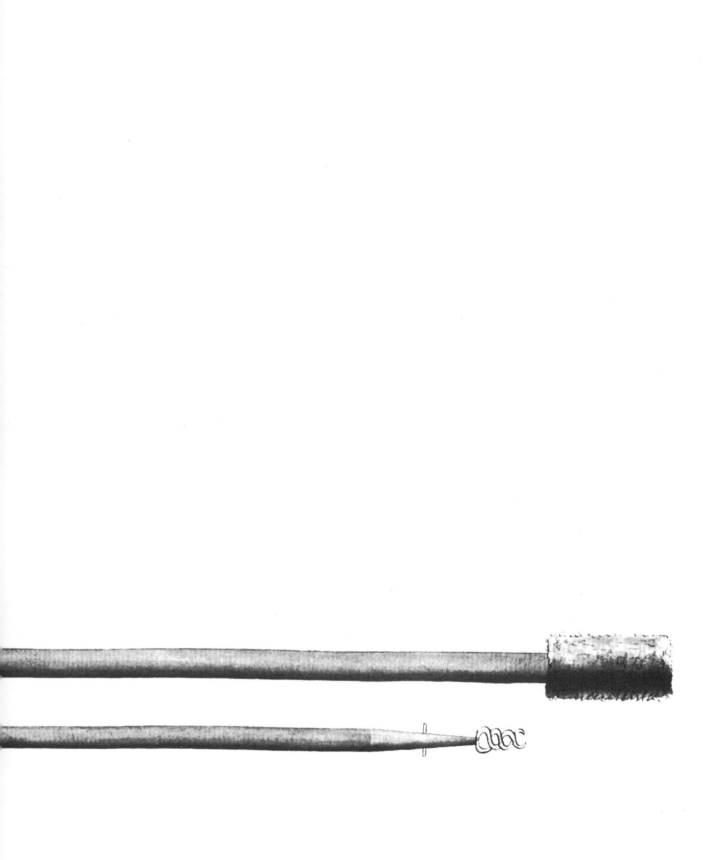

Being a survey of camp equipage ————

To Sustain Life and Provide Comfort

Chapter 6

"Camp equipage," during the Revolutionary War, was a widely inclusive term. It covered almost every personal item that wasn't an arm or an accoutrement. Canteens and knapsacks were classed as camp equipage. So were tents, camp beds, tables and chairs, and in some instances even racks for muskets. Whatever their size or nature, these were the objects designed to sustain the soldier's life and to provide for his creature comforts. A few were issued on a personal basis, one to each soldier, but more were intended for use by a squad or even a larger group. The personal items might be carried by the soldier himself, but on a long march or in battle, most camp equipage was loaded on wagons as part of the baggage.

Canteens

Certainly one of the most personal of all items of camp equipage was the canteen. This was the vessel which held the Continental soldier's liquid refreshment and from which he drank directly as a general rule. The idea of several persons drinking from the same bottle was not as repugnant to Revolutionary soldiers as it is today. The principles of hygiene were not so well understood. Still there was often the simple matter of having enough to drink. Water was sometimes scarce, and a hot, weary soldier prized it highly. If he could have diluted it with some of his rum ration, he would have cherished it even more dearly. He wanted it for himself. Army authorities recognized the essentially personal nature of a canteen, and when possible they strove to provide one for each soldier. In most cases they apparently succeeded, but there were notable failures. In 1778, for instance, C. C. Pinckney complained about the cruelty of providing only one small canteen to every six or eight men among the troops in the South. If these canteens held a quart as most of them did, that meant only four ounces of water per man for perhaps a whole day's march, a very tiny amount for a hot climate. Other examples of shortages were less spectacular, but they existed nonetheless. (1)

The most common type of canteen of the Revolution was a wooden keg shaped somewhat like a very short barrel. The ends or heads were solid wood, between 6 and 9 inches in diameter. The sides were made of staves 3-4½ inches long in general. These staves were held in position by hoops. Usually these hoops were wood, most often willow or hickory with a buttonhole and eyelet joint. It is possible that some hoops of tinned iron and even brass were used also, though metal hoops did not become really popular until after the war. Usually there were also three metal loops for the sling strap, and always there was a mouth opening, often in a thickened portion of a stave. White oak was the preferred material for canteen construction since it did not make the water taste as strongly as did cedar, the other common wood. But other woods seem to have been used as well, including even pine. (2)

In addition to the standard canteen there were a number of variants. In one the staves were replaced by a single thin piece of wood which was bent around the heads and nailed fast. This method of construction apparently developed during the War but never became widely popular until the beginning of the 1800's. Tin canteens were

Glass bottle used as
a canteen during
the Revolution.
George C. Neumann
Collection.

also used. These were shaped somewhat like a flask, either oval or slightly kidney-shaped in cross section. Such tin canteens were popular in the British Army and so were obtained by capture. One record from Maryland, however, indicates that they were actually made in this country as well, despite the shortages of tinned iron. In an emergency other forms of bottle could also be used for carrying water, and there is good evidence that at least a few Continental soldiers actually used glass or ceramic containers, sometimes sewed in leather fittings, to carry their prized refreshment. *(3)*

Knapsacks and Haversacks

Water was a necessity for each soldier, but so was a device for carrying his extra clothing, his food, and other items of personal equipment for his individual needs. For this purpose the soldier normally used a knapsack or a haversack, or possibly a combination of the two. In later times the haversack was thought of as a carrier for food and eating utensils, while the knapsack was used for clothing and other personal items. During the Revolution, however, the terms were used loosely and often interchangeably. Essentially both were large envelopes of canvas or linen that the soldier usually wore under his left arm or slung slightly to the rear with the strap passing over his right shoulder. Some Continentals may also have worn the knapsack squarely on the back in the modern manner. This was the new British fashion, and it undoubtedly influenced American custom before the end of the War. The British also sometimes used goatskin instead of canvas or linen, and they left the hair on the outside. Without doubt some Continentals carried such hairy knapsacks, too. (4)

In the Archives of Maryland under the date of February 9, 1776, there is a contemporary sketch of a "new invented Napsack and haversack in one That is adopted by the American Regulars of Pennsylvania, New Jersey & Virginia...." It shows the knapsack portion made of canvas, painted red, and lined with linen. The haversack is made of Russian linen and is unpainted so that it could be washed. The combination pack was designed to be worn under the left arm with the painted canvas section on top to protect the unpainted haversack from the weather. Food and eating utensils could be placed in the haversack from the top. The knapsack was filled through a slit in the underside

Knapsacks, haversacks, and canteens of the Revolution drawn by H. Charles McBarron, Jr.

1. *Tumpline and strap.*

2. *Tumpline pack made up.*

3. *Tumpline pack in place.*

4. *"New-invented" combination knapsack-haversack carried by Maryland, Pennsylvania, New Jersey, and Virginia troops, as shown by a drawing in the Maryland Archives dated February 9, 1776. Each envelope is 21 inches long and 13 inches deep, made of duck painted red and lined with linen.*

5. *The combination knapsack-haversack folded for carrying.*

6. *The combination worn with the blanket roll in between the two envelopes.*

7-10. *Series of knapsacks designed to be worn squarely on the back. 7 is a white goatskin type worn by some British troops at the beginning of the War. 8 is a canvas knapsack, often painted the facing color of the uniform. 9 is the back of a knapsack showing the strap arrangement. 10, a brown goatskin knapsack of the type worn by the British Army prior to the Revolution.*

11. *British dragoon knapsack of white linen.*

12. *A wooden canteen with barrel rim.*

13. *Tin canteen always worn on cords instead of straps.*

14. *British Army haversack of brown linen.*

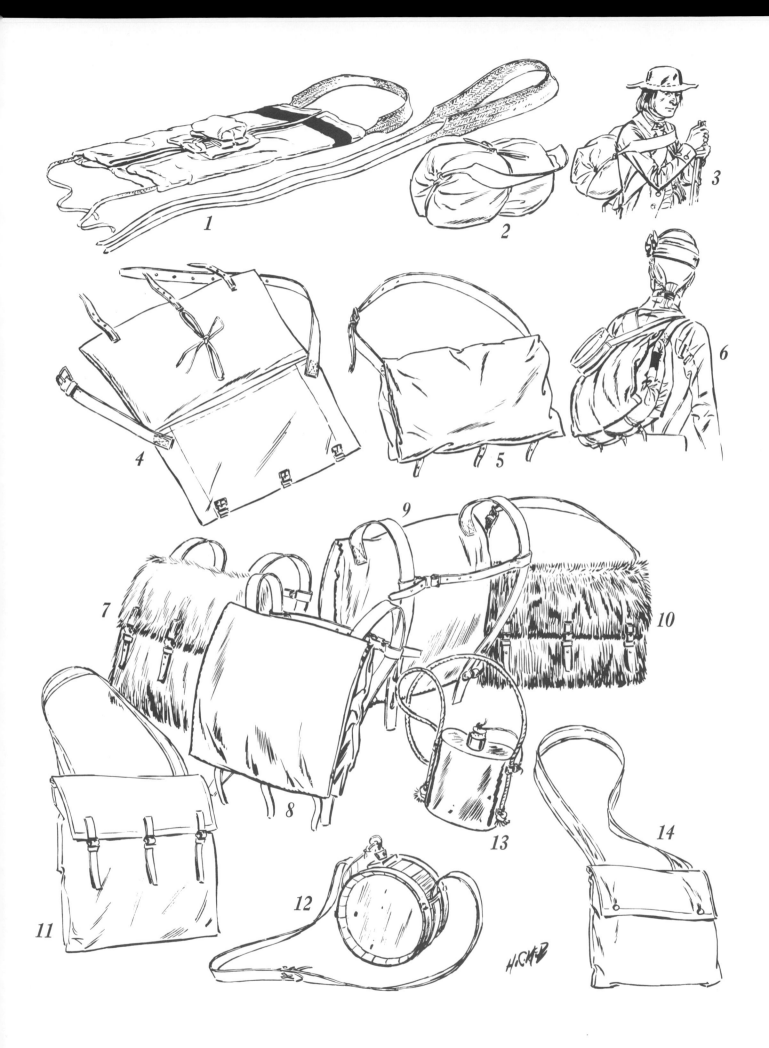

which was then tied shut with a thong. When worn, the soldier's blanket was probably carried between the two sections, supported by the straps underneath. *(5)*

A slightly more primitive manner of carrying personal gear was the tumpline. This was simply a strap that passed around the chest and secured a pack made up with the soldier's blanket rolled around his clothing and smaller items of gear. Large numbers of these tumplines were listed as missing by New Hampshire troops after the Battle of Bunker Hill, and it is probable that they continued to be used thereafter when regular knapsacks and haversacks could not be obtained. *(6)*

Rations

The food that the Continental soldier placed in his haversack or wrapped in the center of his tumpline pack was normally issued directly to him as an individual rather than to a company or regimental mess. When food was plentiful the daily ration was good. The Army around Boston, for instance, was supposed to issue the soldiers the following daily ration:

1. One pound of bread.
2. Half a pound of beef and half a pound of pork; and if pork cannot be had, one pound and a quarter of beef; and one day in seven they shall have one pound and one quarter of salt fish, instead of one day's allowance of meat.
3. One pint of milk, or if milk cannot be had, one gill of rice.
4. One quart of good spruce or malt beer.
5. One gill of peas or beans, or other sauce equivalent.
6. Six ounces of good butter per week.
7. One pound of good common soap for six men per week.
8. Half a pint of vinegar per week per man, if it can be had. *(7)*

Even at Valley Forge the hoped-for rations included 1 1/2 pounds of flour or bread, 1 pound of beef or fish, or 3/4 pound of pork, and 1 gill of whiskey or spirits; or 1 1/2 pounds of flour, 1/2 pound of pork or bacon, 1/2 pint of peas or beans, and 1 gill of whiskey or spirits. But naturally these rations varied according to the quantity and type of foods available in camp. Sometimes they were much reduced and hunger became a very real factor. *(8)*

Hearth on the Philadelphia, showing camp kettle and frying pan. U.S. National Museum.

Cooking Utensils

Whatever the ration available, it was usually issued raw. It was up to the soldiers themselves to cook it. Bakeries might on occasion be set up to provide bread instead of flour, but ordinary foods were left to the skill of the men. Cooking utensils were issued as a part of the normal camp equipage with a set hopefully for every six or eight men. Such a group or mess would get together and select the best individual cooks in their number to prepare the food for the rest. Sometimes whole companies would go together and appoint a small number of cooks for the entire number. This happened most often in winter encampments. When the Army was on campaign it was more usual for the men to cook and eat in small units. (9)

*Iron camp kettle
from the Philadelphia.
U.S. National Museum.*

*Soldiers cooking with
the two types of broilers
made from barrel hoops
excavated at Morristown.
Drawn by
H. Charles McBarron, Jr.
Courtesy Stanley J. Olsen.*

In order for the soldiers to do the necessary cooking of their food they were issued camp kettles. Officers received kettles with covers; enlisted men got open kettles. Sometimes these were cast iron kettles with wire handles and short legs; sometimes they were tinned iron, much thinner and without legs. The goal was to provide every six or eight men with one such kettle, but there is evidence that sometimes the ratio rose as high as ten or twelve men to one kettle. (10)

These kettles were used for cooking the peas or beans, for making soups or stews, and for boiling the meat in the approved fashion of the times. Most other methods of cooking were looked on with disfavor, and officers were instructed to inspect the messes of their men to be sure that they were preparing their food properly. Provisions, they were told, "ought always to be boiled or roasted, never fried, baked or broiled, which modes are very unhealthy." The men were also to be taught to use vinegar freely as an aid to health. (11)

Despite these injunctions the men did indeed broil their meat upon occasion. Ramrods made very good spits for small pieces, and excavations of Revolutionary War campsites have turned up homemade broilers of bent strap iron rescued from old barrel hoops. Obviously the officers were not so strict about their inspections as they might have been. Nevertheless only the kettle became an official issue item for cooking.

Camp kettles were sometimes carried on the person; sometimes hauled by wagon. When they were carried they were frequently fitted with a linen carrying case and strap so that they could be slung from the shoulder like the knapsack and canteen. (12)

Group of forks and spoons excavated in the American campsites at Morristown. National Park Service, U.S. Department of the Interior.

149

Horn drinking cup.
Crosby Milliman Collection.

Eating Utensils

Once the provisions had been issued and prepared there was still the matter of eating them, and this required more items of equipment. A plate was a necessity and so was a spoon and perhaps a knife and possibly even a fork. The soldier might provide these utensils for himself, but there are records of the purchase of wooden bowls, trenchers, and both wooden and pewter spoons for issue to Maryland troops, and it is quite likely that other states also provided eating utensils even though the records are silent on the subject. Drinks also required a utensil. The canteen might prove entirely adequate as a drinking vessel when only water or very diluted spirits were concerned, but many a soldier preferred to drink his gill of whiskey or his quart of beer without any dilution. Such men wanted a cup or tumbler, and it is safe to assume that the average Continental carried one in his haversack with his other eating utensils. Probably it was made of horn. Such horn cups were easy to make. All it required was a section of cow horn with a wooden plug at the smaller end. Horn cups were also light and much less fragile than the costlier ceramic drinking vessels. The necessary knife for cutting the bread and meat might be a sheath knife, a pocket knife, or even on rare occasions a special camp table knife. Many soldiers, especially riflemen, carried belt knives that they used both for fighting and for general purposes about a camp, including eating. Most regular infantrymen and artillerists carried large jack-knives, and these could be used for eating as well as for the other purposes for which they were intended. Some pocket knives were even designed with fork combinations especially for eating. *(13)*

Enlisted men and junior officers might make do with the issue camp kettles, homemade broilers, wooden trenchers, spoons, and pocket knives for their messes. Higher-ranking officers fared much

Left:
Horn container for flints
or other small objects.
Right:
A salt container of horn.
Crosby Milliman Collection.

better. Washington, for instance, carried an elaborate mess chest with him in the field. Compactly designed, it included four kettles with detachable wooden handles, a folding grill, eight bottles for spirits, six pewter plates and three platters, containers for seasonings, two knives and four forks, and two tinder boxes. And this was only part of his mess equipment. Orders exist for many more plates and cannisters. *(14)*

Pocket knives
excavated at a
British campsite
in New York City.
Courtesy of
the New-York
Historical Society,
New York City.

American combination
pocket knife and fork.
Joseph Aiken Collection.

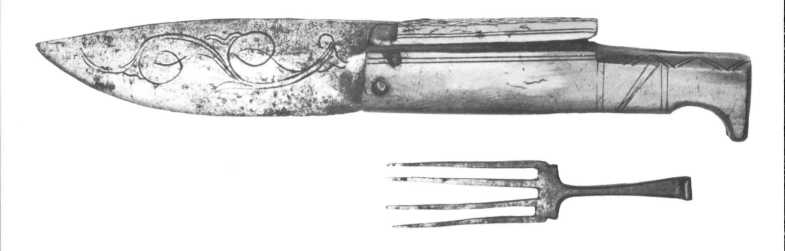

George Washington's
mess chest.
U.S. National Museum.

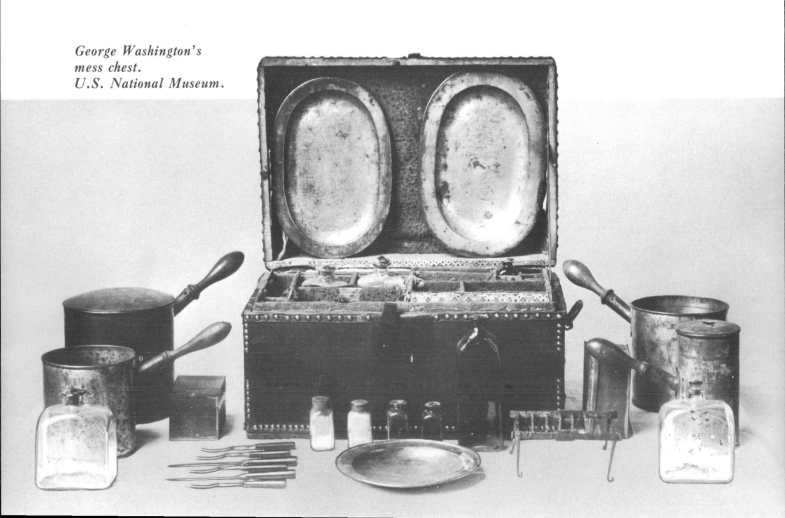

Tents

When Washington lived with his men in a winter encampment he usually selected a large house in the neighborhood for his headquarters. In fact he did this even on campaign when it was feasible. At these times he normally ate in the house and entertained his officers there. Often in the field, however, there were no houses near the chosen campsite. Then Washington used his special dining tent for his own meals and for official functions. This was a large oval affair, 80 feet in circumference with side walls 5 feet 6 inches high and a roof sloping steeply up to the ridge. This he called his dining marquee. The roof was supported by two poles or "standards" at either end of the ridge pole and numerous small poles around its circumference. The edges of the roof were scalloped and edged in red. The side walls were separate and attached to the short poles. In addition to his dining tent Washington also had at least two others, a smaller sleeping tent which was 8 feet long and a baggage tent. (15)

Tents of the Revolutionary War varied greatly in size and design, though almost all were wall tents and either oval or rectangular. According to a contemporary British description:

> The sizes of the officers tents are not fixed; some regiments have them of one size, and some of another: a captain's tent and marquee is generally 10½ feet broad, 14 deep, and 8 high: the subalterns are a foot less; the major's and lieutenant-colonel's, a foot larger; and the colonel's 2 feet larger.
> The subalterns of foot lie two in a tent, and those of horse but one. The tents of private men are 6½ feet square and 5 feet high, and hold 5 soldiers each.
> The tents for the horse are 7 feet broad and 9 feet deep; they hold likewise 5 men, and their horse accoutrements. (16)

*"Modern Tents,"
Plate 1, from Grose's
Military Antiquities of
1801. His caption
reads: "Fig. 1. The
tent poles of a private
tent. 2. A private tent.
3 and 4. Fly tents.
5. An officer's marquis.
6. One of a very
modern construction,
chiefly calculated for
subalterns; the door by
being placed in the
centre of the side,
leaves an area between
the beds which are
placed at each end.
7. A captain's tent or
marquis with a
chimney. 8. A captain's
marquis shown in a
different point of view.
9. A field officer's
marquis. 10. His
servant's tent in the
rear. 11. Tent or tents
of a colonel of militia."*

MODERN TENTS. Pl 1

154

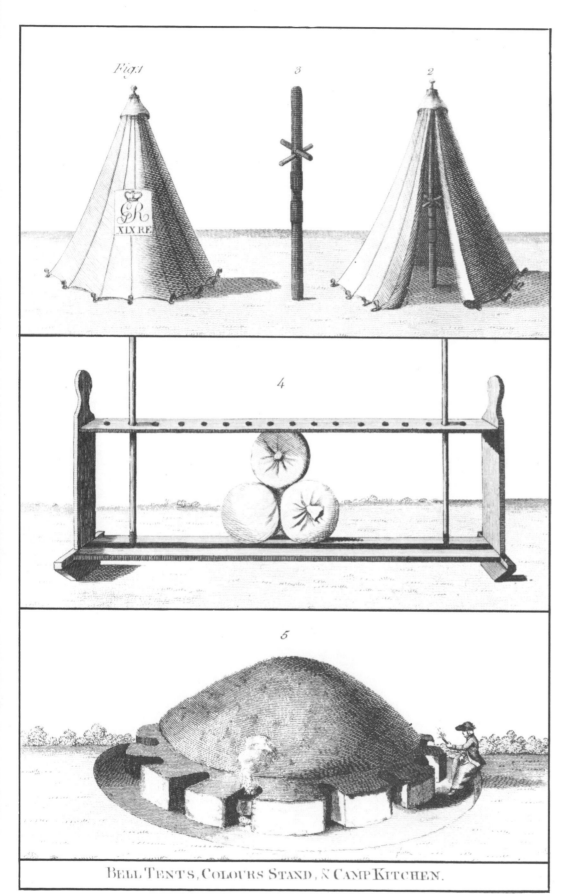

BELL TENTS, COLOURS STAND, & CAMP KITCHEN.

"*Modern Tents,*"
Plate 3 from Grose.
"*Fig. 1. A bell-tent
viewed in the front.
2. The same seen in the
rear. 3. The centre
pole with the cross for
supporting the arms.
4. The stand for the
drums, colours, and
officers espontoons.
5. A camp kitchen with
a woman cooking.*"

155

"Modern Tents,"
Plate 2 from Grose.
"Fig. 1. A horse for
supporting the firelocks.
2. The manner in which
the notches for receiving
them are cut. 3. The
side of one of the
supporters. 4. Manner
in which the arms are
placed. 5. Laboratory
tents belonging to the
artillery. 6. A field-
officer's tent or
marquis."

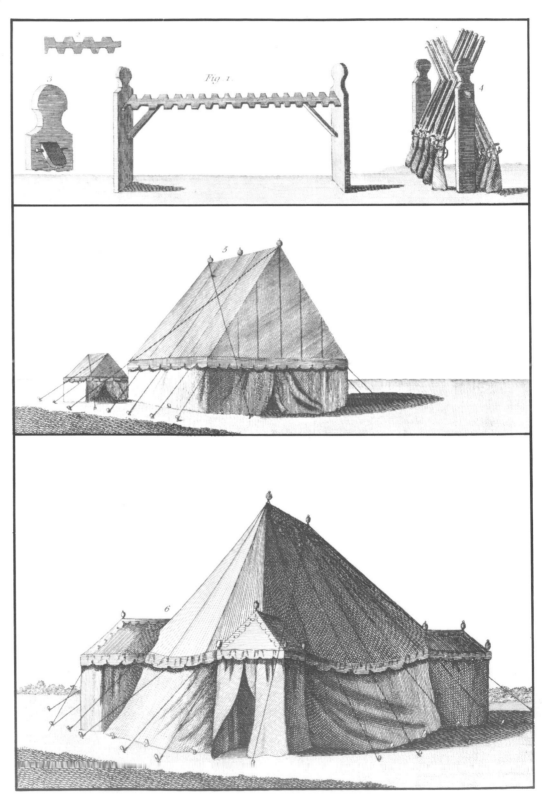

There was also one smaller circular tent called a bell tent or a bell of arms. This had a single central pole with two dowels driven through it about four feet above the ground. Soldiers did not customarily take their arms into their sleeping tents. Instead they racked them in bells of arms with their barrels supported by the dowels of the center pole. *(17)*

There were other racks in a camp also. Sometimes a long horizontal musket rack was used in place of the bells of arms. Presumably these were then covered with a rectangular tent or at least a piece of canvas. Another long rack with a shelf and a pierced transverse member held the flags, the officers' pole arms, and the drums in their canvas cases. *(18)*

Americans followed these British patterns and practices as best they could. Frequently, however, there were not enough tents. Smaller tents had to make do, and more soldiers had to be crowded into each one. At the end of the 1777 campaign, for instance, the field officers of each regiment were allowed one privates' tent each, while other commissioned officers were crowded four to such a tent, and non-commissioned officers and privates were quartered with eight in each tent. Things were still worse in the southern army in 1778 when Captain/C. C. Pinckney reported twelve privates to a tent for those lucky enough to get in. Others were forced to sleep outside in the rain and heavy dews. Whatever their design or size, tents in America were normally used only during the campaign season. In winter quarters the soldiers preferred to build log huts with fireplaces and wooden bunks for six or eight men. *(19)*

Camp Furniture

In either tent or hut there were few sleeping comforts for enlisted men. In the huts it was customary to build wooden bunks, and the men sought leaves or straw to make their rest more comfortable. In tents they frequently wrapped themselves in their blankets and slept right on the ground. Officers slept somewhat more comfortably. Bags filled with straw were sometimes provided for mattresses, and higher-ranking officers frequently carried folding camp beds with them in the field. These interesting pieces of furniture folded up like a cot for ease in carrying, but when set up for sleeping they formed sturdy narrow beds with canvas supports for the mattress. Some even boasted canopies with curtains to keep out drafts and mosquitoes. *(20)*

Officers often carried other pieces of furniture as well. The camp stool, for instance, was a standard item of equipment. Washington had eighteen or more of them, and most officers boasted at least

George Washington's camp bed folded and open. Mount Vernon Ladies' Association of the Union.

one or two. In some instances they seem to have been items of issue though most were undoubtedly privately purchased by the officers themselves. They were usually simple x-shaped frames with a fabric or leather seat. (21)

Tents, camp beds, camp stools, mattresses, and the like were all carried in baggage wagons. So were almost all of the personal effects of the officers who were relieved from the necessity of carrying knapsacks or haversacks. Instead they invested in a variety of trunks, portmanteaus, packing cases, and valises to hold their clothing, toilet articles, telescopes, and other bits of personal gear. There was no special military pattern for any of these containers. The standard wood, leather and hair boxes of the day were pressed into service. The only requisites were that they be big enough to hold the necessary items and that they be sturdy enough to withstand the rough treatment meted out by army wagonmasters. (22)

Private soldiers, too, worried about the rough treatment of their knapsacks when they were carried by wagon. They carefully wrapped all fragile items in the middle of their bundles with clothing and blankets to take up the shock when the packet was tossed into a wagon or thrown out on the ground. They took good care of their other bits of camp equipage, too. Whether individually issued or charged to a whole squad, good equipage meant better living. Weapons and accoutrements were for fighting. Tools were for work. But camp equipage was designed for the soldier's comfort. It paid him to take care of it, and when he could he did.

One of three small leather pack cases which belonged to George Washington. Inside is a center compartment framed in light wood. The front pocket is collapsible. The case is 13 inches high and 15 inches wide. Mount Vernon Ladies' Association of the Union.

Small leather campaign trunk
studded with brass tacks
belonging to George Washington.
It measures 33 ¾ inches in width.
The brass plate on top
is marked "GEN^L WASHINGTON N° 3."
Mount Vernon
Ladies' Association
of the Union.

Small leather campaign chest
bound in iron and studded
with brass tacks
which belonged to George Washington.
It is 27 ⅜ inches wide,
and on this one the brass plate
is marked "GEN^L WASHINGTON N° 4."
Mount Vernon
Ladies' Association
of the Union.

Pine packing case
about three feet square
with iron hasp and rope handles
which belonged to George Washington.
Cases such as this
may well have been used for
campaign gear.
Mount Vernon Ladies' Association
of the Union.

Notes to Chapter 6

1. C. C. Pinckney to Moultrie, May 24, 1778, William Moultrie, *Memoirs of the American Revolution,* 2 vols., New York, 1802, I, 213. Donald Yeates to Governor and Council, February 15, 1781, Browne, *Archives of Maryland,* XLVII, 72.

2. J. Griest to Council, Browne, *Archives of Maryland,* XII, 164. *Ibid.,* XVI, 48. William S. Cornwell, "The Museum's Collection of Military Canteens," *Bulletin* of the Rochester Museum of Arts and Sciences, June 1964.

3. Council of Safety, February 3, 1776, Browne, *Archives of Maryland,* XI, 138; Council to Vanbebbes and Harrison, July 6, 1776, *ibid.,* 557; Deputies to Council, March 26, 1776, *ibid.,* 290. Cornwell, "Canteens," *passim.*

4. Donald Yeates to Governor and Council, February 15, 1781, Browne, *Archives of Maryland,* XLVII, 72. Gerrard Hopkins to Du Vall, July 30, 1776, *ibid.,* XII, 146.

5. Manuscript Archives of Maryland, Baltimore, Red Book 4, #13.

6. Bouton, *New Hampshire State Papers,* VII, *passim.*

7. Bolton, *Private Soldier Under Washington,* pp. 78, 79.

8. *Ibid.,* pp. 80, 81.

9. *Ibid.,* pp. 77-85.

10. Council of Safety, February 3, 1776, Browne, *Archives of Maryland,* XI, 138. Donald Yeates to Governor and Council, February 15, 1781, *ibid.,* XLVII, 72. C. C. Pinckney to Moultrie, May 24, 1778, Moultrie, *Memoirs,* I, 213.

11. Knox's instructions to artillery officers, quoted in Birkhimer, *Artillery,* p. 76.

12. Donald Yeates to Governor and Council, February 15, 1781, Browne, *Archives of Maryland,* XLVII, 72. General Orders, Headquarters at Stanton, August 23, 1777, Washington, *Writings,* IX, 125, 127.

13. J. Griest to Council, Browne, *Archives of Maryland,* XII, 164.

14. *General Washington's Military Equipment,* 3rd ed., Mount Vernon, Va., 1963, pp. 20, 21.

15. These tents are now divided among the Smithsonian Institution, Valley Forge, and the National Park Service (Yorktown Battlefield).

16. Smith, *Military Dictionary,* under "Tent."

17. *Ibid.* Francis Grose, *Military Antiquities, Respecting a History of the British Army,* 2 vols., London, 1801, II, 28-40.

18. *Ibid.*

19. C. C. Pinckney to Moultrie, May 24, 1778, Moultrie, *Memoirs,* I, 213. September 13, 1777, George Weedon, *Valley Forge Orderly Book, 1777-1778,* Samuel W. Pennypacker, ed., New York, 1902, p. 49.

20. Donald Yeates to Governor and Council, February 15, 1781, Browne, *Archives of Maryland,* XLVII, 72. *Washington's Military Equipment,* pp. 26-29.

21. *Ibid.,* pp. 22, 23. Donald Yeates to Governor and Council, February 15, 1781, Browne, *Archives of Maryland,* XLVII, 72.

22. *Ibid.*

Scalpel,

Being
a survey of
the medical
and
surgical
supplies

Saw and Spirits

Chapter 7

A sick soldier is a useless soldier. Worse than that, each one is a burden that requires the attention of several other people. In the Revolution, these included surgeons, mates, nurses, orderlies, hospital guards, and other specially detailed personnel. It is in the best interest of any army to cure its wounded and diseased men as quickly as possible, return them to active duty or discharge them and relieve the burden on the hospital staffs. Like any good officer George Washington was well aware of this fact. With an average of 18 per cent of the Army sick at all times, not to mention several serious epidemics which greatly increased this figure, plus the quantities of wounded which resulted from each campaign, it was a major concern, and he frequently wrote Congress about medical needs. Yet few armies in the last two centuries have been so poorly prepared or organized for the care of the sick as the Continental Army. (1)

The Hospital Department

There were many causes for this. One was the haphazard and slow recognition of the problem. In the beginning Congress looked to the Massachusetts provincial government to supply both doctors and medicines for the Army at Boston. Fortunately the Bay State patriots had been foresighted in this and purchased a group of fifteen medicine chests in March of 1775, just before hostilities broke out, and these were presumably available to the volunteer surgeons who joined the troops in the days after Lexington and Concord. It was not until July 27, after the shock of Bunker Hill, that the Continental Congress finally got around to passing "The Act for the Establishment of the Hospital for the Army." In so doing it used the word "hospital" as meaning an entire medical department, not just a building, and at the head it placed a "Chief Physician and Director General of the Army Hospital." It was a step in the right direction, but it was a vague act. It seemed to apply only to the installation at Cambridge, Massachusetts, and when the conflict spread to New York and the South, the whole question of hospitals for these areas had to be argued and settled. So did the matter of the relationship of these hospitals or medical departments to each other. (2)

Faced with this problem Congress vacillated and dallied while disputes between the directors of the various hospitals increased. On April 7, 1777, almost two years after the war had begun, Congress decided on four district "hospitals" corresponding to the military divisions of the country: the Eastern, comprising that portion of New York east of the Hudson plus the New England states; the Northern, consisting of upper New York and southern Canada; the Middle, which gathered the states of New Jersey, Pennsylvania, Delaware, and Maryland; and the Southern, which included the remaining states from Virginia through Georgia. At the head was the centralized control of the Director General, who quickly became one of the most powerful men in the Army. He examined all applicants for medical appointments, selected minor departmental officials, was the final arbiter of professional practices, controlled the purchase and distribution of all supplies, and performed a host of other important functions. Apparently it became so powerful a position that it worried Congress, and on February 6, 1778, that body decentralized the authority, making each district hospital almost autonomous. This must have seemed like a good idea to sectionally minded congressmen, but it didn't work well in practice. It led to duplication of efforts and competition for the scarce drug supplies which drove up prices. Also there were awkward days or even weeks when an army on the march passed from the jurisdiction of one hospital into that of another. When that happened there was medical chaos and neglect. In spite of these drawbacks Congress stuck with this organization for more than two years. Then, on September 30, 1780, it restored the Director General to all his former authority. *(3)*

A second major cause of the dreadful straits in which the sick or wounded Continental found himself was the character of the men selected as Director General. Of the four men who held the post at various times the first three all proved to be poor choices and had to be removed for the public good. One was an accused traitor, one a poor administrator, and one a profiteer. It was not until Dr. John Cochran was appointed in 1781 that a truly capable administrator held the job, and by that time hostilities were almost at an end. *(4)*

Types of Hospitals

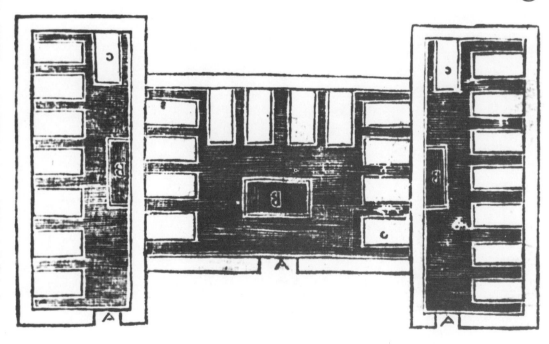

Plan for a hospital from Dr. James Tilton's Economical Observations on Military Hospitals...

Despite the changes in the overall organization of the Hospital Department there were at most times three types of actual hospitals in the sense of physical medical establishments which served the troops. One was the general hospital which was operated by the Continental medical establishment. In the early part of the war this might be located in private homes, barns, or churches. None of these

Elevation of a hospital from Tilton.

structures was ideal for the purpose. Houses were too small and cramped. Barns were bigger and airier, but they were apt to be dirty, and they lacked heat. Churches had the advantage of pews that could easily be converted into beds, but again there was the heat problem. College halls and public buildings were also used, but they did not prove entirely satisfactory, either. In the end a special hospital was built with Continental funds at Yellow Springs, Pennsylvania, primarily for convalescent patients. *(5)*

Next to the general hospital came the flying hospital. This, too, was manned by the Continental military establishment. It was normally a spring and summer affair, following campaigns and necessarily mobile to meet emergencies. It might be established in tents or, if the Army camped long enough, in a hut with recommended dimensions of 15 x 25 feet with a 9-foot ceiling and containing six beds as well as a doctor's bench and an operating table. *(6)*

Closest to the average soldier was the regimental hospital managed by the regimental surgeon and his mates. When the regiments were in towns or cities these hospitals might be in private houses, but in winter encampments they were normally in specially constructed huts of three sections with the center room a recommended 31 1/2 x 19 1/2 feet and the two wings 35 1/2 x 16 feet. The plan was illustrated by Dr. James Tilton in his *Economical Observations on Military Hospitals and the Prevention of Diseases Incident to an Army.* A building of this sort was expected to hold twenty-five patients. Theoretically these were to be new cases or minor diseases. Once a disease had been diagnosed as a major case, the sufferer was supposed to be sent to a general hospital for intensive care. Transportation problems, however, often prevented this scheme from operating as planned. So did the jealousy of regimental surgeons and the reluctance of the soldiers to leave friends and familiar faces. *(7)*

Drugs and Medicine Chests

*Medicine chest of the eighteenth century
such as might have been used during the Revolution.
From contemporary descriptions
it seems to be slightly smaller
than the standard half chest.
West Point Museum.*

By no means the least important cause of American suffering during the Revolution was the acute shortage of medicines, equipment, and instruments. The great bulk of all these items had always been imported from England, and the war promptly cut off this source except for a few drugs that trickled through via the West Indies. Inflation and the reluctance of Congress to appropriate money for drug purchases made druggists reluctant to sell such medicines as they did have to the Continental hospitals, and inadequate transportation further compounded the difficulties. At times the shortages became critical, and it was not until after the French alliance that anything approaching an adequate supply reached either the regimental surgeons or the general or flying hospitals. *(8)*

When drugs and other supplies could be had, they were normally packed in medicine chests. Large chests were issued to district hospitals and slightly smaller ones to regimental surgeons. If one may judge from the lists of contents, these were big chests, for they contained eighty-one different medicines, when they could be had, some of them in quantities as large as six pounds. There were also quantities of surgical dressings, lint, bandages, fracture pillows, splints, sponges, twine, flannel, etc., plus surgical instruments, pharmaceutical equipment for making pills and powders, and

Medicine chest with top trays removed to show arrangement of drug bottles and packets. A syringe can also be seen in the tray resting on the lid. West Point Museum.

miscellaneous supplies including gallipots, bottles, boxes, and wrapping paper. Half chests are also mentioned as being issued to regiments at different times, and possibly there were smaller boxes as well. *(9)*

Despite the great number of drugs listed for these chests only a few were really considered essential and included in quantity when they were available. Peruvian or Jesuits' bark was one. It was actually cinchona, from which quinine was later discovered. Cantharides (Spanish flies) was also popular for making blistering plasters, but the biggest group of all were the purgatives. Jalap, ipecac, and rhubarb were the botanical favorites, and Epsom salts and Glauber's purging salts were the chemical choices. Tartar emetic was preferred for inducing vomiting. Cleansing the system through the use of these agents was considered beneficial for a number of ailments. *(10)*

Medical kit of Dr. Solomon Drowne
of the Continental Army.
It contains a box of scissors
and scalpels, drugs in
both raw and processed forms,
curved needles and suture material,
scales and weights,
a mortar and leg splints.
Armed Forces
Institute of Pathology Photograph.

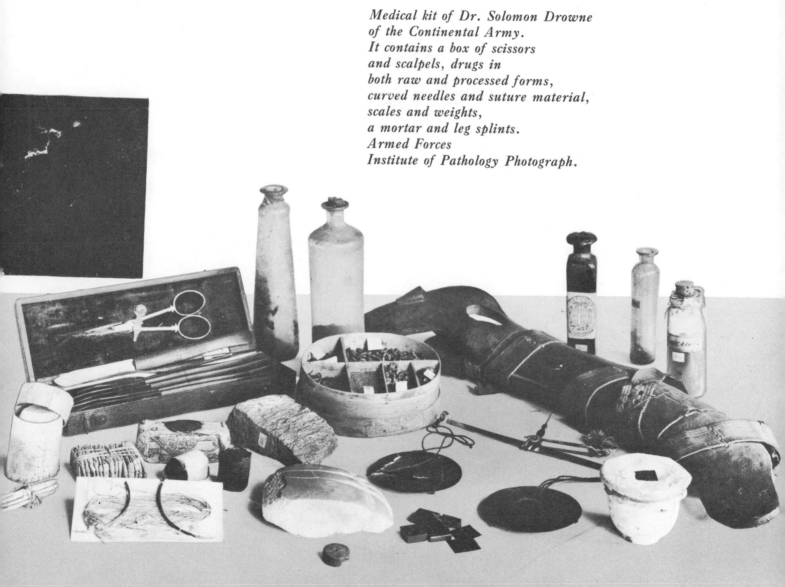

Other common ailments called for more specific remedies. Venereal disease, for instance, was dosed with an elixir of spring water, sumac roots, and gunpowder. If this failed to bring prompt relief, a mixture of salts and turpentine was drunk. Fresh milk was also considered of great benefit to sufferers from social diseases, and though they were frequently punished for having contracted such a malady by having their pay stopped they were usually allowed sufficient funds to purchase milk. Snakebites were treated by doses of olive oil and applications of mercury ointment, and kidney ailments were dosed with a glass of horseradish roots and mustard seed in gin. *(11)*

Gum opium was also used when it could be had for its narcotic effects. So was laudanum. Such opiates were scarce, however, and often the unfortunate patient who was forced to undergo a probing or amputation could hope only for a stiff drink of rum or gin and perhaps a bullet to bite on. Then burly hospital attendants held him down, and the surgeon did his painful work. *(12)*

Many of these drugs were sent to the surgeons in bulk or unprepared states. Thus pharmaceutical equipment was needed to make them ready for use. Balance scales and weights were provided for measuring ingredients, and mortars and pestles were used for pulverizing them. Often there were two sets of mortars and pestles, one large and one small. References include mention of ceramic, brass, and limestone mortars. Pestles were probably of the same materials. Spatulas for making boluses or soft pills, pill-rolling tiles, and various knives completed the usual equipment. Both raw and prepared drugs were normally stored in bottles of various shapes and sizes or in paper packages. A few were kept in boxes. *(13)*

Surgical Instruments

Surgical instruments were also stored in the medicine chests. These were much simpler and cruder tools than those which blossomed forth in the surgical kits of the Civil War less than a century later. Also they were fewer in number. There were bullet probes, bullet extractors, forceps, catheters, lancets, amputating and trepanning sets, surgical knives resembling long-bladed scalpels, retractors or surgical hooks, tourniquets, syringes, and crow-bill tooth extractors. Finally there were curved needles, thread, and scissors. *(14)*

Of all this equipment the lancet was probably the most used. Bleeding was the universally approved cure for a great many ailments, and it was the lancet which opened the vein. Huge quantities of blood were removed from the patients. A man stricken with pleurisy, for instance, could expect to have twelve ounces of blood drained from his jugular vein while he was ordered to breathe deeply and cough. If his chest pains did not diminish within twenty-four hours, he could expect another bleeding. Rheumatic patients were bled ten ounces

Field operating kit
of the Revolution.
The instruments it contains
are forceps, a bullet extractor,
two retractors,
and three amputating knives.
Armed Forces
Institute of Pathology Photograph.

from the afflicted area, and sufferers from many other diseases got similar treatment. The practice of bleeding a patient had the great advantage that it was a treatment that could always be given no matter how scarce medical supplies might be. As long as the surgeon had his lancet he could minister to the sick, and a remarkable number managed to recover. (15)

The amputation kits, too, saw all too frequent service. Massive infections, gangrene, and shattered bones all called for the removal of the affected limb. Even multiple fractures normally resulted in such drastic surgery. Simple breaks might be treated with crude setting and splinting, and

Lancet of two blades in a brass case. Donald W. Holst Collection.

even then crooked arms and legs often resulted. If several bones of a limb were broken, especially with compound fractures, the surgeon could only amputate. Without anesthetics this was a gruesome operation. Shock was a major hazard, and the use of unsterilized instruments and dressings fostered serious infections. Only the exceptionally hardy survived. *(16)*

Indeed, survival was the key question in the whole hospital experience. Many soldiers dreaded the hospitals and suffered in silence rather than seek medical aid. Once they were admitted, they faced critical shortages of drugs, primitive treatments, including bleeding, which might actually make them worse, and crowded conditions in frequently airless rooms which often placed men afflicted with contagious diseases right next to wounded soldiers from the battlefield. It has been estimated that a Revolutionary War soldier going into battle had a 98 per cent chance of escaping death. If he entered a hospital his chances of survival were only 75 per cent. Many doctors served selflessly and heroically to minister to the soldiers. Despite administrative failures and medicinal shortages they did the best that they could within the limits of their skill and knowledge. For the Continental soldier, however, the situation remained bleak. *(17)*

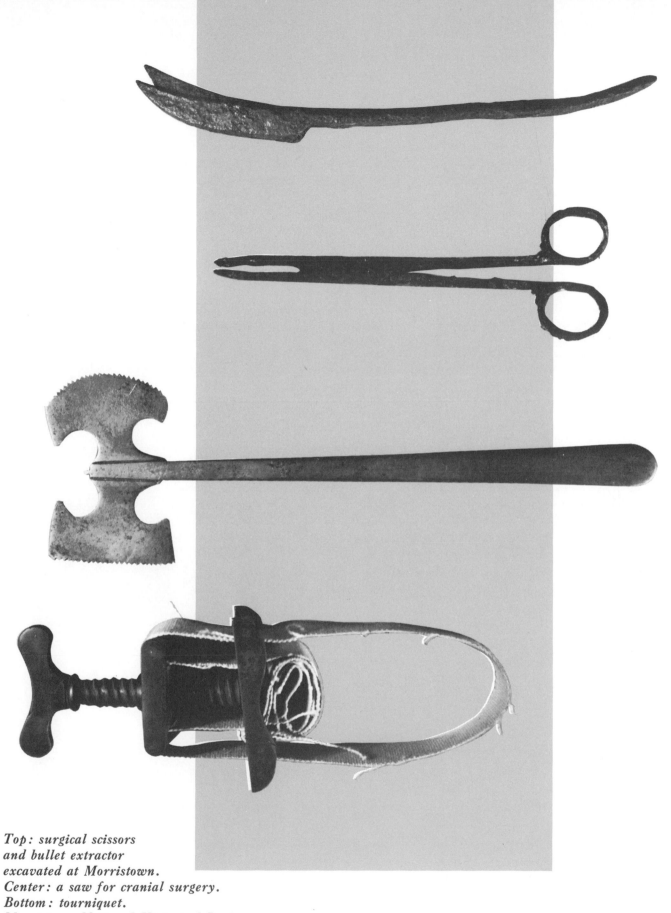

Top: surgical scissors and bullet extractor excavated at Morristown.
Center: a saw for cranial surgery.
Bottom: tourniquet.
Morristown National Historical Park.

Notes to Chapter 7

1. Howard Lewis Applegate, "The American Revolutionary War Hospital Department," *Military Medicine* (April 1961), pp. 296-306. Howard Lewis Applegate, "The Medical Administrators of the American Revolutionary Army," *Military Affairs,* XXV, No. 1 (Spring 1961), 1-10. George B. Griffenhagen, *Drug Supplies in the American Revolution,* U.S. National Museum *Bulletin* 225, Washington, 1961, *passim.* See also Harvey E. Brown, *The Medical Department of the United States Army, 1775-1873,* Washington, 1873. Howard Lewis Applegate, "The Need for Further Study in the Medical History of the American Revolutionary Army," *Military Medicine* (August 1961), pp. 616-618. Isobel Stevenson, "Beginnings of American Military Medicine," *Ciba Symposia,* I, No. 11 (February 1940), 344-359.

2. July 19-27, 1775, Ford, *Journals of the Continental Congress,* II, 191-211. Applegate, "Hospital Department," pp. 296, 297. Applegate, "Medical Administrators," p. 1.

3. April 7, 1777, Ford, *Journals of the Continental Congress,* VII, 231-237. February 6, 1778, *ibid.,* X, 128-131. September 30, 1780, *ibid.,* XVII, 878-886. Brown, *Medical Department,* p. 23. Applegate, "Hospital Department," pp. 297, 298.

4. Applegate, "Medical Administrators," *passim.*

5. Applegate, "Hospital Department," p. 299.

6. *Ibid.* James Tilton, *Economical Observations on Military Hospitals and the Prevention of Diseases Incident to an Army,* Wilmington, 1813, pp. 47-50. General Orders, January 13, 1778, Washington, *Writings,* X, 300.

7. *Ibid.*

8. Griffenhagen, *Drug Supplies, passim.*

9. Ford, *Journals of the Continental Congress,* III, 442, n. 10. Griffenhagen, *Drug Supplies,* pp. 130-133, *et passim.*

10. *Ibid.,* p. 129. Howard Lewis Applegate, "Remedial Medicine in the American Revolutionary Army," *Military Medicine* (June 1961), pp. 451-453. Howard Lewis Applegate, "Preventive Medicine in the American Revolutionary Army," *Military Medicine* (May 1961), pp. 379-382.

11. *Ibid.*

12. *Ibid.*

13. Griffenhagen, *Drug Supplies, passim.*

14. *Ibid.*

15. Applegate, "Remedial Medicine," p. 451. Baron van Swieten, *The Diseases Incident to the Armies with the Method of Cure,* Philadelphia, 1776, *passim.*

16. John Jones, *Plain Concise Practical Remarks on the Treatment of Wounds and Fractures,* Philadelphia, 1776, *passim.* Applegate, "Remedial Medicine," pp. 451, 452.

17. Applegate, "Need for Further Study," p. 617. Louis M. Duncan, *Medical Men in the Revolution, 1775-1783,* Carlisle, Pa., 1931, *passim.*

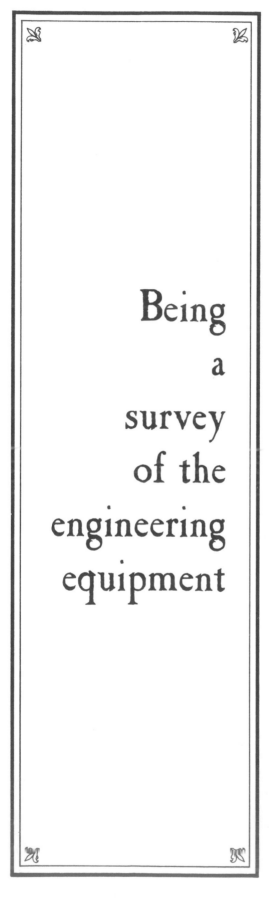

Being
a
survey
of the
engineering
equipment

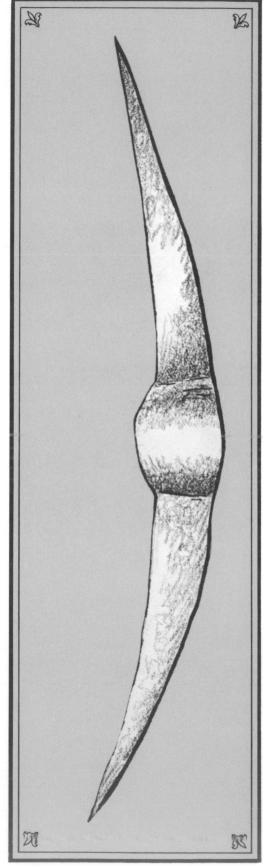

For
Fort
and
Camp

The Regular of the Revolution was not a digging soldier in the modern sense. The days of trench warfare and foxholes were still far in the future. Yet the Continental soldier did do some digging and erect some field fortifications. When he was going to hold a strong position or remain in one place for a long period of time he fortified it with formal works of wood and earth. At Yorktown he threw up

Chapter 8

siege lines called parallels and dug slanting approach trenches to get within striking range of the British works. Engineer officers directed the digging and fortifying, but it was the Regular soldier from the infantry and artillery who did most of the digging and made most of the accessories of fortification.

Field Fortifications

The usual field fortification of the Revolutionary War was made primarily of dirt. It started with a wide deep ditch. This not only created an obstacle for enemy troops to cross but it also provided the dirt to make the walls of the fort. Most of this dirt was piled on one side of the ditch to form a parapet about as high and wide as the ditch was deep and broad. A height of eight or ten feet was usual for a good fort or redoubt. This meant that a firing step had to be built on the inner wall of the parapet to allow the defenders to shoot over it. A little dirt was often thrown on the side of the ditch towards the enemy to make a gently sloping surface called the glacis. (1)

The outer wall of the parapet sloped back at the natural angle of repose, the angle at which piled dirt would naturally settle. The inner wall was straighter, and this required some form of support to hold the dirt in place. If the parapet were pierced with embrasures for artillery, these openings also had to be lined so that they could be kept nearly vertical. These supports or wall linings were of various sorts. They might be wooden palings, but more often they were especially designed structures called fascines, saucissons, and gabions. Even sand bags were occasionally used in the modern manner. The fascine was a bundle of sticks tied in three or four places. The usual fascine for facing the inside of a parapet wall was 10 feet long and 12 or 15 inches in diameter. It was recommended that fascines be bound with willow wythes every two feet. To make fascines, six stout sticks were cut and bound together to form three x-shaped supports with their lower ends stuck into the ground. The boughs for the fascines were then laid between the upper arms of these x's and tied. Six men were usually detailed to the task, two to cut the boughs, two to gather them, and two to bind them. Such a team could make twelve fascines an hour. When finished the fascines were staked to the parapet wall they were made to support with five long stakes. Extra-long fascines were called saucissons. (2)

*Reconstructed Grand French Battery
at Yorktown,
Colonial National Historical Park,
showing saucissons and gabions in use.
National Park Service,
U.S. Department of the Interior.*

The gabion was quite a different form of wall support. Sometimes it could even form a light wall itself, and it was sometimes used in that way to protect a battery. These gabions were wicker-work cylinders made of small branches and usually filled with dirt. They were made in various sizes depending upon the task for which they were designed. The biggest were used in sieges to protect soldiers digging approach lines. They were often 5 or 6 feet high and 3 feet in diameter. Gabions used in field forts were usually 3 or 4 feet high and 2 1/2 or 3 feet thick. There were even some very small gabions made to place on top of a parapet to protect the heads of soldiers firing over it. These were only about a foot high and flared from 8 or 10 inches in diameter at the bottom to 12 inches at the top so that they would create firing loopholes when lined up alongside each other. All gabions were made by driving stakes into the ground in a circle of the proper diameter and then weaving boughs around them. (3)

There were also other wooden elements in fortification. Some dirt forts were strengthened by pickets or fraising. Pickets were upright poles set like a stockade. Fraises were poles set horizontally or at an angle in the sloping outer parapet wall. And, of course, there were also completely wooden forts with the traditional stockade or with double walls of logs filled with dirt. Outside most of these fortifications the soldiers created an obstruction called an abatis. This was nothing more than a tangled mass of felled trees with their branches facing towards the enemy and as much intertwined as possible. It was the eighteenth-century equivalent of a barbed wire entanglement. (4)

Finally there was a special device called a cheval-de-frise. This consisted of a heavy piece of timber, perhaps 5 or 6 inches square and 10 or 12 feet long. Through this were driven 6-foot wooden rods about 1 1/2 inches in diameter usually shod with iron and crossing each other at right angles. These chevaux-de-frise were used to stop up holes in the wall and to block streets. (5)

Entrenching Tools

To build these fortifications and siege works the Continental soldiers had a variety of tools. There were shovels, spades, picks, mattocks, axes, and fascine knives which were carried by the various regiments as well as saws, hammers, and less common implements. All were purchased in quantity for the Continental Army, and after June 18, 1776 all such tools belonging to the Regular Army were ordered to be marked "CXIII" with either a stamp or brand. The purpose, of course, was to identify Continental property, but the significance of the Roman numeral is unknown. Some have suggested that the "C" stands for "Continental" rather than five hundred and that the remaining numerals are thirteen for the number of colonies. It is interesting speculation, but it is only a guess. When Washington issued the order he failed to explain what was on his mind. In any event the order remained in effect only some six months, for on January 30, 1777, all tools as well as arms and accoutrements were ordered marked "U.S.," "U. States," or "United States." (6)

Students have given little attention to the entrenching tools of the Revolution. There have been no books about them, and actually little survives in the way of documentary data. There is, however, one

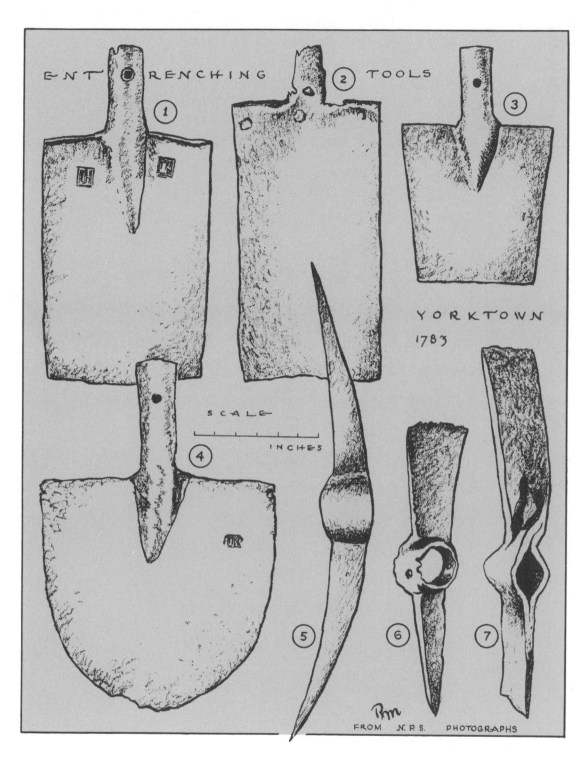

Entrenching tools excavated at Yorktown.
Drawing by
Robert L. Miller.
Courtesy Company of Military Historians.

real treasure trove of information that permits the modern scholar to know exactly what these Revolutionary War tools looked like. When the siege of Yorktown ended in victory, General Washington ordered that all the works built by the Americans be razed and the land restored to proper farming conditions. As they did this the happy American soldiers apparently threw away their tools in wholesale lots, for National Park Service excavations at the site have recovered quantities of them. Buried since 1781, they offer absolute documentation of American engineering and entrenching tools.

Among these tools there are three types of spade, one type of shovel, one pick, and two different sorts of mattock. None of them bear the "U.S." or "CXIII" mark, so perhaps that was customarily branded on the handle rather than stamped on the blade or head. Most of these tools seem to be of European manufacture, and many are stamped with the mark of a manufacturer or inspector, something which one would not normally expect on an American-made piece. Some are definitely French Army equipment.

Among these tools the most common type of spade (no. 1 on page 181) has a blade 8 inches wide and 11 3/4 inches long with a widened flange at the top to support the foot and a socket pierced with one hole for a rivet through the handle. Many of the spades of this pattern have large rectangular maker's marks with unidentified initials on the blades. The second form of spade is a much older variety of a kind often found on seventeenth-century sites. It has a blade 7 3/8 inches wide and 13 1/2 inches long of two-piece construction designed as a shell around a wooden core. The iron pieces are welded together at the bottom and riveted through the wooden core at the top (no. 2). Some of these are stamped with a large incised letter "G" near the handle and they may well be of American manufacture. The third type of spade has an unusually modern appearance with a short wide blade 7 1/2 inches wide and 7 3/4 inches long. There is no flange at the top and no mark was found on the single specimen of this kind which was recovered (no. 3). Normally all three types of spade would have been fitted with a straight wooden handle about 3 feet long with a short crosspiece forming a "T" at the top.

All the shovels that were found seem to follow one pattern which is both wider and flatter as well as rounder at the point than modern shovels (no. 4). These shovels closely resemble those illustrated in Suirery de Saint Remy's *Memoires d'Artillerie,* which appeared in various editions between 1697 and 1745, and since many of them bear still discernible French proofmarks in addition to maker's marks, it may be assumed that they are standard French Army issue. The usual specimen has a blade 11 1/4 inches wide and 11 inches long. These shovels might have had either a short handle similar to those on the spades or a long straight handle in the modern fashion.

The picks are all of one pattern and closely resemble modern picks in all details of design and construction (no. 5). Again, many bear French proofmarks, though some are completely unmarked. The average specimen measures 23 1/2 inches in a straight line from point to point.

Of the two types of pickaxe or mattock, one has a sharp point at one end and a broad blade at the other (no. 6). This pattern closely follows an illustration in Saint Remy and again may be assumed to be French. The socket or eye, in addition to being tapered, bears a pair of holes for a transverse rivet. The average specimen is 14 1/4 inches long. The second form of mattock has two broad blades with their axes at right angles and a definite "twist" line from the forging (no. 7). The eyes for the handles are also often diamond-shaped rather than elliptical as is the case with modern American mattocks. The average length of these heads is 18 inches. No marks have been noted in the study of this form thus far.

A representative collection of these entrenching tools is currently on display in the museum at Yorktown in Colonial National Historical Park, and a few pieces have been lent to the Smithsonian. The rest are available to students in the study collection at Jamestown. There is also a collection of entrenching tools at Fort Ticonderoga, but since this site was occupied for a longer period they cannot as definitely be identified as having been used by the Continental Army.

Axes and Hatchets

Just as important as entrenching tools to the Continental soldier was his axe. In fact it may even have been more important, for it served a wider variety of functions, both offensive and defensive as well as general utility. This was the tool which cut down trees to clear campsites and fields of fire or to create obstructions, provided logs for building huts or strengthening fortifications, and performed the multitude of cutting and chopping tasks necessary for existence in the open. Offensively it was carried by special troops called pioneers, who were chosen to approach an enemy position ahead of the regular attacking force, clearing away his abatis, opening holes in his fraising, and

*Axe head
excavated in an outwork
near Fort Ticonderoga.
The haft is modern.
Author's Collection.*

generally clearing the path for those who followed. These men traditionally carried axes as a symbol of their calling and as the prime tool for their work. Other axes were carried in wagons with the rest of the tools and issued for special purposes when needed.

The felling axe of the Revolution was the product of more than a century of evolution in the wooded country of America. The early settlers had brought an inefficient axe with a rounded top over the eye and no thickened poll to counterbalance the long blade. It tended to wobble in its stroke, and there was no weight to drive the blade deep into the wood. Since axe work was so important in the wilderness here, the axe quickly began to change in design. By the time of the Revolution the blade had shortened and broadened, and there was a heavy poll opposite it that might be a third or a half as long as the blade below the eye. Normally there were short pointed ears projecting back along the handle at the level of the eye, and the forward line of the blade, instead of flaring outward as does that of a modern axe, tended to be straight or even to curve to the rear. Hafts were straight. The typical curves of modern axe handles did not develop for another century.

Hatchets were used as well as axes, but these were normally personal items, as much weapons as tools, and not generally considered engineering equipment. They are discussed in the chapter on edged weapons. There were also broadaxes and adzes for squaring timbers and other tools of all sorts, but they were of less importance than these principal engineering items.

Fascine Knives

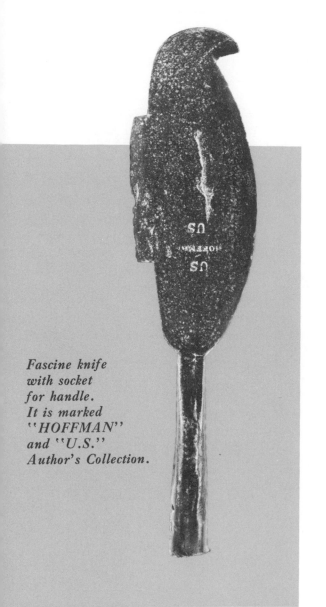

Fascine knife with socket for handle. It is marked "HOFFMAN" and "U.S." Author's Collection.

There was one other cutting tool issued to Continental soldiers for engineering purposes, however, and this was the fascine knife. It looked much like the modern brush hook except that it often had a low axelike blade at the back as well as the usual blade along the swelled front and under the hook. Some examples were socketed and others had a tang so that they could be fitted with a short handle for one-handed wielding. A specimen marked "US" in the author's collection measures 16 1/2 inches from the top of the hook to the bottom of the socket. Two other fascine knives were recovered when the Continental gunboat *Philadelphia* was raised from the bottom of Lake Champlain, and they are now on exhibit in the Smithsonian. As the name suggests, these knives were the tools that the soldiers used for cutting the boughs they needed for making fascines, saucissons, and gabions.

These were the principal engineering tools and devices of the Continental soldier. With them the pioneers and other privates

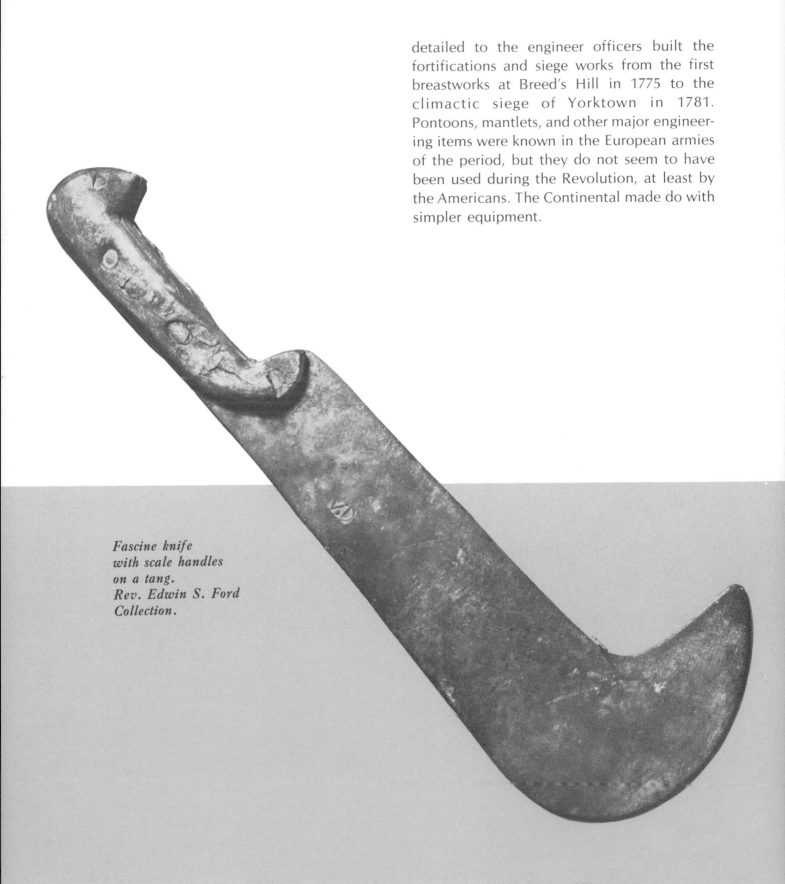

detailed to the engineer officers built the fortifications and siege works from the first breastworks at Breed's Hill in 1775 to the climactic siege of Yorktown in 1781. Pontoons, mantlets, and other major engineering items were known in the European armies of the period, but they do not seem to have been used during the Revolution, at least by the Americans. The Continental made do with simpler equipment.

*Fascine knife
with scale handles
on a tang.
Rev. Edwin S. Ford
Collection.*

Notes to Chapter 8

1. Smith, *Military Dictionary*. John Muller, *A Treatise containing the Elementary Part of Fortification,* 2nd ed., London, 1756, pp. 205-214 *et passim.* Marshal de Vauban, *De l'Attaque et de la Défense des Places,* La Haye, 1737, *passim.* J. G. Tielke, *The Field Engineer; or Instructions upon every Branch of Field Fortification...,* trans. by Edwin Hewgill, 2 vols., London, 1789, *passim.*

2. Smith, *Military Dictionary.* Muller, *Fortification,* pp. 228, 230, 239.

3. *Ibid.*

4. Smith, *Military Dictionary.*

5. *Ibid.*

6. General Orders, Headquarters, New York, June 18, 1776, Washington, *Writings,* V, 156. Headquarters, Morristown, April 17, 1777, *ibid.,* VII, 428. January 30, 1777, Ford, *Journals of the Continental Congress,* VII, 74.

Being a survey of the musical instruments

Chapter 9

Music was a necessity for any army of the eighteenth century, and the Continental Line was no exception. Not only did music boost morale, it also assisted marching in cadence, contributed to the pomp

That They Shall Have Musick

of ceremonies and, in the case of the "Rogue's March," increased the psychological factor in punishment. Most important of all, however, it offered the means of signaling and conveying orders more effectively than the human voice.

Fifes and Drums

The principal instruments for these purposes were the fife and drum. Every company was expected to have at least one drummer and one fifer, and a regiment might have as many as twenty plus a fife major and a drum major. These men, especially the drummers, sounded the signals of the day from reveille to tattoo, or taptoe, as it was frequently called at that time. They called the soldiers together, sounded the "General" as a signal to strike the tents when the army

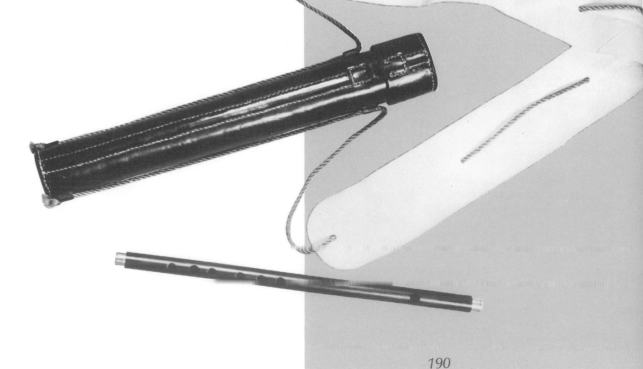

Fife and fifecase of eighteenth-century pattern. Colonial Williamsburg.

was to move, ordered the march itself, regulated the speed of the step, called halts, and provided the music for formal marching. They sent out fatigue parties, indicated meal time and church services, and called parleys with the enemy. In short, they did everything that the bugle came to do in armies of the next century—and a good bit more. Buglers seldom provided march music, and they never presided at military punishments. Fifes and drums, however, regularly officiated when undesirable persons were drummed out of camp with a mock parade. Sometimes drummers were even called upon to go further and actually inflict corporal punishment on soldiers sentenced to flogging, and there are references to the red flannel bags in which the drummers would carry the cat-o'-nine-tails used for this purpose. This was not a common duty, however. It seems to have occurred in only some units and at certain times. The main duty of the drummer and fifer remained music and signaling. *(1)*

The instruments used by Continental fifers and drummers were quite different from those commonly used today. The usual fife, for instance, was made of wood without a mouthpiece. Boxwood was a popular material, but other hard close-grained woods may also have been used. Some fifes, too, were made of iron. One such instrument, made from the barrel of a fowling piece, has been excavated at Colonial Williamsburg. The barrel had simply been cut off in front of the touchhole, plugged in one end and drilled for the various holes. Another series of iron fifes made originally as such has also been found. One was excavated on the Brandywine Battlefield and is now in the Smithsonian. Another was dug up at Saratoga and is displayed at Saratoga National Historical Park. The history of these fifes is obscured, however, by the fact that a third identical specimen has been uncovered at Fort Union, New Mexico, in circumstances that indicate a late nineteenth-century date. This immediately raises the question of

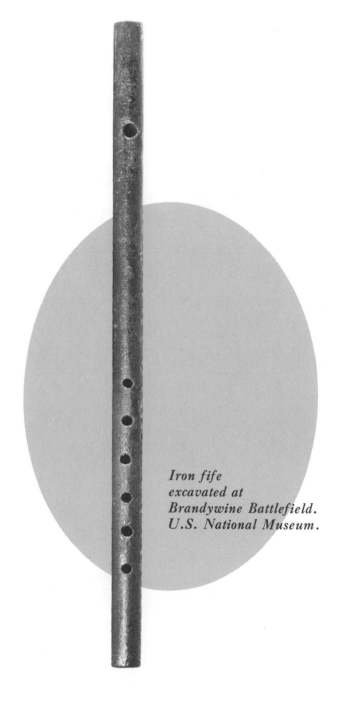

Iron fife
excavated at
Brandywine Battlefield.
U.S. National Museum.

Revolutionary War drum.
The body is painted
light blue with
red and yellow stripes.
Chicago Historical Society.

whether the two found on Revolutionary War sites might have been lost during centennial celebrations in the 1870's or whether the Fort Union specimen was an heirloom. To date this question has not been resolved.

The drums of the Revolution came in two principal types, snare or side drums and bass drums. The eighteenth-century snare drum was a somewhat bigger instrument than those used by modern bands. It was made of wood with a cylindrical shell perhaps 13-14 inches deep and 14-17 inches in diameter. Two hoops, one at either end, held the heads in place and made the drums look another two or three inches deeper. Tension was provided by ropes laced through holes in the hoops with sliding leather tugs for tightening. The lower hoop was also usually cut out on either side for the ends of the snare, which consisted of several strands of gut drawn tightly across the lower head. This snare gave a slightly more brilliant tone to the drum, and it was loosened when

Reproduction of an
eighteenth-century
bass drum
with
belt and beaters.
Colonial Williamsburg.

a duller tone was desired as in the case of a dead march for a funeral. Bass drums were perhaps 23-24 inches deep and about 22 inches in diameter, and they had no snare. They were carried horizontally across the chest and beaten with two wooden strikers which caused them to give off a far different sound from that produced by today's padded beaters and shallow, large-diameter bass drums.

Trumpets and Bugle Horns

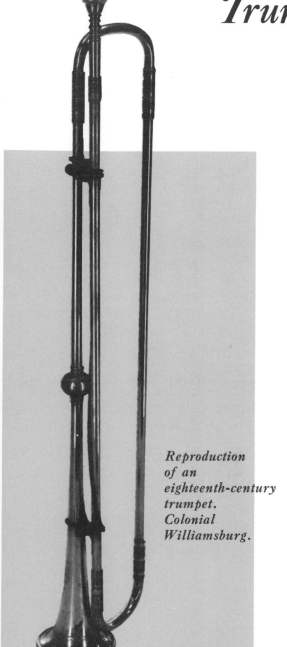

Reproduction of an eighteenth-century trumpet. Colonial Williamsburg.

Fifes and drums provided music and signals very effectively for infantry and artillery regiments which served on foot, but they were utterly impractical for mounted units. Horsemen needed an instrument that could be held and played with one hand, thus leaving the other free for controlling the horse. For this reason most cavalry used either the trumpet or the bugle horn for its signals. The trumpet was the standard instrument for the British horse. It was made usually of brass and looked much like an elongated version of the valveless trumpet that is often mistakenly called a bugle today. There was a separate mouthpiece and the tubing made just one loop. The principal musical characteristic, which is true for all trumpets, is that the bore was cylindrical. It remained the same diameter for two-thirds of its length before flaring out to form the bell. In use, cavalry trumpets were wrapped with a colored cord by which they could be slung around the trumpeter's neck. (2)

Bugle horns were quite different. Descended from the old Saxon hunting horns, they retained their resemblance to that instrument. The tubing still made one loop, but it was a large circle instead of the oblong form of the trumpet. Most important, its bore was

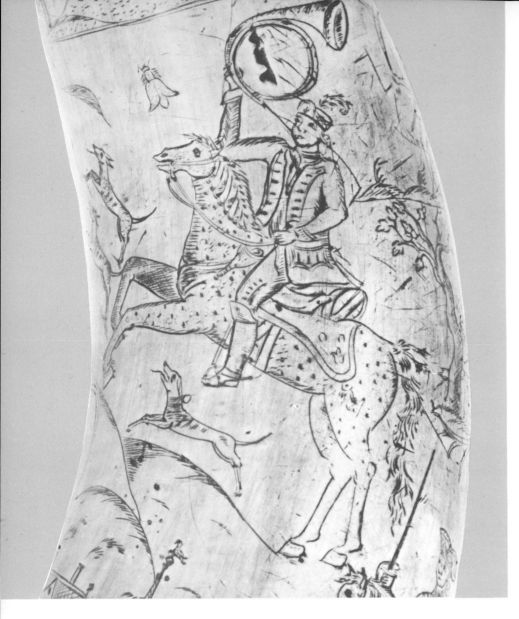

*Light horseman
sounding a bugle horn.
From a
contemporary
powder horn.
Joe Kindig, Jr.
Collection.*

conical, gradually increasing in diameter for most of its length. The type of bore is still the criterion that differentiates between a trumpet and a bugle, and the conical form gives a mellower, less strident tone than the piercing, brassy trumpet. There was also a form of the bugle horn without a loop. In this version the tubing was still conical, but it was shorter and formed a simple arc. Apparently this was a less popular design, but Robert Hinde illustrates it in his *Discipline of the Light Horse* (1778) as an instrument of the British cavalry, and American rifle insignia of the early 1800's show it along with the more common hunting-horn type.

At the time of the Revolution, trumpets were normally used by regular cavalry, bugle horns by light infantry and riflemen who often acted in extended order and desired a signal instrument that carried better than the fife and drum. They also seem to have been used by some light horse troops. In general the Continental Army seems to have followed this pattern except for the riflemen, who appear to have shunned the use of any formal instrument. Instead, Daniel Morgan used a turkey call as a signal to rally his Corps of Riflemen at the Battle of Saratoga, and similar expedients seem to have been substituted for other occasions.

The differentiation between the trumpet for horse and the bugle for light infantry, however, apparently held, though it is not always possible to be certain. Laymen, then as now, often used the terms as if they were synonymous. (3)

Another possible instance of the confusion of instruments by a layman in this same area is the record of "three French horns" issued to Pulaski's Independent Legion in 1778. Since the Legion had no band and since there were also at least two trumpets for the horse troops, it can be assumed that these were for the light infantry. French horns of the period resembled the bugle horn except for their longer tubing which formed additional small loops or crooks. A non-musician could easily fail to see the difference. On the other hand, French horns could indeed have been pressed into service as bugles. The sound would have been approximately the same. At this date it is impossible to know the facts. (4)

French horn
of eighteenth-century
style
with crooks
for changing keys.
Colonial Williamsburg.

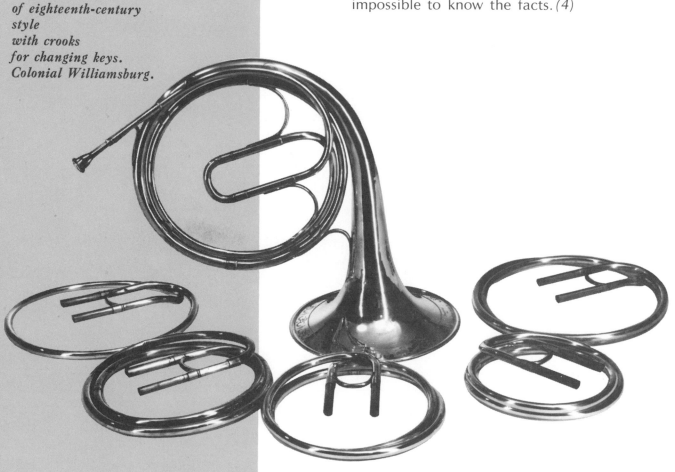

Bands of Musick

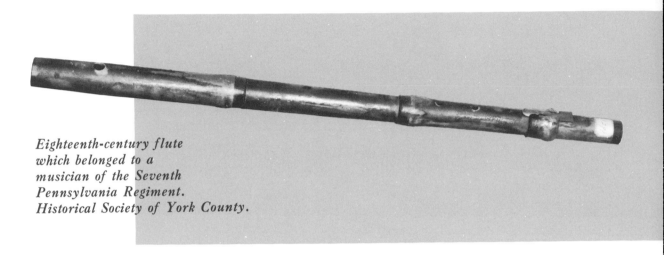

*Eighteenth-century flute
which belonged to a
musician of the Seventh
Pennsylvania Regiment.
Historical Society of York County.*

The fife, drum, bugle, and trumpet were the principal musical instruments of the Continental Army, and for many years it was thought that they were the only instruments. This is far from the case. Some regiments actually had "bands of musick" as well. Among them were the Third Continental Artillery Regiment, Samuel Webb's Additional Regiment, and Christian Febiger's Regiment, and there may well have been others. Since the instruments, instruction, music and other special costs of these bands were paid for by the officers from their personal funds, there are few official records about them. Febiger himself paid all the costs of his nine-man band, and when he tried to obtain reimbursement from the Board of War, he was refused on the grounds that all regiments might ask for bands if his request were granted. Generally the musicians seem to have been taken from the regular fifers who were persuaded to learn the other instruments for such additional inducements as the officers could provide. (5)

In one of his pleas for some financial help, Febiger provides several insights into the methods of recruiting a band, the inducements offered, and the value of such a musical group:

...Early in the War, I had often attempted to raise a Band from British or German deserters or prisoners; but I soon found no dependence could be put on these people. — I determined to try natives. Mr. Sheldon my Fife-Major and several other young men native of this State, whose times expired late in '79: — intended to re-enlist — but to no purpose, until I proposed to form a band and if they would re-enlist during the War if I lived that long or as long as I lived to command whether War and peace and received their training, instruments, and extra clothing as a bounty for so doing, I would immediately enlist them — they agreed....The men are enlisted to serve as musicians or fifers and to do duty as such. Their music had more influence on the minds and motions of the militia last summer in this State [Virginia] then [sic] would the oratory of a Cicero, and in the recruiting business they are at least as useful as a well-spoken recruiting Sergeant....I engaged a Master and 8 — one is dead. And one from a hurt he received is invalided — I have put soldiers, fifers in their place and [of the?] continuing number — 7 are equal to any Band in this country the other two improving. (6)

Nine men seems small for a military band today, but it was about average for the period. And it should be remembered that the drummer also joined them to swell the number somewhat.

Instrumentation varied from unit to unit. In Febiger's band there were four clarinetists (who doubled on violin for orchestral work), two bassoon players who also learned the bass viol, and two French horn players. Other popular instruments included the flute, the hautboy or oboe, the trumpet, the trombone, and the serpent. Most of the instruments were generally similar to their modern counterparts though the external appearance varied somewhat. The trumpet and the French horn, however, were valveless, and the serpent has since disappeared. Even in its day, the serpent was somewhat of a hybrid. It had a typical brass instrument mouthpiece, but it was made of wood covered with leather, and the different notes were obtained by covering and uncovering a series of holes. It was thus part brass, part woodwind, and its tone was shallow, lacking in resonance. Still it functioned as the principal bass instrument in a military band of the period. (7)

If Colonel Febiger's musicians were really as good as any band in the country, they must have been very good indeed. Other bands were at least passable, and the Third Artillery Regiment band, for one, seems to have been quite accomplished if one may judge from its repertoire. On February 17, 1783 it played a concert at Portsmouth, New Hampshire that included "several overtures, simphonies, military music, several songs, and several duettos on the French horn." These were undoubtedly difficult pieces and a far cry from the simple fife and drum tunes that are usually thought of as the sole music of the Continental Army. They offer a worthy beginning for the long series of Army bands that has followed. (8)

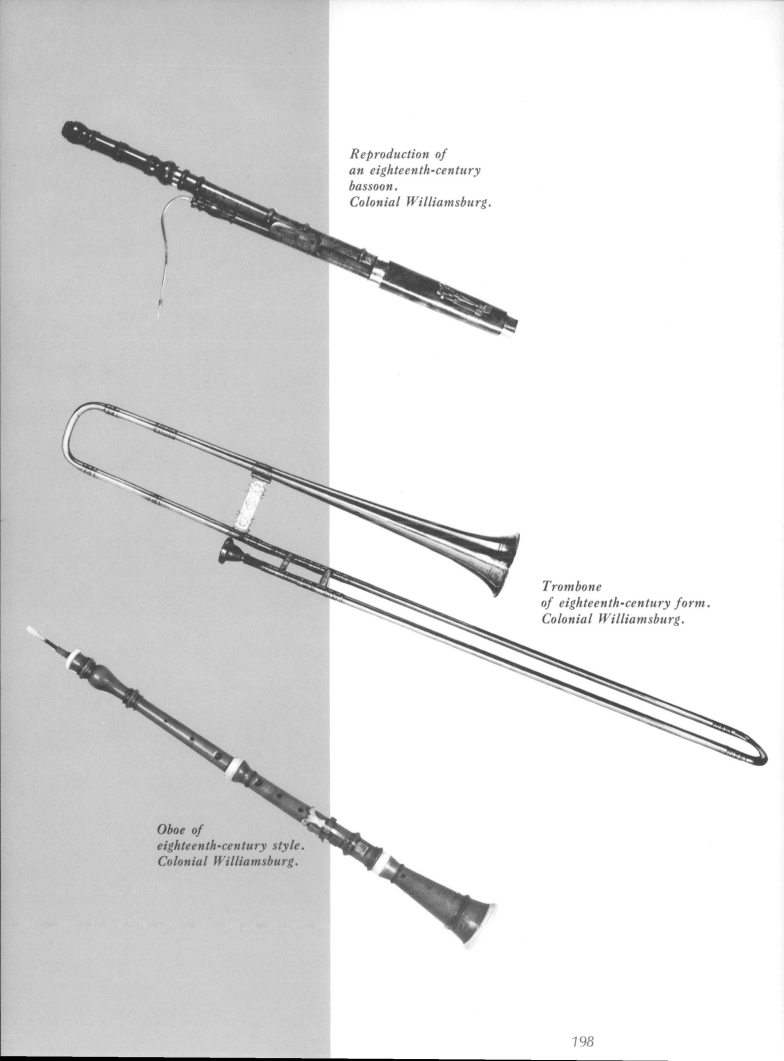

*Reproduction of
an eighteenth-century
bassoon.
Colonial Williamsburg.*

*Trombone
of eighteenth-century form.
Colonial Williamsburg.*

*Oboe of
eighteenth-century style.
Colonial Williamsburg.*

Brass band
at Colonial Williamsburg
showing methods of
holding the instruments.

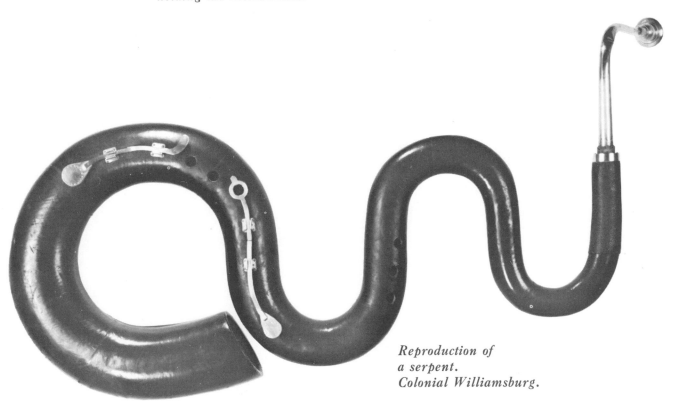

Reproduction of
a serpent.
Colonial Williamsburg.

Notes to Chapter 9

1. Von Steuben, *Regulations,* pp. 50, 51, *et passim.* Thacher, *Military Journal,* p. 180. William C. White, *A History of Military Music in America,* New York, 1944, pp. 18-32.

2. Smith, *Military Dictionary,* unpaged article on "Trumpet." Simes, *Military Guide,* article "Trumpet" in the "Dictionary." Epaphras Hoyt, *Practical Instructions for Military Officers,* Greenfield, Mass., 1811, pp. 170, 171, 373.

3. *Ibid.* James Wilkinson, *Memoirs of My Own Time,* 3 vols., Philadelphia, 1816, I, 237, 238.

4. Holst and Zlatich, "Dress and Equipment of Pulaski's Legion," pp. 100-102.

5. Febiger to Washington, March 14, 1782, Washington, *Papers,* vol. 193, p. 30. Oscar Sonneck, *Early Concert-life in America, 1731-1800,* New York, 1949, p. 319. In the music research files at Colonial Williamsburg kindly made available by Musick Master George P. Carroll are a number of letters from the Febiger papers which bear on this subject. Of most importance is a letter to the Board of War dated March 7, 1780. These papers are also available on microfilm at the Virginia State Library.

6. Febiger to Washington, March 14, 1782, *Washington Papers.*

7. Febiger to Board of War, March 7, 1780, Febiger papers. H. W. Schwartz, *The Story of Musical Instruments,* New York, 1943, *passim.* Henry G. Farmer, *History of the Royal Artillery Band,* London, 1954, pp. 1-87. Henry G. Farmer, *Military Music,* London, 1950, pp. 18-34.

8. *New Hampshire Gazette,* February 15, 1783, quoted in Sonneck, *Concert-life,* p. 319.

To Keep Horse

and Man Together

Being a survey of the horse equipment

It takes more than a horse to outfit a cavalryman. The horse is the most obvious piece of equipment, if it may be so considered, but it in turn needs a whole group of accessories to make it function

Chapter 10

and to keep it in good condition. Reins and headstall are required to provide control, a saddle for a firm seat, stirrups for stability and leverage, spurs for inducing movement, curry combs, horseshoes, picket poles, and a host of other minor implements for maintaining the mount in a presentable and efficient condition. In addition the cavalryman or mounted officer needed to carry his weapons, extra clothing, and personal gear just as the foot soldier did, and so additional horse equipment such as holsters, carbine buckets, valises, saddle bags, and portmanteaus were designed for the purpose. There was, in fact, a tendency to overload the horse with the accumulated equipment, weapons, and man that it was expected to carry.

Epaphras Hoyt, who gained his experience as a cavalryman during the Revolution, described his idea of the ideal cavalry rig shortly after the War:

Their accoutrements consist of saddles, bridles, holsters, halters, and surcingles....
The best saddles are those that are about nineteen or twenty inches in length, with wide pads that come down about the horses' sides almost as low as the skirts, to rest as near the back-bone of the horse as possible without hurting him, for the nearer the rider sits to his horse's back the safer is his seat. From hence it is evident that the pommel must rise enough to preserve the withers from being pressed, and that a horse with high withers must have a high pommel....the cantle ought to be high, which will keep the rider firm in his seat, the skirts of such a length that they will come three or four inches below the tops of the rider's boots; the girth and surcingle at least three inches in width, the stirrups of the best leather...the breast-plate not too wide, and the saddle cloth of a moderate size. To the saddle should be added a mail pillion. Curb bridles with double reins and nose-bands are the best for cavalry; the bitt should be full and thick in the mouth, especially at the ends where they join the bars....Upon the snaffle rein should be fixed a sliding loop, which will play easily upon the reins; the length of the curb reins should be equal to the length of the snaffle reins from the bit to the loop when it is held in the hands, as the trooper is mounted.
Usually there is a valise for personal belongings, curry combs, etc. (1)

*Continental cavalrymen mounted
with their arms and equipment.
The dress corresponds with
descriptions of
Baylor's Third Continental Dragoons.
Drawing by Clyde A. Risley.*

Bridles

The bridles that Hoyt mentioned were little different from military types today if one may judge from pictures in contemporary books on equitation and paintings such as the David Morier series of British horse regiments painted in 1751. Apparently there were two principal types, one used when separate curb and snaffle bits were used and one of the so-called Pelham style which was frequently employed when a Pelham bit which combined snaffle and curb reins

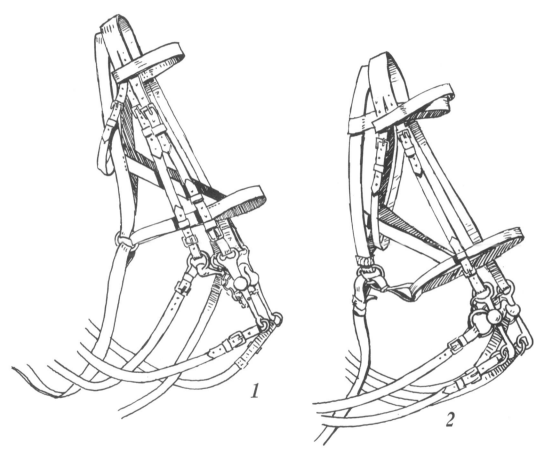

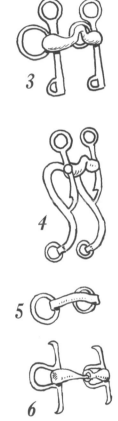

Halters and bits.
Drawing by Clyde A. Risley.

1. *English halter and double bridle based on contemporary description.*

2. *French halter from de la Parterie's Institutions Militaires with Pelham-style bridle and bit.*

3. *Pelham-style bit based on specimen in Washington's Headquarters Museum, Newburgh.*

4. *Curb bit found at Fort George and now belonging to New-York Historical Society.*

5. *Check snaffle bit, New-York Historical Society.*

6. *Snaffle bit found at British campsite, New-York Historical Society.*

7. *Jointed curb bit found at Stony Point.*

was used. Both kinds of bit have been found in Revolutionary War sites in this country. The only description given of bits in contemporary literature aside from whether they are snaffle or curb revolves around the fact that they should be full in the mouth where they join the side bars, and this requirement occurs almost universally. Apparently it was heeded, for although both jointed and solid bits have been found, single as well as Pelham types, all have been decidedly full in the mouth. *(2)*

Saddles

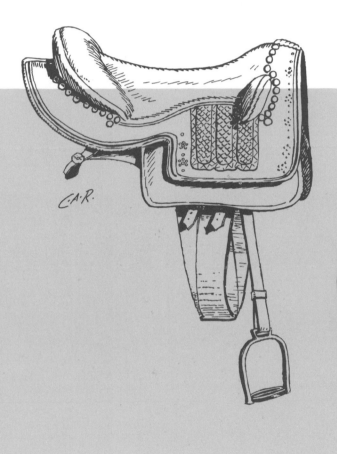

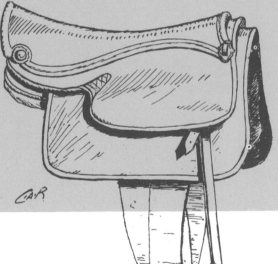

British officer's saddle (left)
and flat saddle (right)
after Diderot.
Drawing by Clyde A. Risley.

Of all the pieces of equestrian equipment, however, the saddle was probably the most important and the most complicated. Not only did it provide the rider's seat, but it also supplied the support for the stirrups and offered the frame for hanging the trooper's weapons and the containers for his personal gear. Saddles varied somewhat in their external appearance, but most were basically of the same construction. Underneath was a frame of wood called a saddle tree. This was the important element that gave the saddle its shape and determined whether it would fit both horse and man properly. Generally there were four elements, a pommel arch that formed the front of the saddle, a cantle arch for the rear, and two side pieces that connected the two arches. The pommel arch had to rise high enough to protect the horse's withers. The cantle arch offered support to the rider to keep him from sliding back. Together they assured that the saddle would not press directly on the horse's spine where the skin was close to the bone and so would rub off easily and create sores. Over the frame went the variously designed padding, covers, skirts, etc., which gave the individual saddles their character. Then there were the various straps to secure the saddle in place. The girth and surcingle which passed under the horse's belly kept it from slipping sideways; a breast strap and a crupper kept it from sliding forward or back. The girth attached to the tree underneath the skirt. The surcingle passed over the top of the saddle and was buckled on after the saddle was in place and the girth tight. In this way it not only helped hold the saddle in place but also helped hold the holsters, shabraques, and pads in place and kept the flaps and side panels of the saddle down.(3)

In general there were four types of saddle popularly used

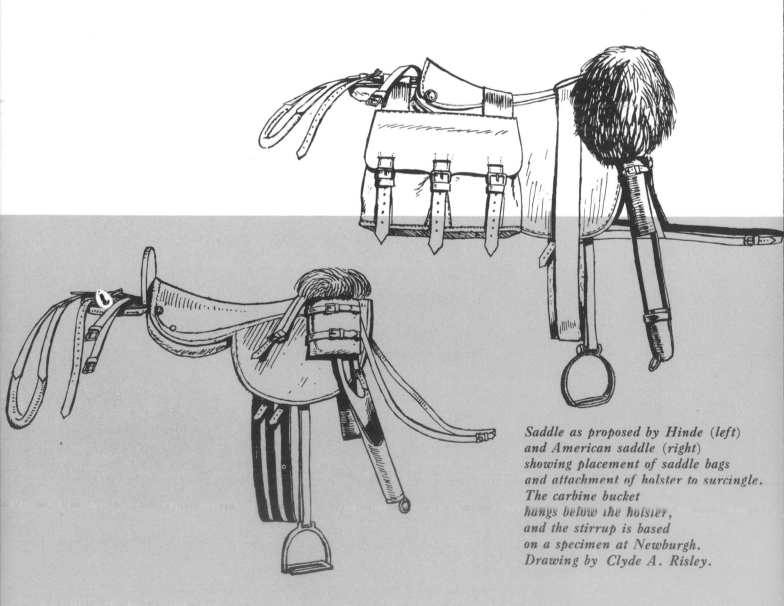

Saddle as proposed by Hinde (left)
and American saddle (right)
showing placement of saddle bags
and attachment of holster to surcingle.
The carbine bucket
hangs below the holster,
and the stirrup is based
on a specimen at Newburgh.
Drawing by Clyde A. Risley.

during the Revolution. Two were British, one French, and one Central European. Most common was the British flat saddle developed from the popular hunting saddle of the period and not too different from the English saddle of today in its general contour. A companion to this was an officers' version with padded cantle and leg rolls at the front. The plates for Diderot's famous *Encyclopédie* illustrate both of these forms as "English saddles." Also, in the Smithsonian Institution there is a saddle attributed to General de Kalb that is similar to the English officers' type but covered in quilted red cloth and somewhat more fully padded. Robert Hinde in his *Discipline of the Light Horse* (1778) shows a modification of the common flat saddle with a vertical arch framed in iron and covered with leather behind the cantle to protect the rider's back from being bumped by the gear tied on behind. This was, however, merely a proposal, and there is no indication that any were ever so equipped or that they came to America. *(4)*

There is also a good possibility that French saddles found their way to America along with the other military gear provided by that country. If so, they differed from the English types in having

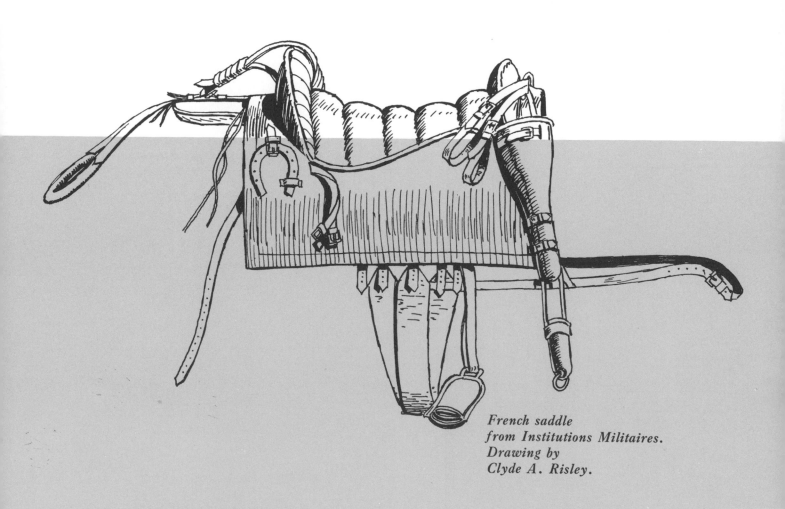

*French saddle
from Institutions Militaires.
Drawing by
Clyde A. Risley.*

209

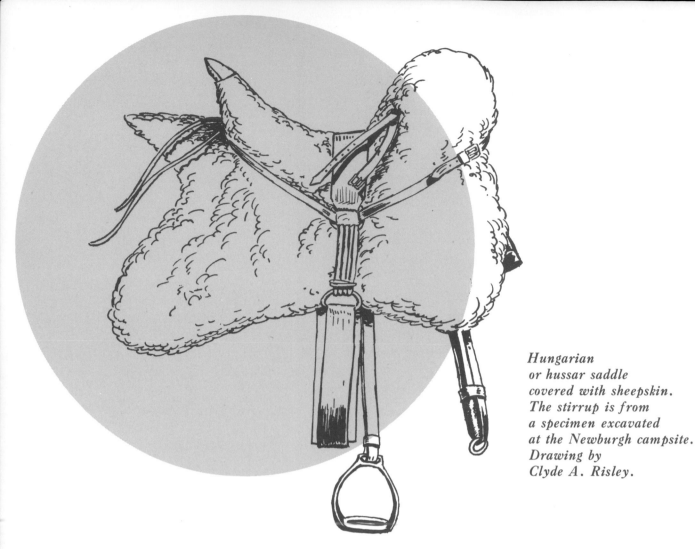

*Hungarian
or hussar saddle
covered with sheepskin.
The stirrup is from
a specimen excavated
at the Newburgh campsite.
Drawing by
Clyde A. Risley.*

padded seats and higher padded cantles and pommels. The skirts also were square, fuller, and provided with straps on the off side for attaching spare horseshoes. *(5)*

The fourth type of saddle and one that is frequently mentioned in the documents is the hussar, Hungarian, or sheepskin saddle. Pulaski's Independent Legion, for one, was issued such saddles. They had high cantles and pommels, and instead of leather, sheepskins with the hair side out were used to cover the frame and to provide the skirts. According to indications in the correspondence between Washington and Pulaski, these sheepskins were obtained directly from the butcher and thrown over the saddle traces with only the surcingle to hold them in place. *(6)*

In addition to these more or less standard forms of saddle, there were undoubtedly a great variety of other types used by American soldiers. Officers, for instance, often brought with them saddles they had used in civilian life, adapting them when necessary to hold holsters and portmanteaus or valises. Also, it is known that in 1778 Sheldon's Second Continental Dragoons received an issue of horse equipment captured from the Brunswick Dragoons during the Saratoga campaign. These may have been English saddles, but then again, they may also have been German types and so have added another form of saddle to the heterogeneous supply of the Continental Army. *(7)*

Below the saddle hung the stirrups. These were suspended by straps called stirrup leathers that fastened directly to the frame. The stirrups themselves (or stirrup irons as they are sometimes called) were actually made of iron. Usually they consisted of a simple arch formed as a single rod with a slot or loop at the top for the leathers to pass through and a tread that might be oval or rectangular. Often the tread also consisted of a rod which formed the outline of the shape plus another rod running through the center. In rarer instances it was fashioned as a flat plate with holes cut in it.

Holsters and Carbine Buckets

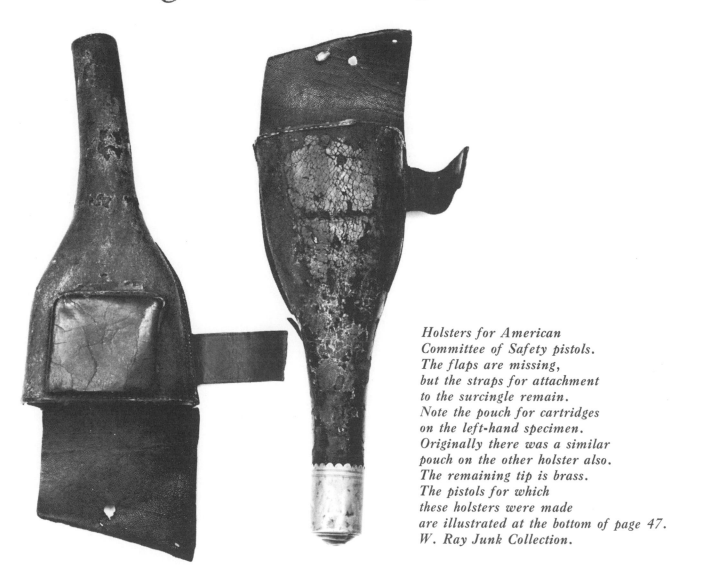

Holsters for American Committee of Safety pistols. The flaps are missing, but the straps for attachment to the surcingle remain. Note the pouch for cartridges on the left-hand specimen. Originally there was a similar pouch on the other holster also. The remaining tip is brass. The pistols for which these holsters were made are illustrated at the bottom of page 47. W. Ray Junk Collection.

At the front of the saddle were the holsters for carrying the pair of pistols recommended for every trooper and mounted officer. These were made of stout leather and shaped as closely as possible to the outline of the pistol. Normally there was a cap at the muzzle end made of pewter or more usually brass, and there was a cover at the open end to protect the weapons from rain and snow. Sometimes these covers were leather, sometimes cloth, and a further covering of bearskin was desirable as additional protection. On rare occasions these holsters were made singly and attached by straps to staples on the pommel of the saddle. More usually they were made as a pair joined by a broad strap that could be thrown over the pommel. Additional straps to go around the surcingle and the breaststrap helped to hold them in place. The pistols were placed in these holsters with their butts forward so that they could be drawn readily with either hand.

Another piece of equipment for carrying a weapon was the leather carbine bucket. This was hooked to the saddle on the right or off side and hung from two straps just below the holster. It was in reality a little socket that held the muzzle of the carbine. An iron ring at the tip of the bucket was designed to receive one end of a picket pole for tying the horse up when he was not being ridden. When the trooper was dismounted he usually carried his carbine on a broad leather strap that passed over his left shoulder and attached the carbine by a snap on a sliding loop so that it hung muzzle down on his right side. When he was mounted he unsnapped the carbine, inserted the muzzle in the bucket, and passed a strap from the pommel of his saddle around the small of the stock to secure it. The carbine was thus completely free of the rider and could be left on the saddle when he dismounted if this was desired.

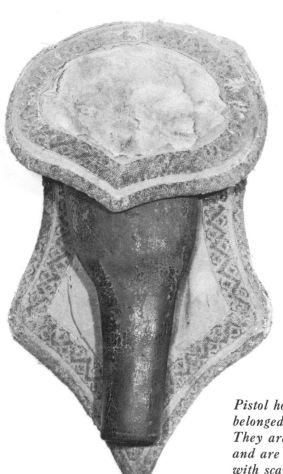

*Pistol holsters which
belonged to George Washington.
They are made of black leather
and are trimmed
with scarlet braid.
Mount Vernon Ladies' Association
of the Union.*

1. Early holster with strap for
   attachment to a staple on the
   saddle pommel from Warren Moore
   Collection.

2. American holster with pewter tip
   and a broad suspension strap slit
   to receive the surcingle. The
   covering is linen. Charles J. West
   Collection.

3. Probably the most common form of
   holster. Thongs are provided for
   tying to the saddle, and there is
   a loop at the back for the surcingle.
   The lower strap may have
   engaged the breast strap. There is
   a bearskin cover on the flap, and
   the tip is brass.
   Drawing by Clyde A. Risley.

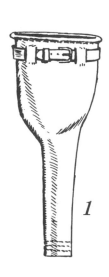

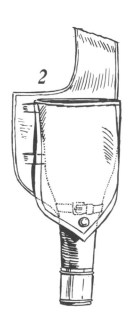

Valises and Saddle Bags

At the rear of the saddle were straps for attaching the blanket roll or cloak. At times they also held on a portmanteau full of personal gear plus such other things as a curry comb, mane comb, hoof pick, and nose bag for the horse. Instead of the portmanteau or valise, however, Congress early recommended the use of a pair of saddle bags connected by two broad straps. Actually, these leather bags were more commodious than the portmanteau. They were rectangular in form, and normally they had a flap that fastened with two or three straps and buckles. Their broad suspension straps passed over the horse's back, one just behind the saddle and one directly across the seat, so that the bags hung one on either side just below the rear of the saddle. *(8)*

Saddle bags.
Both pair are made of russet leather
and fit the description
favored by Congress
with two broad supporting straps.
The left-hand pair are
in the Clyde A. Risley Collection.
The upper specimen
is based on a fragment
formerly owned by Norm Flayderman.
Drawing by Clyde A. Risley.

Horseshoes

Leaving the items designed for the rider and turning to those for the horse himself, it should be noted that shoes were as important then as they are now both to protect the hoof and to afford surer footing. The principal difference between the horseshoe of the Revolution and that of today lies in the fact that the horseshoes of the Continental Army were handmade rather than mass-produced, forged rather than stamped. They might be flat or grooved, "fullered," as it was called, and they might or might not have heel caulks. Both width and thickness varied considerably, though recoveries from Revolutionary War sites indicate that they were apt to be both broader and thinner than modern shoes.

Spurs

The final bit of horse equipment was worn not by the horse but by the rider. This was the spur. By the middle of the eighteenth century the spur had receded from the bulky form with huge rowell and had assumed a fairly modern appearance. The arch was reasonably small, the neck short, and the rowell of modern size with short points.

Typical eighteenth-century spurs.
Drawing by Clyde A. Risley.

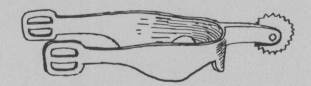

Revolutionary spurs might be made of iron for the simpler types, but brass was common and silver was used for the better specimens. Sometimes the arches were hinged, but usually they were solid. The combination of one stud and one buckle was common for attaching the strap that passed over the instep, while two studs were usual for the lower strap. Sometimes, however, there were simply double loops at the ends of the arms for straps to be sewed fast or otherwise attached. George Washington, for one, had silver spurs with such loops from which short lengths of chain held both buckles and studs. The necks might be straight but more often curved slightly downwards. Doubly curved necks are also encountered occasionally. Rowels might be star-shaped or take the form of a wheel with a serrated edge.

The men who wore these spurs and used the other pieces of equipment from saddles to bridles fought in many different organizations and under many different circumstances. The Continental Army boasted four specific regiments of light dragoons plus Lee's Battalion and also horse troops in both Pulaski's and Armand's legions, and then there were the field officers of other branches of the service who often served on horseback. Some used their horses as engines of attack, as mobile fighting platforms. To others, horses were primarily transportation. Officer or enlisted man, dragoon or legionnaire, however, their needs were the same—a firm seat, together with guidance and care for their mounts. And these were the types of horse equipment they employed to attain their ends.

Notes to Chapter 10

1. Hoyt, *Military Art,* pp. 9, 10.

2. *Ibid.* Maj. G. Tylden, *Horses and Saddlery,* London, 1965, pp. 205, 206.

3. *Ibid.,* pp. 112-129.

4. *Ibid.,* pp. 122-129. Robert Hinde, *Discipline of the Light Horse,* London, 1778, p. 526. Denis Diderot, *Recueil des Planches sur les Sciences, les Arts Libéraux, et les Arts Méchaniques avec leur Explication,* 11 vols., Paris, 1762-1772.

5. M. de la Porterie, *Institutions Militaires pour la Cavalerie et les Dragons,* Paris, n.d. (1764?)

6. L. Rousselot print entitled "Hussards, Reglement de 1786," No. 51, Paris, n.d. Washington to Pulaski, February 14, 1778, Washington, *Writings,* X, 457, 458.

7. Washington to the officer commanding at Albany, New York, January 1, 1778, Washington, *Writings,* X, 246.

8. George Clinton, *Public Papers of George Clinton,* ed. by Hugh Hastings, 8 vols., New York, 1899-1904, II, 829, 830. Tylden, *Horses and Saddlery,* pp. 124, 125.

Chapter 11

Being a survey of the clothing and uniforms of the Continental soldier*

*This chapter was written by Marko Zlatich and Detmar H. Finke.

To Clothe The Naked Soldier

The Continental Army, like any regular army before and since, attempted to present as formidable and warlike an appearance as possible. However, to say that its officers and men were in uniform would come short of the mark. It is even true that certain regiments and large numbers of individuals were reported "Not fit for Duty for want of cloathing," but this was usually a temporary status between campaigns. The Continental soldier was clothed, but rarely uniformly, since no uniform regulations were prescribed until 1779, and even after that, a faulty supply system and other circumstances mitigated against the full realization of these regulations. One of the circumstances that operated throughout the war was that clothing often wore out while in service and logistical support being what it was, new supplies never caught up with the troops. This is common in all wars and the primitive transportation system in a country 3,000 miles long from north to south did nothing to help matters. Therefore, only a brief sketch of what the uniform was supposed to be contrasted to what actually was received is the subject of the following. (1)

System of Clothing Supply

When the Continental Army first mustered at Cambridge, few men had uniforms of any sort. In 1775, Congress was aware of the need for clothing the army, but it had to start from scratch. Stocks of cloth had to be purchased as no stores of ready-made uniforms existed, beyond what could be captured from the enemy. Purchasing agents were appointed in New York, Massachusetts, and Connecticut, the most industrially advanced colonies, and in December 1776 James Mease was elected Clothier General to direct the Continental Clothing Department. Thereafter, assistant clothiers general were appointed in Boston and Albany to collect and distribute locally. Other agents were sent to France and Holland to arrange for the importation of cloth and ready-made clothing.

Uniforms of Continental troops.

Drawing by
H. Charles McBarron, Jr.

1. *An American rifleman based upon a German drawing of the 1780's which shows the figure all in white linen.*

2. *An American rifleman based on a sketch by a Bavarian officer; the uniform seems to be cotton tinted green with white fringe.*

3. *The ideal Continental uniform striven for but seldom achieved.*

4. *An American soldier based upon one of the figures in Van Blarenbergh's eyewitness painting of the surrender at Yorktown. The coat is brown, the trousers light blue, stockings yellowish, and everything ragged.*

5. *Ordinary seaman in a costume such as some of Glover's Marblehead Regiment may have worn.*

6. *Marine in green coat faced white.*

7. *An American rifleman after a British caricature.*

8. *An American soldier based on French engravings of the period.*

9. *Dragoon with the brass helmet which was illustrated frequently by John Trumbull.*

However, it was never possible for Congress to provide sufficient habiliment for the troops of the Continental establishment. Even with supplies from France and Holland the states were held responsible for issuing bounty clothing or the equivalent in cash to new recruits. After 1779, when Congress realized the utter futility of conducting the clothing business under James Mease, the responsibility for their own regiments devolved back on the states, who had to clothe their quotas on active duty and were authorized to purchase stores on the account of the United States. The inevitable result was that neither the Congress nor the states bought much clothing. Yet, on March 23, 1779, Congress approved an ordinance regulating the Clothing Department with a Clothier General subject to the orders of the Board of War and the Commander-in-Chief. State and regimental clothiers were to see that proper returns, fitting, and distribution were to be instituted at the local level.

Even when clothing was available, more often than not, it was incomplete, ill-made, or ruined from long exposure. At other times, as in the crucial month of December 1780, funds were lacking to expedite large shipments from France. Vast stores rotted for lack of transportation or were sold by agents and profiteers as the price of finished textiles skyrocketed. The sincere efforts of the fourth Clothier General, John Moylan, could not suceed until his office was made responsible to the Superintendent of Finance, Robert Morris, who disbursed cash on the basis of an annual estimate. As a result, more clothing than ever before was issued, but shortages persisted to the end of the war because sufficient funds were not available.

The system abounded with paradoxes. It was sometimes abused for personal profit and it also caused the ruin of several fortunes. Clever commanding officers, such as Samuel B. Webb of Connecticut, manipulated it so that their men always had more than enough clothing, while the same lack of accountability caused other regiments to be almost without clothing.

Types of Clothing

The articles of clothing most common to the Continental soldier were the same as those issued to European troops, except that the mode of warfare adopted by the Americans forced certain modifications, and produced one outstanding contribution. This new item was the hunting shirt. Made of linen or any other form of homespun cloth, it was loose, easy to remove, and allowed a freedom of movement not unlike the farmers' or workmen's smocks. Utterly utilitarian, it was considered by Washington to be an ideal military garment. With its fringe on cape or collar, seams, and edges, it could be dyed almost any military color,

Variations in American rifle dress.

Drawing by
H. Charles McBarron, Jr.

1. Blanket coats given the Army by Montgomery in the Quebec campaign, 1775-76.

2. Ranger Company of Philadelphia, 1775.

3. Rifleman as shown in the sketch by Du Simitiere for the design of the Great Seal.

4. Morgan's Rifleman as drawn by John Trumbull.

5. The white linen hunting shirt of the Fourth Regiment, Dutchess County Militia, now preserved at Newburgh.

6. Indian dress as described in the "Life of Horatio Jones," Buffalo Historical Society Publications, VI, 419.

7. Blanket worn Indian fashion.

8. Breechcloth and leggings as worn by some riflemen.

9. Moccasin.

10. Rifle dress as described by a member of the Quebec campaign.

and cuff and collar facings could be added as regimental distinctions. When worn over other clothing it served as an overcoat. Some hunting shirts were pullovers while others resembled frocks in that they were open down the front. Originally worn as uniforms by rifle units, these shirts were also adopted, at one time or another, by most of the Continental Army.

The more traditional military garb of the eighteenth century, however, consisted of:

Head Gear

The commonest form was the cocked hat with a rosette or cockade on the left side, under a loop fastened to a button, tassels at each corner, and cloth edging or binding. Feathers were prescribed for officers, but were also sported by enlisted men in the artillery and other elite units. The brim of the cocked hat was approximately 5 inches wide at the back and 3 1/2-4 inches in the front, but hats having brims of only 2 inches were also popular. Regiments with grenadier and light infantry companies were sometimes able to turn the men out in smart caps of leather or stiffened cloth. Knitted wool caps were also issued in great quantities, but their appearance is unknown. Whenever possible, the cavalry had helmets of hard leather or brass.

Coats

The military coat of the period was made of wool or broadcloth and came with lapels, cuffs, collar and skirts which could be turned back. The lapels were generally worn buttoned back and the coat fastened by hooks and eyes; however, in cold weather, the lapels could be buttoned across down to the waistband. It was the practice of the times to face the collar, cuffs, and lapels with a different color from that of the coat to provide a regimental distinction; such coats were then known as regimentals. When supplies of colored cloth, i.e., red, white, buff, yellow, etc., were short, only the collar

Hats and postures.
Drawing by
H. Charles McBarron, Jr.

1. The round hat.

2. Diagram of the round hat with dotted line showing the cock of the brim.

3. Diagram of the cocked hat with lines upon which the brim was cocked up. The crown was always circular and usually 4 inches high.

4. The manner of saluting without weapons.

5. Position of greatest attention, 1751, with heels one step apart.

6. Position of maximum attention, 1777, with heels four inches apart.

7. Method of wearing the cocked hat. The front angle was placed directly over the corner of the left eye.

8. Cedar twigs were sometimes worn in the hat to denote rank. With Mercer's troops, for instance, it designated a lieutenant.

9. Position of present arms.

10. Light infantry cap based on a sketch of Lieut. Judah Alden by Kosciusko.

11. Dragoon helmet based on one worn by Moses Titcomb now in the Essex Institute.

12. Cockade.

13. The formal marching step.

14. Officers in cocked hats. General officers often wore their hats almost straight across the front.

225

*Tailor's pattern
of the Tench Tilghman coat
in the collection of the
Maryland Historical Society.
Drawing by Donald W. Holst.*

and cuffs were faced. The length of the coat depended upon the amount of cloth on hand but usually extended to just above the knee. Shorter coats, e.g., coatees, were about as long as present-day jackets, just covering the buttocks.

Early in the War, Congress agreed with Washington that the base color of the foot soldiers' coats was to be brown with regimental facing distinctions of other colors. This was the same color that Massachusetts and Connecticut had chosen for the regiments they raised for the Continental Army. Thus, Congress merely confirmed what was already established fact.

The troops coming from Pennsylvania and southward seemed to prefer blue as the ground color, and Congress complied with their practice by authorizing the purchase of blue cloth. From 1777 to the end of the War, this was the basic color of the infantry coat, although gray, green, various shades of brown, red, and light blue were also worn by individual regiments. The use of variant colors seems to have been the result of the latitude allowed regiment commanders to decide the type of regimentals between 1775 and 1779. Shortages of blue cloth also accounted for some of the diversity which occurred even within the same regiment. At any given time, a review of the Continental Army would produce a truly motley effect, with coat colors varying from battalion to battalion and company to company. Because officers were responsible for purchasing their own uniforms, they often appeared in attire which differed from that of the men under their command.

Smallclothes

Made of less substantial cloth than the coats, the smallclothes came in as many colors as the coats, but white was generally preferred. These garments consisted of waist-coats, vests, breeches, overalls, and trousers. Worn under the coat, the waistcoat was single-breasted and had flaps covering the pockets at the waist. It was usually without sleeves, although sleeved varieties were also encountered. This garment was also called a vest. Breeches were full in the rear but tight in the crotch and were frequently made of leather, which provided longer wear but caused great discomfort. Washington considered the overall, a long-legged garment covering the entire leg and lower torso to be a superior item of clothing, and it was adopted by most regiments after 1778. Woolen overalls were preferred for winter service; linen overalls for summer.

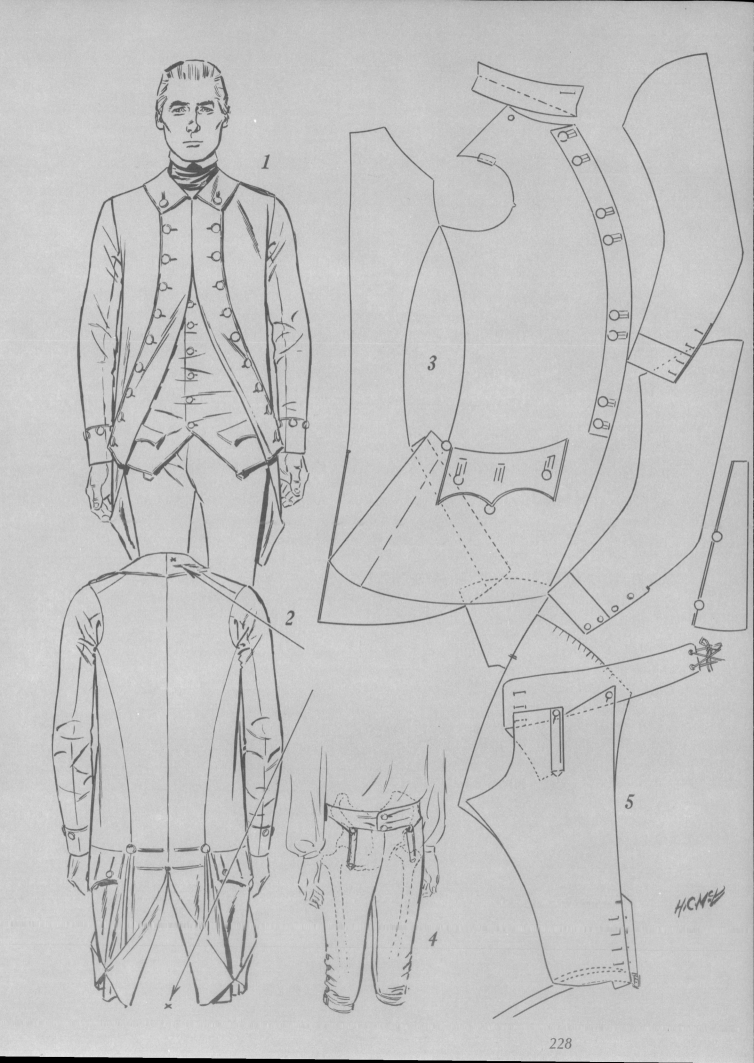

1

2

3

4

5

HICKEY

228

Patterns of coat and breeches.

Drawing by
H. Charles McBarron, Jr.

1. *Coats were long-waisted and tight in the sleeve. There was no padding and stiffening as it is known today.*

2. *The back length of the coat, as shown by the arrows, was divided into eight equal parts; five lengths to the waist and three for the skirts.*

3. *Diagram pattern for a Revolutionary War uniform coat.*

4. *Breeches were worn with the waist band no higher than the hip bone and often lower. They were held up by tight lacings in the back.*

5. *Diagram pattern of a pair of Revolutionary War breeches. These were very full in the seat.*

Foot and Leg Wear

Stockings were made of knitted wool, wool cloth, linen, and even silk. They came in a variety of colors, styles, and textures. Shoes, for the most part, were of the buckle type, although laced shoes were also available. Mounted officers and cavalry were generally to wear boots when on horseback. On campaign, the foot soldier could rely on such extra leg coverings as leggings which protected the leg from ankle to hip, gaiters whose protection extended to the knee, spatterdashes that covered to the calf, and, finally, wrappers of odd bits of cloth tied to the legs in lieu of or in addition to any of the foregoing. In the wilderness, moccasins, breechclouts, and other items of Indian costume were adopted whenever supplies of regular clothing were lacking or conditions of warfare made it necessary.

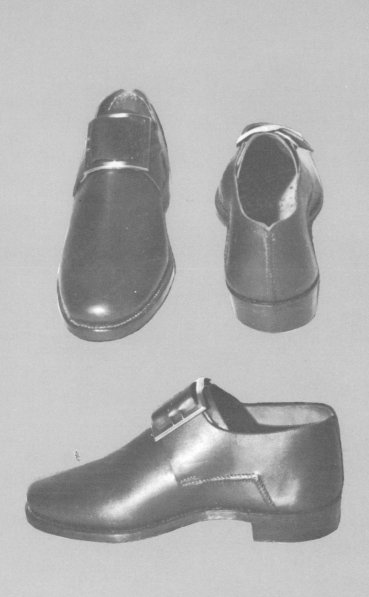

*Continental Army shoes
reconstructed by
Ernest W. Peterkin
from fragments
recovered on the Philadelphia.*

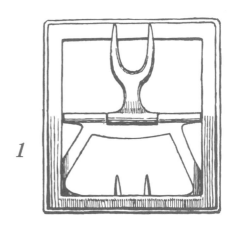

1

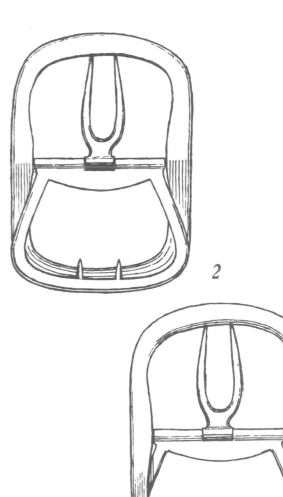

2

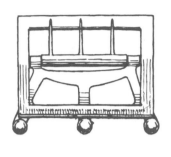

3

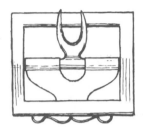

6

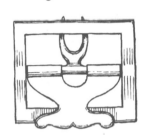

4

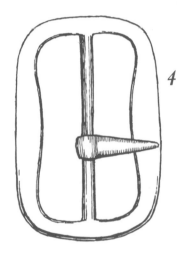

5

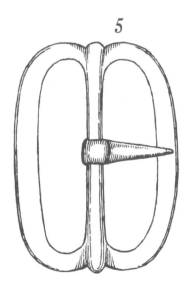

Typical buckles (actual size).

> *Drawing by*
> *Peter Copeland and*
> *Donald W. Holst.*

1. *Shoe buckle from the Philadelphia.*

2. *Front and back of British-pattern shoe buckle.*

3. *Front and back of stock buckle.*

4. *Waist-belt buckle of the commonly found pattern.*

5. *Waist-belt buckle from Valley Forge.*

6. *Front and back of a knee buckle.*

231

Miscellaneous

Other items of dress were watch coats of especially thick wool (which were worn on guard in the winter), overcoats, cloaks, and blankets. The rigors of campaigning and shortages of supply also made it necessary for the soldier to adopt such a multitude of odd expedients and combinations for clothing that it would be impossible to list the many possible variants. To this must be added the items of civilian wear brought by the recruit and never exchanged for issue clothing, clothing which was donated by patriotic citizens, and state supplies provided during periods of particular want. Foraging and confiscation also added to the soldiers' personal wardrobes.

Of all items of clothing in the Continental stores, shirts or shirting cloth such as linen seem to have been in greatest need. Shirts were of the pullover variety and normally were white, but brown and checked shirts were also frequently in evidence. A stock of leather or dyed linen was worn around the collar for added protection and military smartness. Officers' shirts were made of finer linen with cambric ruffles at the neck.

In short, the Continental soldier wore whatever was at hand and whether of regimental, civilian, or a combination of styles, this became his uniform at the moment. A survey of some of the uniforms worn by various Continental staff and line organizations will provide the balance of this study.

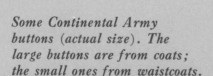

Some Continental Army buttons (actual size). The large buttons are from coats; the small ones from waistcoats.

1. *Sixteenth Continental Infantry.*

2. *Twenty-fifth Continental Infantry.*

3. *First Maryland Battalion.*

4. *Eighth Massachusetts Regiment.*

5. *USA button of the common form. After 1779 the USA button was supposed to be worn on the coat by all regiments with state buttons on hats.*

6. *First Connecticut Regiment.*

7. *First Pennsylvania Battalion.*

8. *Rhode Island Regiment.*

9. *Delaware Regiment.*

10. *New Jersey Regiment.*

11. *Continental Artillery. The infantry buttons were made of pewter; the artillery button was supposed to be brass, but pewter specimens have also been found.*

Uniforms for General and Staff Officers

Uniforms for general officers were prescribed by a General Order in June 1780 as blue coats with buff facings and linings, yellow buttons, and white or buff smallclothes. Aides-de-camp and other staff members with military rank were to wear the uniforms of their rank and unit; aides who did not belong to a specific unit, the same uniform as the general officers. Such members of the staff as had no military rank were to wear plain coats, hats with a cockade, and swords. A portrait of Dr. Barnabas Binney, a surgeon in the Hospital Department, shows him in a plain blue coat with silver buttons and a white waistcoat and stock.

Uniforms of the Various Branches

Corps of Sappers and Miners and Corps of Engineers

These troops were ordered in June 1780 to wear a uniform consisting of blue coats with buff facings and red linings, and buff smallclothes.

Infantry

January 1776-January 1777. With the uniform of most of the regiments of the Northern Army already determined as noted above, issues began to be made out of the Continental Store at Cambridge. That at least some of the twenty-seven Continental regiments on the first establishment received uniform regimentals is borne out by deserter descriptions. However, these were so variegated they defy description in this limited space. Troops coming up from the Southern states, Pennsylvania, Virginia, Maryland, Delaware, and North Carolina, to join Washington's army were mainly attired in bounty clothing provided by their states. The most popular form of dress of the Virginians was the hunting shirt. Regimental orders in the Sixth Virginia Regiment for April 3, 1776 list short-fringed hunting shirts for officers, plain ones for enlisted men, white cuffs for sergeants, and dark for drummers; hats for both officers and men were to be cut round, bound with black and the brims to be two inches deep and cocked on the left side with a button, loop, and cockade.

The Continental regiments raised by North Carolina were to be supplied with coats, waistcoats, breeches, hunting shirts and spatterdashes, according to resolves of December 1775. The Maryland, Delaware, and Pennsylvania Continentals arrived equipped in much the same way. David Hall's Delaware Battalion had on blue coats faced with red, the color combination most frequently used for Revolutionary War uniforms.

1777-October 1778. During this period, the bulk of the clothing came from local stocks and was made from American cloth. These supplies rapidly dwindled, and urgent requests had to be made to the American agents abroad to procure uniforms for the whole army. Mr. Mease's method had been to issue clothes in Philadelphia to each regiment passing through the city until his supplies were exhausted, leaving nothing for future use. In September 1778, 20,000 suits of uniforms were received in Boston from France. These were of two types; blue faced red, and brown faced red, with a proportionate quantity of white waistcoats and breeches. Major Samuel Nicholas, the commandant of the Marine Corps, was designated to convoy this clothing to the Army, a mission he carried out successfully. To apportion the French uniforms to the several Continental battalions a lottery was devised with Washington's aides drawing as proxies for the units from the various states. Blue faced with red was drawn for North Carolina, Maryland, New Jersey, and New York; while brown faced with red was drawn for Virginia, Delaware, Pennsylvania, Massachusetts, New Hampshire and Colonel Moses Hazen's regiment.

Stockings and shirts were plentiful, but hats and blankets were insufficient to meet the demand.

1779. In this year, the first general orders regarding uniform colors and styles appeared in October and were distributed throughout the army. All coats were blue, but the facings changed according to this pattern:

> 1. New Hampshire, Massachusetts, Rhode Island, and Connecticut: white facings, drummers' and fifers' coats white faced with blue.
> 2. New York and New Jersey: buff facings, drummers' and fifers' coats buff faced with blue.
> 3. Pennsylvania, Delaware, Maryland, and Virginia: scarlet facings, drummers' and fifers' coats scarlet faced with blue.

4. North Carolina, South Carolina, and Georgia: blue facings, buttonholes edged with narrow white lace or tape, drummers' and fifers' coats blue faced with white.

These uniform colors were to continue in effect nearly to the end of the War.

1783. The remnant of the Continental Line was ordered by Washington into blue uniforms faced red, with white smallclothes.

Drummers and Fifers

Following European customs, the uniforms of the regimental musicians were to be the reverse of those of the regiment. Colonel Christian Febiger's Second Virginia Regiment was authorized a uniform of blue faced red and Congress granted Febiger permission to clothe his drummers and fifers in red faced blue. The regulation of October 1, 1779 also confirms this by specifying reverse colors for drummers and fifers.

Light Infantry

Usually, the only distinction of the light infantry was their leather caps with red and black plumes. However, a former Massachusetts light infantrywoman described a uniform she received when she enlisted sometime in 1781 as the usual New England uniform of blue coat lined with white, a white waistcoat, and white breeches or overalls. In addition the coat had white wings on the shoulders and white cords on the arms and pockets. Her cap with a cockade on one side had a red-tipped plume on the other, and a white turban around the crown. A portrait sketch by Kosciusko of Lieutenant Judah Alden of the Light Infantry Company of the Second Massachusetts shows him wearing a helmet with a small crest with hair, narrow flat visor, and low pointed cap plate.

Artillery

1776-1779. Deserter descriptions confirm that the uniform of the artillery was black faced with red, plain yellow buttons, white waistcoats and breeches, white stockings and black garters, cocked hats with hair cockades and white tassels.

1779-1783. Washington's regulation of October 1779 prescribed a blue uniform coat faced and lined scarlet, yellow buttons and bindings, the coats to be edged with narrow, yellow worsted lace or tape, and the buttonholes bound with the same.

Cavalry

First Regiment of Light Dragoons. When raised by the Act of the Virginia Convention of June 12-13, 1776, the officers were to furnish their own horses, saddles, and equipment. On December 18, 1776, the Council of State directed that each enlisted trooper be "furnished with a coat, cap, a pair of leather breeches, and a pair of Boots and Spurs at the Public expence." Previously, the Council had authorized the

Keeper of the Public Store to sell clothing and equipment to the officers recruiting their troops to the extent that at least some of the regiment had blue coats, leather breeches, gilt buttons, and boots. Neither horsemen's caps, helmets, nor hats were provided out of public stocks. Lefferts shows a trooper in a short blue coat faced and lapelled with scarlet, scarlet waistcoat, black-breasted leather helmet, and the rest the same as was actually purchased in Virginia.

The actual uniform prescribed in regimental orders of April 1777 and secured by August 1778 consisted of: short brown coats with green lapels, cuffs, and collars, green waistcoats, leather breeches, gilt or yellow buttons of regimental pattern, black leather caps with perpendicular fronts and green turbans with yellow tassels. Trumpeters, saddlers, and farriers had a reverse uniform of green and brown.

Clothing was provided by Virginia from its public store at Richmond in 1780 and very little seems to have been received thereafter. The uniform can be reconstructed as being short blue or black coat lapelled green and lined blue, black stocks, blue overalls for foot and horse, some leather breeches, a visored black leather helmet with a black cockade on the left side, stable jackets and linen shirts. This uniform prevailed through 1782. During this period, the regiment suffered much from want of helmets and had to do service in hats.

Second Regiment of Light Dragoons. The lack of documentary and written evidence about the uniform is partially compensated for by contemporary portraiture and paintings showing members of the regiment. As the only cavalry unit remaining to the end of the war, the Second was a favorite of John Trumbull, and officers and troopers of the regiment are prominent in several of his most important works. Based upon the work of Trumbull, the uniform of 1780-1783 was a blue coat faced, lapelled, and trimmed buff, buff smallclothes, white belts, and metal helmets with light blue turbans having yellow tassels. On dismounted duty, brown or dark-colored overalls were worn.

Third Regiment of Light Dragoons. The uniform for the period 1776-1778 is unknown. The first record is a bill for cloth delivered the regiment by the Williamsburg, Virginia Public Store, May 29, 1779. A uniform of white jackets faced, lapelled, and lined with blue is indicated by the types of cloth received. A portrait of Lieutenant Roger Nelson belonging to the Monmouth County Historical Society confirms this in addition to white double-breasted waistcoat, black leather belt with silver plate, and silver epaulettes and buttons.

The Commonwealth of Virginia again provided cloth from its stores when the regiment joined the Southern Army in 1780. At this time, green facing cloth was issued along with leather breeches, white stockings, white shirts, and stable jackets. A drawing in the *Allgemeine Taschenbuch* of a Continental light horseman depicts the uniform which agrees with the 1779 uniform in most details and adds a black jockey cap with foxtail and red turban.

Fourth Regiment of Light Dragoons. As the officers had gone to "considerable expence" to secure scarlet uniforms, Washington gave Clothier General James Mease the necessary permission to allow 240 coats of red faced blue captured from the Eighth and Twenty-fourth British Foot to be turned over to the regiment for uniforms. Hunting shirts, leather breeches, stockings, shoes, and helmets of an undetermined style rounded out the regimental attire for the years 1777-1779.

For the period 1780-1782, deserter descriptions are the only source, as a number were described in a uniform coat of green faced red, red waistcoat, leather breeches, green overalls, helmets trimmed with bearskin, and green cloaks with red capes.

Partisan Corps

Lee's Legion. Lee's biographer, Thomas Alexander Boyd, in his *Light-horse Harry Lee* (New York, 1931) describes Lee before the battle at Paulus Hook on July 15, 1779, as wearing a bright green jacket, high frilled stock, lambskin breeches, polished boots, and a leather cap topped by a "resplendent horsehair plume." When crossing the Dan in 1780, Boyd relates that the Legion appeared in short green jackets, tall caps "draped with bearskin," breeches, and white linen overalls. However, in 1782 Charles Willson Peale painted Lee in a buff uniform jacket faced green with silver buttons and epaulette, and a buff waistcoat.

Armand's Legion. Charles Willson Peale's portrait of General Armand, executed in 1782-1783, gives many details of the Legion uniform as worn from 1779 to 1783, although it is not known how much would pertain to the horse and how much to the foot. The coat is blue with buff cape and unbuttoned lapels. The waistcoat is also blue and is lined with buff and has buff edging and three rows of small gilt buttons. Armand wears a black helmet with a wide bearskin roach, leopard-skin turban, and white feather on the left side. Gold shoulder knots with a silver star on each and a scarlet stock complete the uniform.

Pulaski's Legion. The exact style of this uniform is as yet unknown, but its basic elements for the years 1778-1780 have been recorded. Both horse and foot had blue coats, and helmets with black turbans, a star, white feathers, and horsehair crests. The cavalry wore leather breeches and sleeved waistcoats, boots, and blue or gray cloaks. Trumpeters had green lace trimmings and sergeants wore silver lace. The infantry had gaiters and white smallclothes. In 1778 drummers wore red coats and all ranks had white buttons marked "USA."

Von Heer's Corps. When proposing the formation of a squadron of provost guards in 1777, Captain von Heer requested that the troopers be outfitted as dragoons and wear green or blue coats faced black. For the balance of the war, the dress of a trooper in von Heer's Corps was a blue coat faced yellow, leather breeches, and a "casquet," a metal frame shaped to the skull and worn over the crown of a hat as protection against saber blows.

Wagoners

The wagoners were to wear brown or gray coats, with linen vests and breeches, white buttons marked "USA," and uncocked narrow-brimmed hats with narrow white binding. The few deserter descriptions available for wagoners show that clothing similar to this was indeed worn, but the evidence is too sparse to permit any sweeping conclusions.

Such were the uniforms of the Continental Army as they have been recorded and prescribed. If actual issues fell short of the desired articles, it was but one more hardship the soldier bore with admirable fortitude. He carried on as best he could and despite the lack of uniformity he managed to attain an appearance that both friend and foe described as "soldierly."

Notes to Chapter 11

1. This chapter is based on original material from the Washington Papers in the Library of Congress; from the Revolutionary War Papers in the War Records Division, and from the Papers of the Continental Congress in the Diplomatic, Legal, and Fiscal Division, both of the National Archives. The principal printed sources consulted were Fitzpatrick's *Writings of Washington*, Force's *American Archives*, Ford's *Journals of the Continental Congress*, and Lefferts' *Uniforms of...the War of the American Revolution, 1775-1783*.

Recognition, Rank and Valor

Being a survey of
the insignia and colors*

Chapter 12

The need for distinctive insignia as a means of enforcing security, order, and discipline became apparent shortly after General Washington took command of the Continental Army before Boston in early July 1775. The lack of uniforms in the Continental Army at this time made it almost impossible to differentiate between the officers, non-commissioned officers, and enlisted men, and the resulting confusion soon forced the adoption of badges of rank to end this inconvenience. These distinctions had to be both clearly visible and easy to manufacture from materials readily available. The distinctive insignia chosen in mid-July for the general officers were sashes, those

*This chapter was written by Detmar H. Finke.

for the other officers were cockades, and those for the non-commissioned officers were epaulettes or strips of cloth on the shoulders of their coats.

The sashes which distinguished the general officers, their aides, and the brigade majors were ribbons of various colors worn across the breast between the waistcoat and the coat. The Commander in Chief wore a light blue ribbon, the major and brigadier generals a pink ribbon, and the aides-de-camp and brigade majors a green ribbon. (1) Towards the end of the same month it was thought proper to further distinguish the major generals from the brigadiers by changing the color of the major generals' ribbons to purple. These ribbons were described by one of the Brunswickers captured at Saratoga in October 1777 as being worn by the American general officers "like bands of orders over their vests." (2)

The distinctive cockade insignia chosen for the other officers were to be worn on their hats. The cockades of field officers were to be red or pink, those of captains yellow, and those of subalterns green. That the order for the distinctions of this kind was enforced was brought out in August 1776, when Lieutenant Holcomb of Colonel Johnson's regiment was confined and tried by a court martial for "assuming the rank of a Captain, wearing a yellow cockade, and mounting Guard in that capacity." As it appeared that Lieutenant Holcomb had acted as he did through misinformation and want of experience he was only cautioned and then released from arrest. To avoid any further such incidents the regulations concerning the officers' insignia were restated in general orders for the cognizance of those officers who had recently arrived in camp. The regulation was the same as that issued in July 1775, with the exception of the captains' cockades, which were now to be white or buff instead of yellow. (3)

The non-commissioned officers were to be distinguished from the enlisted men by epaulettes or strips of cloth sewed on the right shoulders of their coats, red for sergeants and green for corporals. (4)

Both General Washington and some of the other officers seem to have worn epaulettes with their uniforms as well as the ribbons ordered to designate rank in July 1775. This use of the epaulette would seem to have been considered more as a part of their military uniform rather than an insignia of rank.

The distinction of rank for officers by cockades and sashes and for non-commissioned officers by varicolored epaulettes or strips of cloth remained in force until June 1780 when, following representations first made by General Jedediah Huntington to Washington in October 1779, new regulations for the insignia of all ranks and grades of officers were adopted. These regulations were published in general orders in June and July 1780 and were in general retained in force until the end of the war. (5)

The new distinction of rank for the general officers, who as a class were now also distinguished by special uniforms, was by the

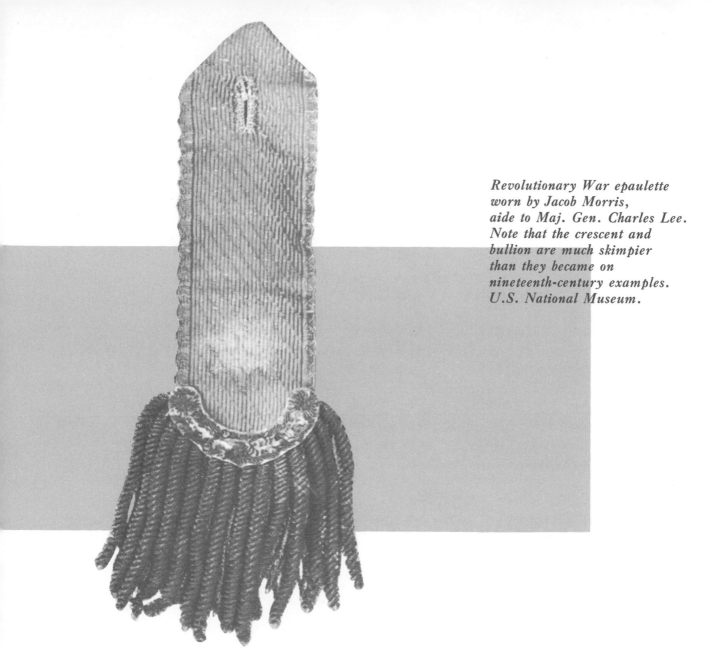

number of silver stars on their gold epaulettes, and by the plumes on their hats. Two stars and a black and white plume indicated a major general, and one silver star and a white plume a brigadier general. No specific insignia for Washington as Commander in Chief is known to have been officially designated in orders. But Washington, as can be seen from his portraits, first wore three small star-shaped rosettes of gold lace on his epaulettes in 1779-80. After about late 1780 he is shown wearing three silver stars in the place of the gold rosettes. Charles Willson Peale in the contemporary portraits of Washington from 1776 to 1781 does not show him wearing a plume of any kind on his hat. (6)

The field-grade officers (colonels, lieutenant colonels, and majors) were to wear two epaulettes, and the company-grade officers (captains and subalterns) were to wear only one epaulette each, captains on the right shoulder and subalterns on the left. These epaulettes were to be of silver for the infantry and cavalry, and gold for the artillery, as had been determined for the trimmings of these arms in general orders in October 1779 and in previous correspondence between Washington and Congress. *(7)*

Two distinct types of epaulettes are known to have been worn during the Revolutionary War. Both types consisted of a lace strap, a crescent, and a fringe of bullion. The basic difference was in the shape and composition of the crescent. In the type of epaulette described by General Washington as being worn by the Prince William and Fairfax County, Virginia militia companies, and worn by Washington himself in his 1776 portrait by Peale and by most of the French officers serving in America during the war, the crescent consisted of one or two rosettes or "round roses" of lace which also covered the jointure of the crescent and the bullion. *(8)* In the second type, worn by Washington from at least 1779 on, and by most other officers during the whole war, the crescent was merely a continuation of the strap, and the jointure of the crescent and the bullion was concealed by a curved strip of lace, usually of elaborate design and often further decorated by metal sequins. *(9)*

Various staff officers, to clearly indicate their duties, were also to wear plumes of various colors in their hats in addition to the above epaulettes. The aides-de-camp of the Commander-in-Chief, a white and green feather; the aides of major and brigadier generals, a green feather; the brigade and subinspectors, a blue feather; the Adjutant General and his assistants, the most colorful—red and green feathers. *(10)*

The common insignia of all Army officers, warrant as well as commissioned and also those staff officers without military rank, were the cockade and the wearing of side arms. The cockade was the same black cockade as was worn by the British Army, until the addition of a white relief or center in 1780 created the "union cockade." This cockade was to be emblematic of the expected union of the American and French armies in that year. It was no doubt also intended as a reply to Rochambeau's courteous gesture of adding a black relief to the white French cockade in honor of the American Army, shortly after his arrival in Newport in May 1780. *(11)*

As early as March 1779, Congress proposed and General Washington agreed that all the infantry sergeants and corporals were to wear white worsted epaulettes; all the artillery sergeants, corporals, gunners, and bombardiers, yellow epaulettes; and the dragoon sergeants, corporals, farriers, and saddlers were to have blue. The sergeants were to wear epaulettes on both shoulders and the corporals one on the right shoulder. What the other artillery and dragoon specialists were to wear is not stated. That it was not always possible to fulfill these orders is brought out in a general order of May 1782 which stated that white strips of cloth might be used to distinguish the infantry sergeants and corporals, if the clothier was unable to procure white worsted epaulettes. *(12)*

Military Decorations

An "honorary mark of distinction" for four years' satisfactory service by privates and non-commissioned officers in the Continental Line was established in Brigadier General Paterson's brigade in mid-June 1782. This mark of distinction was to be "one stripe of white tape, on the left sleeve of the regimental coat, which shall extend from seam to seam, on the upper part of the sleeve, three inches from and parallel with the shoulder seam, so that the tape may form a herringbone figure." To insure that this order was carried out General Paterson presented the brigade with the necessary material to make these chevrons. If a soldier had served eight years he was to receive another stripe set in one inch below the first. (13) In August 1782, Washington issued orders for "honorary badges of distinction" for non-commissioned officers and privates who had served more than three years "with bravery, fidelity and good conduct." This badge was to consist of "a narrow piece of white cloth, of an angular form" and to be placed on the left arm of the uniform coat. For those who had served more than six years under the same conditions another piece of cloth of a similar shape set parallel to the first was to be worn. A few days later this order was amended to permit the stripes to be the same color as the facings of the unit to which the soldiers who were awarded this badge belonged. General Paterson's earlier brigade orders were cancelled and the men ordered to wear the length-of-service badges as prescribed in Washington's orders of August 7 and 11, 1782. (14)

At the same time that the honorary badges for long and faithful service were established, General Washington also created a decoration, "the badge of Military merit" for "unusual gallantry" and "extraordinary fidelity." This badge could only be awarded upon certification of such acts to the Commander in Chief by the individual's regimental or brigade commander. After approving the award, Washington promised that the name and regiment of the person

245

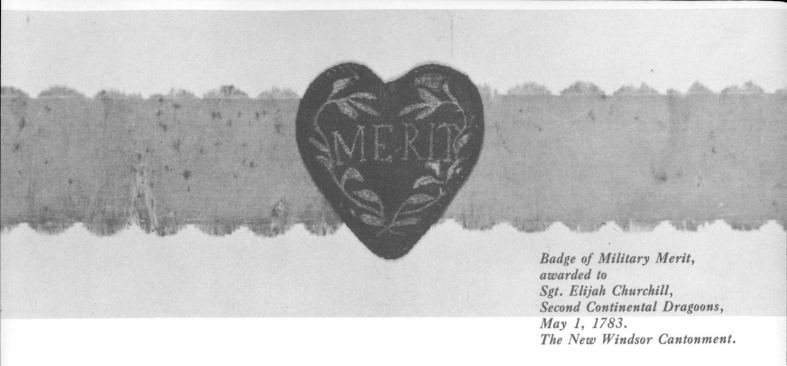

Badge of Military Merit,
awarded to
Sgt. Elijah Churchill,
Second Continental Dragoons,
May 1, 1783.
The New Windsor Cantonment.

receiving this honor and an account of his deed would be enrolled in a "Book of Merit," which was to be kept in the orderly office at the Commander-in-Chief's headquarters. The award itself was to consist of "the figure of a heart in purple cloth, or silk, edged with narrow lace or binding" and worn on the facings over the left breast of the uniform coat. Men given this award were to be allowed to pass all guards and sentries whom officers were permitted to pass. Only three of these decorations for valor are known to have been issued during the entire Revolutionary War. They were awarded to Sergeants Elijah Churchill of the Second Light Dragoons, William Brown of the Fifth Connecticut, and Daniel Bissell of the Second Connecticut Regiment. *(15)*

Colors

During the Revolutionary War, the Continental Army is known to have used three types of colors: a national color (first the Grand Union flag and later the Stars and Stripes), regimental standards or colors, and grand division colors.

The national color, or the flag used to signify united efforts of the various colonies, was primarily used to identify Continental installations or headquarters and as a naval flag. The first color of this type to be used by the Continental Army was the Grand Union flag, which had a field of thirteen alternate red and white stripes, with the British Union, the crosses of St. George and St. Andrew, in the first canton. This flag was flown over the Continental works at Boston on January 1, 1776 to celebrate the birth of the newly reorganized army, and was flown over the fort at the lower end of Manhattan Island, when the Continental Army occupied New York in 1776. *(16)*

A new national color was created by the Continental Congress on June 14, 1777, when it was resolved "that the flag of the United States be made of thirteen stripes, alternate red and white; that the union be thirteen stars, white in a blue field, representing a new constellation." Like the Grand Union flag there is no evidence that the Stars and Stripes were ever carried into battle by a Continental Army unit. The Stars and Stripes like its predecessor was primarily a naval and government installations flag. It is known to have been flown over the American works in the siege of Yorktown in 1781, and over the captured British batteries there. *(17)*

The use of regimental standards of colors to designate individual units was practiced in the American colonies at the outbreak of the Revolutionary War. This is shown in the organization of the Connecticut Army in May 1775, when standards were prescribed for the six regiments organized at that time, to be "distinguished by their colors." The colors of the regimental standards were to be: "for the First yellow, the Second blue, the Third scarlet, Fourth crimson, the Fifth white, and the Sixth azure." As no blue cloth was available at that time it was later resolved that the standard of the Second Regiment was to be green. When the Seventh and Eighth regiments were organized in July 1775, their standards were to be blue for the Seventh and orange for the Eighth. A description of such a color—the one furnished General Israel Putnam's Third Connecticut Regiment—states that it had on the one side the motto "An Appeal to Heaven" and on the other side *"Qui transulit sustinet,"* and it is probable that the other Connecticut colors had the same inscription. *(18)*

Shortly after the reorganization of the Continental Army in January 1776, the Commander-in-Chief of the Army, General Washington, required that every regiment should be supplied with two flags, a regimental standard or color and a "Grand Division" color, both to be small and light, and to bear if possible "some kind of similitude to the uniform of the regiment to which they belong." An example of such a regimental color is that of Thompson's First Continental Infantry from Pennsylvania, which is contemporaneously described as having "a deep green ground, the device a tiger partly enclosed by toils, attempting the pass, defended by a hunter with a spear (in white), on crimson field, the motto Dominari nolo." *(19)*

Just what the design or the color of the "Grand Division" colors was is not known at this time. But they were widely used, as a statement of the colors belonging to the several brigades of the main army of September 1778 shows. Listed as in service at this time were twenty-six regimental standards, one regimental color and forty-seven "Grand Division" colors, distributed as follows: *(20)*

	Standards	Regimental Colors	Grand Division Colors
North Carolina	2 (bad)		
Woodford's	1 (good)		
Muhlenberg	4 (bad)		
Scott	1 (bad)		
Smallwood	None		
2d Maryland	None		
Wayne	2 (bad)		4 (good)
	2 (good)		4 (bad)
2d Pennsylvanian	3 (bad)		
Clinton	1 (good)		4 (good)
	2 (bad)		8 (bad)
Parsons	2 (bad)		8 (good)
Huntington	None		
Nixon	3 (good)		11 (good)
Paterson	None		
Larned	1 (bad)		4 (good)
	1 (good)		
Poor	1 (good)	1 (good)	4 (good)
TOTAL	9 (good), 17 (bad)	1 (good)	35 (good), 12 (bad)

In 1779 the concept of two colors for a battalion or regiment was restated by Steuben's regulations and further clarified by Washington and the Board of War. The two colors were now referred to as the "Standard of the United States," which was to be the same throughout the Army, and the "Regimental Colour," which was to be the same color as the facings of the regiment. From the estimates of articles ordered to be imported from France in June 1779, it would appear that the ground of the "Standard of the United States" was to be deep blue, and that of the "Regimental Colours," crimson, deep blue, white, or buff according to the regimental facings. (21)

While national standards and regimental or battalion colors were supplied to individual Continental units at various times during the war, it was not until July 1782 that the Commissary General of Military Stores, Samuel Hodgdon, in Philadelphia, submitted an estimate for 100 silk standards to fill the needs of the whole Continental Army. Each standard was to contain 4½ yards of silk and to carry the name of the state and the regimental number in gold leaf in a garter of blue, each standard to be supplied with two silk tassels and to have the ends of the staff mounted in brass. But even this late requisition was cut in half and Hodgdon was only authorized to supply 50 standards. Whether these standards to be supplied by Hodgdon in July 1782 were a modified version of the national standard of regimental colors is not ascertainable. But it was probably this type of standard that was left at Newburgh by the field commissary of military stores and obtained by Washington for his troops in early March 1783. *(22)*

Finally, two regiments, Jackson's and Webb's, had each in September 1782 received one of the light infantry colors distributed by the Marquis de Lafayette to the light infantry earlier in the war. According to a contemporary description, these light infantry colors were "emblazoned with a cannon and the device 'ultima ratio.' " *(23)* It was an old device associated by long tradition with the French artillery, which had dubbed its guns *"ultima ratio regum"*—the last argument of kings. With Lafayette's gift it was transferred to a new country and a new tradition. But there was a vital difference. The cannon might remain a final argument for the American Army, but the king was gone. That had been the hope when the young Frenchman presented the colors. By 1782 it was a certainty. Webb's and Jackson's men would carry their handsome new standards in that happy knowledge. The motley army that had surprised Jesse Lukens at Boston seven years before had won the war.

Notes to Chapter 12

1. General Orders, Cambridge, July 14 and July 20, 1775, Washington, *Writings,* III, 339, 352.

2. Ward, *The War of the Revolution,* II, 538.

3. General Orders, Cambridge, July 23, 1775 and August 15, 1776, Washington, *Writings,* III, 357 and V, 437, 468.

4. General Orders, Cambridge, July 23, 1775, *ibid.,* III, 357.

5. Washington to Brigadier Huntington, October 24, 1779, *ibid.,* XVII, 18. General Orders, Short Hills, June 18, 1780, *ibid.,* XIX, 21.

6. *Ibid.* Charles Coleman Sellers, "Portraits and Miniatures by Charles Willson Peale," *Transactions of the American Philosophical Society,* New Series, XLII, Part I (1952), 355-360.

7. P. Scull, Secretary, Board of War to Washington, May 25, 1779, in *Washington Papers.* Washington to Board of War, May 27, 1779, Washington, *Writings,* XV, 160. General Orders, Moore's House, October 2, 1779, *ibid.,* XVI, 387-388.

8. Washington to William Milnor, *ibid.,* III, 265-267. Sellers, "Portraits and Miniatures by Charles Willson Peale," pp. 353-360.

9. *Ibid.* Mendel L. Peterson, "American Epaulettes, 1775-1820," *Military Collector & Historian,* II, No. 2 (June 1950), 17-19.

10. General Orders, Short Hills and Pracaness, June 18 and July 14, 1780, Washington, *Writings,* XIX, 21, 172.

11. *Ibid.*

12. P. Scull, Secretary, Board of War, to Washington, May 25, 1779, in *Washington Papers*. Washington to Board of War, May 27, 1779, Washington, *Writings*, XV, 160. General Orders, Newburgh, May 14, 1782, *ibid.*, XXIV, 253, 254.

13. Henry Whiting, ed., *Revolutionary Orders of General Washington*, New York and London, 1844, pp. 220-222.

14. *Ibid*. General Orders, Newburgh, August 7 and August 11, 1782, Washington, *Writings*, XXIV, 487-488; XXV, 7.

15. Allan P. Westcott, "For Military Merit," *Military Affairs*, V, No. 3, 211-214.

16. Milo M. Quaife, Melvin J. Weig, and Roy E. Appleman, *The History of the United States Flag*, New York, 1961, pp. 26-27.

17. *Ibid.*, pp. 51-53.

18. Force, *American Archives*, 4th series, II, 562, 1038, 1582, 1687.

19. General Orders, Cambridge, February 20, 1776, Washington, *Writings*, IV, 341. Hazard, *Pennsylvania Archives*, 5th series, II, 13.

20. Report by Alexander Scammel, September 5, 1778, Washington, *Writings*, XII, 470.

21. Estimate of articles to be purchased in the Department of the Board of War and Ordnance, June 11, 1779, Papers of the Continental Congress, pp. 417, 419, National Archives.

22. Letter to Timothy Pickering, March 10, 1783, Washington, *Writings*, XXVI, 205. Washington to Secretary of War, March 11, 1783, *ibid.*, 206, 207.

23. General Orders, Verplancks Point, September 5, 1782, *ibid.*, XXV, 130-132.

Regimental Organization

of the
Continental Army*

*This section was written by Detmar H. Finke and William Watson.

Infantry

During the Revolutionary War the basic tactical infantry unit of the Continental Army was the battalion or regiment, usually one and the same in the American Army as it was in the British. The battalions were composed of the field officers, the battalion staff, and a number of infantry companies.

The field officers were normally a colonel, a lieutenant colonel, and a major. The staff usually consisted of an adjutant, a quartermaster, a surgeon with his one or two surgeon's mates, and a chaplain. The companies were composed of a captain, one or more lieutenants, an ensign, sergeants, corporals, a drummer and a fifer or two drummers, and a varying number of privates.

The New England regular forces raised in the late spring of 1775, which were designated by Congress as the Continental Army in June of that year, consisted of twenty-six battalions from Massachusetts, eight from Connecticut, and three each from Rhode Island and New Hampshire. The regimental field officers and staffs conformed to the above organization with the exception that in those units in the Connecticut, Rhode Island and Massachusetts forces where general and field officers also held regimental or company rank, additional majors or captain lieutenants were assigned to carry out the general officers' nominal duties. (1)

The Massachusetts battalions consisted of 10 companies of 59 men each, comprising a captain, a lieutenant, an ensign, 4 sergeants, a drummer, a fifer, and 50 privates. At first, the Massachusetts Provincial Congress had attempted to assign the companies a strength of 100 men each, but this organization had to be rejected when the men from the smaller localities refused to serve under any officers other than those from their immediate neighborhoods. The New Hampshire battalions had the same number of companies and the same organization as those from Massachusetts. The First through Sixth Connecticut battalions were made up of 10 companies each of 100 men commanded by a captain, 2 lieutenants, and an ensign, while the Seventh and Eighth Connecticut battalions had a company strength of only 70 men. The Rhode Island battalions had at first 8 and later 10 companies. The companies had a strength of 60 men each, including the three company officers. (2)

In answer to a request from New York, the Continental Congress on May 25 had authorized the New York Provincial Congress to muster up to 3,000 men for the protection of New York City and posts at Kingsbridge and in the highlands on the Hudson. By late June 1775 the New York Provincial Congress was in the process of organizing 4 infantry regiments of 750 men each, including company officers. Each regiment was to have 3 field officers; a staff consisting of an adjutant, a quartermaster, and a surgeon; and 10 companies, each made up of a captain and 2 lieutenants, 3 sergeants, 3 corporals, a drummer and fifer, and 64 privates. However, recruiting went slowly, and the Second Regiment at Albany on July 24 had only a colonel, a lieutenant colonel, a major; no staff officers; 10 captains, 20 lieutenants, 15 sergeants, and 233 rank and file. (3)

An additional New York unit authorized by the Continental Congress on June 23, 1775 was the "Green Mountain Boys" battalion from the New Hampshire Grants (now Vermont). By order of the New York Provincial Congress this battalion was to have a strength of 500 men and to consist of a lieutenant colonel, a major and 7 companies, each with a captain, a first and a second lieutenant. (4)

On June 14, 1775, the Continental Congress authorized the raising of ten rifle companies, six in Pennsylvania, and two each in Maryland and Virginia. Each company was to consist of a captain, 3 lieutenants, 4 sergeants, 4 corporals, a drummer or trumpeter, and 68 privates. Two additional companies were authorized to be raised in Pennsylvania on June 22, and these two companies with an additional company raised in Lancaster and the original six Pennsylvania companies were organized as a battalion of nine companies with the usual field officers and battalion staff. (5)

The Continental Congress on June 26, 1775 also authorized North Carolina, if necessary, to raise a force of 1,000 men. The North Carolina Provincial Congress in August ordered this force to be organized as 2 regiments of 500 men, each with the regular number of field officers, an adjutant, and 10 companies of 50 men, each with a captain, a lieutenant, and an ensign. (6)

Washington took command of the New England armies before Boston on July 3, 1775. He announced the next day that the Continental Congress having taken into its pay and service all of the troops of the several colonies which had been raised for the defense of the "liberties of America," they were now the "Troops of the United Provinces of North America." Washington spent the rest of the year trying to convince his troops of this. (7)

One of his first problems was to provide for a clear method of identifying the general and staff officers, regimental officers and noncommissioned officers from the great mass of enlisted men. Sashes of different colors were to be worn by the general and staff officers, the regimental officers were distinguished by varicolored cockades in their hats, and the non-commissioned officers by stripes of red or green cloth on their shoulders. *(8)*

Once a means of distinguishing officers was provided, a clear chain of command was established on July 22 by the creation of divisions and brigades. The regiments were assigned, usually in groups of six, to a specific brigade commanded by a brigadier general, and two brigades to a division commanded by a major general. *(9)*

On August 5, Washington, in order to more clearly enforce the directive of Congress that the regiments of the various New England armies were in fact to be no longer considered as troops of the provinces, but as a part of the whole Army of the United Provinces, ordered the establishment of a court with a brigadier general as moderator and six field officers as members to settle the rank of all the regiments in the Continental Army, to number the regiments accordingly, and to settle the rank of all officers in order to prevent disputes among them on that subject. By August 20, the court had reported to Washington that the ranks of regiments and officers were now determined, that the regiments had been numbered accordingly, and that copies of these decisions were transmitted to all brigades by orders. *(10)*

The Continental Army before Boston now consisted of 38 numbered "Regiments of foot in the service of the United Colonies," 2 companies from Colonel Himan's Connecticut regiment at Ticonderoga, and 4 companies of independent Massachusetts infantry. The strength of this force was: field officers, 34 colonels, 32 lieutenant colonels, and 36 majors; staff officers, 15 chaplains, 35 adjutants, 37 quartermasters, 36 surgeons, and 35 surgeon's mates; non-

commissioned officers, 1,345 sergeants and 662 drummers and fifers; rank and file, 19,060, of which 14,442 were present and fit for duty. *(11)*

In order to provide for the regular continuity of the Continental Army before Boston, most of whose enlistments would expire by the end of the year, Congress on September 30 appointed a committee to confer with Washington and the governors and assemblies of the New England colonies on measures for supporting, continuing, and regulating the Continental Army. *(12)*

On the basis of the report made by the above committee, Congress passed a series of resolutions on November 4, 1775. The new army before Boston was to consist of 20,732 men, officers included. It was to be composed of 27 regiments as follows: Pennsylvania, 1; New Hampshire, 3; Massachusetts, 16; Rhode Island, 2; and Connecticut, 5. Each regiment was to consist of 728 men, officers included, and to be divided into a headquarters and 8 companies. Each company was to have a strength of a captain, 2 lieutenants, an ensign, 4 sergeants, 4 corporals, 2 fifers or drummers, and 76 privates. *(13)*

On the same day that Congress prescribed the terms for the new army, it resolved to keep three battalions of foot in South Carolina and one in Georgia at Continental expense for the defense of those colonies. These battalions were to have the same strength and serve under the same regulations as the Continental Army until December 31, 1776. All the officers were to be appointed by South Carolina and Georgia, respectively. *(14)*

During the next ten months a number of battalions were raised in the Continental service to meet operational requirements. The battalions raised were primarily of two types, 27 battalions as ordered by Congress on November 4, 1775, and 14 of a somewhat simplified type adopted in October 1775. The latter had the same

major, all to be appointed by the battalion commander. (16)

Directly for the Canadian theater of operations and primarily from Canadians and Continental troops in that theater whose enlistments had expired, eight battalions were raised of the types authorized either in October or November. In addition, several independent companies of riflemen or rangers and one regiment of four battalions were raised for this service. (17)

Continental troops in North and South Carolina were raised on a different basis from the rest of the states. These two states usually raised their own troops and then had them approved by the Continental Congress. They also appointed all of their own officers. A total of 10 battalions and 3 companies of rangers from the Carolinas were accepted by Congress. (18)

number of field officers as the former, only one staff officer (an adjutant), and the same company organization less one lieutenant, no musicians, and 68 instead of 76 privates. (15)

A surgeon was added to the staff of the October-type battalion in December, and enlistments of both types were usually for one year, although in the spring and early summer attempts were made to enlist men for two or three years or for the duration. The field officers and staff officers were appointed by Congress and the company officers by the state of the battalion's origin. However, when the need arose to raise battalions speedily, Congress also allowed the states to appoint the field officers. In July 1776 the staffs of all battalions were increased by a sergeant major, a quartermaster sergeant, a drum major, and a fife

On September 16, 1776, Congress, acting on a report by the Board of War, resolved that 88 battalions were to be enlisted as soon as possible for the duration of the war. The regiments were to be furnished by the several states as follows:

New Hampshire	3 regiments
Massachusetts	15 regiments
Rhode Island	2 regiments
Connecticut	8 regiments
New York	4 regiments
New Jersey	4 regiments
Pennsylvania	12 regiments
Delaware	1 regiment
Maryland	8 regiments
Virginia	15 regiments
North Carolina	9 regiments
South Carolina	6 regiments
Georgia	1 regiment

The appointment of all officers and the filling of vacancies, except for those of general officers, were to be left to the states. The commissions for the officers of these regiments would be issued by Congress. (19)

Reforms in Regimental Infantry Organization

A committee was appointed by Congress in January 1778 to confer with General Washington at his headquarters on a plan for reducing the number of battalions in the Continental service and for reforming other abuses in the Army. Several months later this committee submitted a report, which was acted on by Congress on May 27. It was resolved that each infantry battalion was now to have nine instead of eight companies. The additional company was to be a light infantry company to be kept up to strength by drafts from the other eight companies and to be organized with other light infantry companies into a corps of light infantry during the campaigning season. The usual three field officers were provided, but each was also charged with the command of a company in addition to his regimental duties. The staff consisted of a paymaster, adjutant, and quartermaster, all to be taken from the line; a surgeon and surgeon's mate, a sergeant major, a quartermaster sergeant, a drum major, and a fife major. The three field officers' companies had only a lieutenant and an ensign, the lieutenant of the colonel's company being designated as a captain lieutenant, while the other six companies were officered by a captain, a lieutenant, and an ensign. The non-commissioned officers and rank and file of each company were 3 sergeants, 3 corporals, a drummer, a fifer, and 53 privates. Each battalion was to have a strength of 585, including officers. The adjutant, quartermaster, and paymaster of a regiment were to be chosen by the regimental officers and to be confirmed by the Commander in Chief or by a general officer commanding in a separate department. No more colonels were to be appointed in the regiments in the future. The regiments would have only two field officers, a lieutenant colonel with the pay of a colonel who would be promoted directly from that grade to that of a brigadier general, and a major.

As the campaigning season began soon after the reorganization of the Continental Army proposed by Congress in May

1778, no changes were undertaken until the winter of 1778-1779. The Army was now to consist of 80 infantry regiments divided among the states as follows: New Hampshire, 3; Massachusetts, 15; Rhode Island, 2; Connecticut, 8; New York, 5; New Jersey, 3; Pennsylvania, 11; Delaware, 1; Maryland, 8; Virginia, 11; North Carolina, 6; South Carolina, 6; and Georgia, 1; all organized according to the resolutions of Congress of May 27, 1778. (20)

Washington and Congress agreed in January 1780 that the number of infantry regiments should be reduced to sixty and the men of those regiments eliminated be incorporated into those remaining. Again a committee proceeded to camp and consulted with General Washington. The results of these consultations were contained in resolutions of Congress for a general reduction and reorganization of the Continental Army enacted in October 1780 to become effective in January 1781. In this reorganization the infantry regiments were reduced to fifty instead of sixty, and the states were requested to furnish them as follows: New Hampshire, 2; Massachusetts, 10; Rhode Island, 1; Con-

necticut, 5; New York, 2; New Jersey, 2; Pennsylvania, 6; Delaware, 1; Maryland, 5; Virginia, 8; North Carolina, 4; South Carolina, 2; and Georgia, 1. One Continental regiment not belonging to any state line, Hazen's, was also retained, and all the foreigners contained in the regiments to be disbanded were to be placed into it. No new officer appointments higher than that of lieutenant colonel commandant were to be made. In those regiments where full colonels were continued, the field officers were to consist of a colonel, a lieutenant colonel, and a major; in all others they were to be a lieutenant colonel commandant and two majors. The staff consisted of an adjutant, a quartermaster, and a paymaster (all three with the rank of lieutenant), a surgeon and a surgeon's mate, a sergeant major, a quartermaster sergeant, a drum major, a fife major, and a permanent recruiting party in the state of origin, consisting of a lieutenant, a drummer, and a fifer. Each of the nine companies was to have a captain, 2 subalterns, 5 sergeants and 68 rank and file. The regimental total strength including officers was to be 699 men. (21)

Artillery

Most of the artillerymen raised as part of the Continental Army were organized in regiments of artillery. These regiments, or battalions, as they were sometimes called, were not tactically employed as regiments, and were often divided for administrative purposes. A number of independent artillery companies were raised and the companies within the regiments were freely and often detached. In actual tactical employment General Washington referred to a certain number of guns for a certain duty rather than to any organizational unit. (22)

When Congress took charge of the army before Boston, it also took over the artillery regiment that Massachusetts had raised. On April 13, 1775, Massachusetts had decided to raise an artillery regiment and had chosen William Gridley, a veteran of the Indian wars and the capture of Louisburg, to command it. The regiment was to have a colonel, a lieutenant colonel, two majors, and six companies. Later the Provincial Congress gave Gridley the right to recruit up to four men from each infantry company and increased the establishment of the regiment to ten companies. On September 20, 1775, Congress affirmed its adoption of the Massachusetts artillery by commissioning Colonel Gridley as Colonel of the Artillery. (23)

There was unrest among the officers of the regiment as Gridley began to show his age and came under the influence of his son, an officer in the regiment. Gridley made known his wish to be replaced. Of the two officers that had a claim of seniority to the colonelcy, Washington and his council of general officers all recommended Henry Knox to replace Gridley. Thus, on November 17, 1775, Congress resolved that it was necessary to replace Colonel Gridley on account of his age and unanimously elected Knox Colonel of Artillery. Knox at the time was involved in bringing to Boston some of the cannon captured at Fort Ticonderoga, doing service as a volunteer, and did not know that he had been chosen. The day after he had been selected to assume command of it, the strength of Knox's regiment was a colonel, a lieutenant colonel, a major, 8 captains, 9 captain lieutenants, 8 first lieutenants, 17 second lieutenants, an adjutant, a quartermaster, a surgeon, a surgeon's mate, a commissary, 2 clerks, 4 conductors, 26 sergeants, 26 corporals, 52 bombardiers, 49 gunners, 18 fife and drum, and 257 matrosses. (24)

Congress ordered the regiment reorganized and expanded on December 2, 1775. The new organization was to be a colonel, two lieutenant colonels, two majors, and twelve companies. Congress at the same time forwarded to General Washington the names of two men for him to consider for the two field officer vacancies opened in the new organization. Washington was to appoint them officers and inform Congress of his action if he found them to be of proper character and ability. *(25)*

The December reorganization did result in some expansion. The regiment with Washington in New York in June 1776 consisted of one colonel, a lieutenant colonel, a major, 10 captains, 10 captain lieutenants, 11 first lieutenants, 20 second lieutenants, a chaplain, an adjutant, a quartermaster, a surgeon, a surgeon's mate, 2 cadets, 34 sergeants, 33 corporals, 62 bombardiers, 59 gunners, 24 fife and drum, and 312 matrosses. Even with this expansion, General Washington still thought that he did not have enough artillerymen. To properly man the guns that he planned to use in the defense of New York, he drafted 600 infantrymen from their battalions for temporary duty with the artillery. *(26)*

On July 24, 1776, Congress accepted Knox's plan to raise another battalion of artillery. Congress wanted the plan executed as soon as possible and asked Washington to recommend officers. However, no action seems to have been taken on the plan at that time, for in November Washington still had only Knox's regiment and wrote to Congress of the need to obtain a regiment of artillery with experienced officers. As with the rest of his army, the enlistments of his artillerymen ran out with the year. *(27)*

Congress reacted to Washington's plea on November 26, 1776 by ordering the raising of a regiment of artillery in Virginia for the Continental establishment. Two companies already ordered raised there were to be included in this regiment, which was to consist of a colonel, a lieutenant colonel, a major, and 10 companies. Each company was to consist of a captain, 3 lieutenants, a sergeant, 4 bombardiers, 8 gunners, 4 corporals, and 48 matrosses. The following day Congress resolved that it would appoint the officers, but it left the subalterns to be recommended by Virginia. On January 26, 1777, General Washington wrote to Colonel Harrison and asked him to complete the recruiting of the regiment as soon as possible. Four months later General Washington wrote to Congress that he was not sure whether Harrison's regiment was under his control, since Congress had raised it specially. He stated further that if Congress had no special project for the regiment, he would like it ordered to join him in the field. Ten months later Congress ordered Harrison's regiment to join Washington. The regiment first appears on the returns of Washington's Army in May 1778. Then it consisted of a colonel, a lieutenant colonel, a major, 10 captains, 9 captain lieutenants, 7 first lieutenants, 6 second lieutenants, an adjutant, a quartermaster, a surgeon, a surgeon's mate, a sergeant major, a quartermaster sergeant, 13 sergeants, 22 corporals, 24 bombardiers, 20 gunners, 19 fife and drum, and 148 matrosses. It had then all of its allotment of field grade officers and captains, but only 77 per cent of its quota of lieutenants. It had a surplus of sergeants but only about 60 per cent of its authorized number of corporals and bombardiers and 30 per cent of its allotment of gunners and matrosses. *(28)*

While General Washington had been waiting seventeen months for the arrival of Harrison's regiment, he faced considerable difficulty getting organized units of artillery. On December 12, 1776, Congress adjourned for eight days to move from Philadelphia, which seemed threatened by the British, to Annapolis. Before adjourning it passed a resolution giving General Washington emergency powers to take action relative to the war until it met again. On December 20, 1776, General Washington wrote Congress that under the powers of that resolution, with the advice of Colonel Knox and his council of general officers, he had ordered that three regiments of artillery be raised. Congress approved his action by giving him the power to raise, officer, and establish the pay of three regiments of artillery in its resolution of December 27, 1776. *(29)*

When the enlistments of Knox's regiment ran out and most of the men returned to Massachusetts, the bulk of Washington's artillery was a detachment of Pennsylvania state artillery under Major Proctor. To strengthen this unit, Washington ordered Harmar's company of the Second Pennsylvania Regiment to join it on January 29, 1777 and two days later asked Pennsylvania to send the bulk of her artillerymen standing idle in the Delaware River forts to reinforce it for the winter. In March General Washington wrote Knox, who was in Boston, that Proctor's regiment was the only artillery that he had and that Pennsylvania would recall it on the slightest threat to the Delaware. In April Pennsylvania did try to withdraw part of its artillerymen, but Washington said on April 14, 1777 he would have to keep them until part of Crane's regiment arrived in about ten days. *(30)*

Pennsylvania had a change of mind over the value of retaining control of Proctor's regiment, and on June 20, 1777, Congress received an offer from the state to place it under Continental jurisdiction. The offer was referred to the Board of War and the delegates from Pennsylvania. Apparently they reached an agreement, because on July 19, Congress granted Continental commissions to the officers of Proctor's regiment to date from the date of the state commissions that they already held. *(31)*

Harrison's regiment became the First Artillery and Proctor's the Fourth Artillery. It is not clear exactly how the Second Artillery, Lamb's, and the Third Artillery, Crane's, were raised. Most likely they were raised according to Knox's plan that Congress had approved on July 24, 1776 as two of the three regiments Washington was authorized to raise. By treating Harrison's regiment differently in his letter of May 24, 1777, General Washington seems to imply that Lamb's, Crane's and Proctor's regiments were the three regiments that Congress had authorized him to raise and organize. Lamb's and Crane's regiments began joining the army by companies late in the spring of 1777, and Washington employed elements of both units in his orders of June 12,

1777. In January 1778, Lamb's, Crane's, and Proctor's regiments totaled 2 colonels, a lieutenant colonel, a major, 22 captains, 20 captain lieutenants, 25 first lieutenants, 42 second lieutenants, 2 adjutants, 2 paymasters, 2 surgeons, 2 quartermasters, 2 cadets, 2 sergeant majors, 2 quartermaster sergeants, 95 sergeants, 69 corporals, 60 bombardiers, 64 gunners, 56 fife and drum, 8 bandsmen, and 355 matrosses. *(32)*

On May 27, 1778, Congress passed a uniform organization for all four of the artillery regiments. Each regiment was to consist of a colonel, a lieutenant colonel, a major, a surgeon, a surgeon's mate, a sergeant major, a quartermaster sergeant, a fife major, a drum major, and 12 companies. Each of the companies was to consist of a captain, a captain lieutenant, a first lieutenant, 3 second lieutenants, 6 sergeants, 6 bombardiers, 6 corporals, 6 gunners, 4 fife and drum, and 56 matrosses. A paymaster, adjutant and quartermaster were to be drawn from the line officers and given additional pay. *(33)*

In September 1780 the regiments with General Washington (the Second, Third and Fourth) were at strength in officers and staff except second lieutenants, of which they had only a third of their quotas. They had 748 matrosses, over 80 per cent of their authorization, but only a half of the allotted sergeants, a third of the allotted corporals and bombardiers, and only a quarter of the allotted gunners. *(34)*

On October 3, 1780, Congress reduced the size of the four artillery regiments to 9 companies of 64 matrosses and non-commissioned officers with the same complement of officers in a reorganization to take effect on January 1, 1781. This was a drop of 3 companies per regiment and 20 enlisted men per company. The regiments were also made a part of specific state quotas of troops. The First Regiment was to be recruited and supported by Virginia, the Second by New York, the Third by Massachusetts, and the Fourth by Pennsylvania. On October 21, Congress added a tenth company to each regiment at the request of General Washington. *(35)*

The two regiments with General Washington in March 1781 were short about two-thirds of their second lieutenants, half of their sergeants, and over half of their corporals, gunners, bombardiers, and matrosses. *(36)*

When General Washington wrote Congress of the action he had taken to raise new artillerymen on December 20, 1776, he noted that the pay scale of the American artillery had not been comparable to that of the French and British and that he had promised all of the men who would re-enlist a 25 per cent pay increase. Possibly the men had been getting the same pay as infantrymen of the same rank and were aware that artillerymen were paid on a higher scale than infantrymen in foreign armies. The pay scale established by Congress for the reorganization of May 1778 gave artillery officers and staff a pay rate of a quarter more than infantry officers of the same rank. Enlisted men at the same time were given a dollar to a dollar and a half more per month than the same rank in the infantry. The pay for the officers may have been higher because they were supposed to be trained specialists, while that of the staff member may have been higher because the regiment that he served was organized with more men than the infantry regiment, the artillery regimental surgeon having more potential patients and so on. But why the matrosses should be paid 8 1/3 dollars per month, while the infantry private got only 6 2/3 dollars is not clear. Washington wrote Major General Schuyler on July 24, 1777 that a few days' drill could make a tolerably intelligent man a capable private artillerist. Perhaps it was only because artillery was an elite corps in other armies and elite corps were paid more. (37)

Artillery Artificers

To support the Continental Army certain artisans and mechanics were needed and were referred to as artificers. Throughout the war use was made of hired civilians and details drawn from the ranks of the infantry for their special skills. On December 2, 1775, Congress voted its approval of the terms that General Washington had given the artificers he was using with his army, commenting that it was probably the best deal that could be had. (38)

During the winter of 1776/77 General Washington issued orders for the recruiting of three regiments of artillery. One of these, Colonel Flower's, was to be a regiment of artillery artificers. Making a group of skilled craftsmen a part of the military seems to have been an attempt to get their services more regularly and at a lower price than the same services performed on contract. On January 16, 1777, General Washington wrote Colonel Flower a letter that appears to be Flower's orders to recruit. First Washington wanted personnel for an artillery shop to be set up in Pennsylvania, 49 carpenters, 40 blacksmiths, 20 wheelwrights, tinners and turners, and 12 harness makers, to be enlisted for one year. Also Flower was to recruit for the war as artillerymen to serve at the present at the laboratories a company to consist of

a captain, a captain lieutenant, 4 lieutenants, 6 sergeants, 6 corporals, 6 bombardiers, a fife and drum, and 28 matrosses. Further, he was to recruit to serve with the artillery in the field a company of a master carpenter, a master wheelwright, a master blacksmith, 2 tin men, 2 turners, 2 coopers, 4 harness makers, 2 nailers, 2 farriers, 6 wheelwrights, 25 carpenters, and 15 smiths. The company was to be headed by the master carpenter, and enlisted for the war. Birkhimer says that Flower's unit was never really a regiment, and characterizes it as a collection of mechanics with a slightly military organization. (39)

On February 13, General Washington stated in General Orders that the artificers were to be considered in service and exempted from being required to serve in the militia. On September 18, Congress indicated that it thought the artillery artificers part of the Army by commissioning Colonel Flower and his officers, in conformance with their ranks, in their new corps. (40)

On January 8, 1778, General Washington wrote Knox that he wanted the companies on duty at Carlisle and Springfield increased to 100 men each and enlisted for the war on the best terms that could be had. Congress acted along similar lines on

February 11 by ordering the pay of the artificer to be set at $20 a month plus the other benefits given to the artillery. Colonel Flower was told to augment his four companies and raise others in accordance with the orders of General Washington, who, if necessary, could raise the pay allowed by Congress. (41)

On May 1, 1779, the Board of War reported to Congress that the pay of the artificers needed to be raised. The report pointed out that the civilians many of the men were working with on the same jobs were making good pay, while the artificers made too little to support their families. The Board also pointed out that many of the artificers were men of good position and property before the war and that it was not uncommon in foreign armies for the artificers to make more than the junior officers in the combat branches. On May 1, 1780, Congress cut artificer companies to one officer and attempted to settle the pay complaints and give the men a reason to work by making the pay vary according to merit. A sergeant could get from $150 to $200 a month; a corporal acting as a foreman, the same as a sergeant; and a corporal, fife and drum and private, from $30 to $150 a month. (42)

When Congress reorganized the entire army on October 3, 1780, it called for the retention of a regiment of artificers to consist of 8 companies of 60 men each. This regiment was to have been part of Pennsylvania's quota of troops but appears never to have been raised. It was unclear whether Congress wished to retain the artillery artificer regiment under Colonel Flower or the quartermaster artificer regiment under Colonel Baldwin. Congress specifically dissolved Colonel Baldwin's regiment on March 29, 1781 and formed the men with unexpired enlistments into a company for Washington to appoint officers for and use as he wished. Apparently Colonel Flower's regiment had suffered from a similar shortage of men, because in April 1781 he stepped down as colonel of the regiment and no one was appointed to replace him. Colonel Flower did continue doing similar work, however, in the position of Commissary General of Military Stores, which he continued to hold after stepping down from his command of the artificers. (43)

Cavalry

Like the infantry and artillery, the basic cavalry unit of the Continental Army was the regiment or battalion. The type of cavalry regiment that was used through most of the war had a colonel, a lieutenant colonel, and a major as field officers; a regimental adjutant and his staff, consisting of a paymaster, a quartermaster, a surgeon, a riding master, a trumpet major, a saddler, and a sergeant major; and 6 troops of 34 to 60 men.

Washington's experience of the utility of horse in the summer 1776 campaign led him to recommend the establishment of one or more mounted units in the Continental Line in early December 1776. Congress soon acted on Washington's recommendation and on December 12 appointed Elisha Sheldon, whose service with his troop of Connecticut light horse in the summer of 1776 had elicited Washington's praise, as lieutenant colonel commandant of a regiment of cavalry in the Continental Line, with the rank and pay of a colonel of foot. Congress also authorized General Washington to appoint the other officers of the regiment. Washington in turn transferred the appointment of the officers to Sheldon, reserving for himself the right to refuse any of the officers so appointed if he thought them unfit for cavalry service. Washington pointed out to Sheldon that he would no doubt appoint only gentlemen of "true spirits and good character" and observed that gentlemen of fortune and reputable families generally made the most useful officers. (44)

General Washington described the organization in the recruiting instructions to Lieutenant Colonel Sheldon on December 16, 1776. The regiment, with Sheldon as lieutenant colonel commandant, had one other field officer, a major; a regimental staff consisting of an adjutant, a surgeon, and a surgeon's mate; and six troops. Each of the troops was to consist of a captain, a lieutenant, a cornet, a quartermaster, 2 sergeants, 2 corporals, a trumpeter, a farrier, and 34 privates. (45)

On December 24, 1776, Congress authorized General Washington, as a part of his six months' emergency powers, to raise a total of 3,000 light horse, and on January 1, 1777 recommended that Colonel George Baylor be appointed to the command of a regiment. (46)

In early January 1777 Washington submitted the pay scale for Colonel Sheldon's regiment and a proposed new organization for all cavalry regiments to Congress for approval. Both of these measures were approved by Congress on March 14, 1777. The new organization for a cavalry regiment consisted of a colonel, a lieutenant colonel, and a major as field officers; a staff comprising a chaplain, a regimental quartermaster, a surgeon and a surgeon's mate, a paymaster, a ridingmaster, a saddler, a trumpet major, an adjutant, the last without pay, and four supernumeraries, also without pay; and six troops, each with a captain, a lieutenant, and a cornet; a quartermaster sergeant, an orderly or drill sergeant, a trumpeter, a farrier, 4 corporals and 32 privates; and an armorer with no pay. (47)

On January 9, 1777, Washington authorized Colonel Baylor to raise a regiment of horse. Washington vested Baylor with the power of appointing his company officers, reserving to himself the appointment of the field grade officers and the right to refuse any of Baylor's choice he did not feel were suited for the cavalry service. In addition Washington withheld the nomination of the officers of one troop to be commanded by his former aide, George Lewis, and solicited two lieutenancies for relatives of personal friends. (48)

The Virginia light horse, a squadron of six troops under command of Colonel Theoderick Bland, was taken into the Continental service by Congress on January 14, 1777. The pay was to commence from November 25, 1776. (49)

A fourth regiment of light dragoons was authorized by Washington in January 1777. This regiment was commanded by Colonel Stephen Moylan. Washington informed Congress in the same month that he was not going to organize any additional light dragoon regiments until he saw how the four for which he had commissioned officers could be horsed and equipped. He felt that this would be very difficult. However, if he should be mistaken, he would immediately raise more cavalry units. He did not raise any others. (50)

In the general reorganization of the Army by Congress on May 27, 1778, a new organization was adopted for the cavalry. The battalion retained the same number of field officers as heretofore; the regimental staff lost the positions of the chaplain and the four supernumeraries, and the paymaster, adjutant, and quartermaster were now line officers doing the extra duty for extra pay. The individual troops were enlarged and now consisted of a captain, 2 lieutenants, a cornet, a quartermaster sergeant, a farrier, a trumpeter, 2 sergeants, 5 corporals, and 54 dragoons. (51)

All four of the Continental light

dragoon regiments were ordered reorganized as Legionary Corps by Congress on October 21, 1780. Each of the corps was to consist of four troops of mounted dragoons and two troops of dismounted dragoons with 60 privates to each troop. The officers and non-commissioned officers were to remain as before. General Washington had advised this change, citing the high cost of horses and forage and the need of mounted troops to work in conjunction with foot soldiers. The dragoons had needed infantry to guard their own camps and it was inconvenient to draw details from the infantry regiments. This legionary organization was retained to the end of the war. (52)

Throughout the war the regiment in the field differed from the organization set by Congress and General Washington. In February 1778 all four of the regiments had a full complement of field grade officers and staff and should have had 18 company officers, 30 sergeants and corporals, 12 trumpeters and farriers, and 204 privates. In

actuality the First Regiment, Bland's, had 10 company officers, 22 sergeants and corporals, 6 trumpeters and farriers, and 80 privates; the Second Regiment, Sheldon's, 8 company officers, 20 sergeants and corporals, 6 trumpeters and farriers, and 104 privates; the Third Regiment, Baylor's, 6 company officers, 6 sergeants and corporals, 3 trumpeters and farriers, and 96 privates; the Fourth Regiment, Moylan's, 15 company officers, 17 sergeants and corporals, 7 trumpeters and farriers, and 69 privates. (53)

The reorganization of 1778 added to the regimental staff and also added 6 lieutenants, 18 corporals, and 120 privates to the six troops. A return typical from 1778 to 1781 of the cavalry serving with the main army is that of the First Regiment in November 1778. The regiment had a colonel, a lieutenant colonel, a major, an adjutant, a quartermaster, a surgeon, a surgeon's mate, a paymaster, 5 captains, 3 lieutenants, 3 cornets, a sergeant major, 10 sergeants, 20 corporals, 5 trumpeters, 2 farriers, and 138 privates. (54)

As the end of the hostilities approached, the Second Legion, Sheldon's, was the only one of the cavalry regiments with the main army. In July 1781 it was short 3 lieutenants, 3 cornets, a surgeon, a riding master, a quartermaster sergeant, a trumpet major, 4 sergeants, 7 corporals, 2 trumpeters, a saddler, 3 farriers, and 105 privates. The return of only 137 horses shows that less than half of the 255 privates returned were mounted despite the fact that the legionary organization called for two men mounted for every man on foot. The regiment had a similar return in February 1782 and presumably remained about the same until disbanded. (55)

The three regiments that were sent to join the Southern Army were less able to meet the organization called for. In the campaign of 1780 the First Regiment of Continental Light Dragoons was completely decimated and the officers sent back to Virginia to recruit another regiment with the few remaining men incorporated with the Third Regiment. In their efforts to raise the regiment the officers were hampered by a lack of money and a ceiling on the price they could pay for horses set by the state. Lieutenant Colonel White used his own funds and was able to recruit 200 men but was short horses and arms. On June 25, 1781, the First Regiment could send only 60 men to join the light corps Lafayette was organizing to screen his force in Virginia. On November 9, 1782, the First and Third regiments were again consolidated into a battalion of 5 troops. At the end of the war the three regiments that had served in the South together mustered less than 200 men. (56)

Partisan Corps

The partisan or free corps was a military institution common to most European armies in the mid-eighteenth century. These were usually small bodies of light troops under a separate leader operating more or less independently for the purpose of reconnaissance, securing the march of the main army, or for attacking hostile posts and convoys. During the Revolutionary War both sides made use of such partisan corps. Congress made many attempts to raise such units, some successful, as Ottendorf's, Armand's, Pulaski's and Lee's, and others unsuccessful, such as the German deserter unit of Colonel Klein, and the proposed French unit from Martinique.

An early partisan unit was that of Baron Ottendorf, authorized by Congress on December 5, 1776. Baron Ottendorf's corps, referred to as an independent company, was to consist of 150 privates, sergeants and corporals included. It was to be composed of 3 companies, one of light infantry of 60 men, and two of hunters or riflemen of 45 men; each company was to have a captain and 2 lieutenants. Ottendorf with the rank of major would command the whole and at the same time be the captain of the light infantry company. An adjutant, to act additionally as quartermaster and paymaster with the rank of lieutenant, was also to be appointed. On June 11, 1777, Washington gave command of Ottendorf's corps to Lieutenant Colonel Charles Armand Tuffin, Marquis de la Rouerie, a French volunteer. (57)

During the winter Armand's command dwindled. A return of the corps for November 1777 shows that it had 2 captains, 5 lieutenants, an adjutant, a quartermaster, a surgeon, 5 sergeants, a fifer, or drummer, and 42 privates. During the winter Armand set out on his own to recruit a unit without authority, enlisting even prisoners of war. *(58)*

On May 17, 1778, the Board of War recommended to Congress that Armand, then "commanding the Independent Corps, formerly raised by Major Ottendorf," be authorized to complete this corps by recruiting deserters from the foreign troops in British service, Frenchmen, and any others not owing allegiance to the British crown for a term of three years or for the duration of the war.

Congress acted on the Board of War recommendation on June 25, 1778 and took the independent corps raised by Colonel Armand in consequence of General Washington's permission into the Continental service. Washington was authorized to officer this corps with foreign officers or others who already held commissions in the Continental service and could not be taken care of in other units. The corps was to have a colonel, a major, an ensign major (standard-bearer with pay of lieutenant), and 3 companies. Each company was to have a captain, a captain lieutenant, 2 lieutenants, 8 sergeants, 8 corporals, 2 drummers, and 128 privates. As shown on the army's returns,

the corps fell considerably short of Congressional organization. In August 1778 it had a colonel, a lieutenant colonel, 4 captains, 3 lieutenants, an adjutant, a quartermaster, a surgeon, a surgeon's mate, a sergeant major, a quartermaster sergeant, a drum major, 12 sergeants, 4 fife and drum, and 121 privates. *(59)*

Up until the latter part of 1778 the various troops that had been called Armand's corps were all foot soldiers, but at that time a troop of dragoons was added to the three foot companies. In January 1779 the corps consisted of a troop of dragoons of 3 officers and 42 men, 2 companies of fusiliers of 2 officers and 46 men, and a company of chasseurs of 3 officers and 80 men. *(60)*

Congress ordered Armand's corps recruited to full infantry strength on February 4, 1779. At that time it had very few Americans, most of the troops being German prisoners of war who had deserted to Armand's recruiters and were very quick to desert again. From a strength of over 200 privates in January 1779, the corps had dwindled to 60 foot and 60 horse by early 1780. *(61)*

On April 7, 1778, Congress rewarded Captain Lee of the First Continental Light

Dragoons for his conduct in the previous campaign by promoting him to major and authorizing him to expand and recruit his command to two troops to be an independent corps. Congress promoted the lieutenant and cornet of the troop to troop commanders in the new corps and left the appointment of the rest of the officers to General Washington. On May 28, 1778, Congress expanded Major Lee's corps to three troops with the usual allowance of officers and authorized General Washington to appoint a quartermaster for the corps to rank as a cornet. (62)

In November 1778 Lee's corps actually consisted of a major, an adjutant, a quartermaster, a surgeon, a paymaster, 2 captains, 3 lieutenants, 3 cornets, a sergeant major, 6 sergeants, 12 corporals, 3 trumpeters, 2 farriers, and 95 privates. (63)

On July 13, 1779, Congress ordered Captain McLane's company to join Lee's corps and be joined with his dismounted dragoons to form a fourth troop. In August 1779 Lee's corps consisted of a major, a quartermaster, a surgeon, 3 captains, 4 lieutenants, 4 cornets, 14 sergeants, 16 corporals, 6 trumpeters, 2 farriers, and 149 privates. Lee's Corps at that time had in its four troops the same enlisted strength as the 6-troop cavalry regiment of the time actually had, with one field officer, a much smaller staff and many fewer specialists. On February 14, 1780, Congress ordered Major Lee to recruit 70 dismounted dragoons in addition to those now in his corps and reorganize his corps in 3 troops. (64)

On March 28, 1778, Congress authorized Brigadier General Pulaski to raise and command an independent corps of 68 cavalrymen and 200 light infantrymen. The corps was to be raised in such a way and composed of such men as Washington thought proper, and if he chose, Washington was allowed to dispense with the prohibition against enlisting enemy deserters. Pulaski was to recruit and supply the men and would be paid $130 a man. General Washington

authorized Pulaski to recruit up to a third of his light infantry from deserters on the understanding that they would be primarily German. Later Washington was disturbed to find that deserters were being enlisted as mounted troops and that many of them were British, who were thought less reliable. (65)

On February 2, 1779, Congress ordered Pulaski and his corps to join Major General Lincoln and the Southern Army. Apparently, at this time Pulaski's corps was understrength, because two days later Congress directed General Washington to order its light infantry recruited to full authorized strength.

Pulaski was killed before Savannah and on November 7, 1780, Congress ordered the remains of Pulaski's corps incorporated into the corps of Lee and Armand. (66)

In the reorganization of the Army of October 1780 that was to take effect January 1, 1781, both Lee's and Armand's partisan corps were retained by the Congress. Both were to have the same organization: three troops of horse and three troops of foot. Each of the troops was to have 50 privates with the officers appointed by Washington and approved by Congress. (67)

Congress made Armand's recruiting easier by authorizing him to recruit up to six men from each line regiment. On May 16, 1781, Armand's corps had a full complement of officers but despite provisions to ease recruiting had only enough men for two of the authorized six troops. By October 21, Armand had obtained equipment to supply the planned unit but his command consisted of 2 captains, 3 lieutenants, a cornet, 2 volunteers, 3 sergeants, a trumpeter, and 36 privates. (68)

By November 25, 1783, Armand had augmented his unit to 340 officers and men, or full complement, but rather than leading them to battle, he informed them that they were discharged and no longer subject to the articles of war. The Revolution had been won. (69)

Notes to Regimental Organization of the Continental Army

1. French, *The First Year, passim.*

2. Force, *American Archives,* Series 4, II, 411-413, 648, 744, 766, 767, 1145, 1163, 1580, 1613, 1614.

3. *Ibid.,* 1324, 1325, 1334, 1675. Ford, *Journals of the Continental Congress,* II, 2.

4. *Ibid.,* 105, 123.

5. *Ibid.,* 89, 90, 173, 103, 104.

6. *Ibid.,* 107.

7. General Order, July 4, 1775, Washington, *Writings,* III, 308-311.

8. Detmar H. Finke, "Insignia of Rank in the Continental Army, 1775-1783," *Military Collector & Historian,* VIII (Fall 1956), 71-73.

9. Washington, *Writings,* III, 354-356.

10. *Ibid.,* 402, 403, 435, 436.

11. Return of August 18, 1775, *Revolutionary War Rolls,* 1775-1783, National Archives.

12. Ford, *Journals of the Continental Congress,* III, 265.

13. *Ibid.,* 321, 322. Washington, *Writings,* IV, 145, 147, 204, 205.

14. Ford, *Journals of the Continental Congress,* III, 325.

15. *Ibid.,* 285, 335.

16. *Ibid.,* IV, 416; V, 565.

17. *Ibid.,* IV, 39, 40, 75, 101, 102, 239, 254, 255; V, 471, 518.

18. *Ibid.,* IV, 14, 59, 235, 237, 331, 333; V, 462, 521, 624.

19. *Ibid.,* V, 762, 763.

20. *Ibid.,* X, 39, 40; XI, 538, 543; XIII, 298.

21. *Ibid.,* XVI, 36, 37, 333, 354, 357; XVIII, 893, 895, 959, 960.

22. Washington, *Writings,* V, 406.

23. French, *The First Year,* p. 73. Ford, *Journals of the Continental Congress,* II, 256.

24. French, *The First Year,* pp. 521, 522. Ford, *Journals of the Continental Congress,* III, 358. Return of November 18, 1775, *Revolutionary War Rolls,* National Archives.

25. Ford, *Journals of the Continental Congress,* III, 399.

26. Return of June 28, 1776, *Revolutionary War Rolls,* National Archives. Washington, *Writings,* V, 318.

27. Ford, *Journals of the Continental Congress,* V, 607. Washington, *Writings,* VI, 280.

28. Ford, *Journals of the Continental Congress,* VI, 981, 983, 985, X, 253. Washington, *Writings,* VII, 63; VIII, 117. Return of May 30, 1778, *Revolutionary War Rolls,* National Archives.

29. Ford, *Journals of the Continental Congress,* IV, 1045; VI, 1027. Washington, *Writings,* VI, 400.

30. Washington, *Writings,* VII, 76, 82, 289, 410.

31. Ford, *Journals of the Continental Congress,* VIII, 482, 564.

32. Washington, *Writings,* VIII, 117; IX, 235. Return of January 24, 1775, *Revolutionary War Rolls,* National Archives.

33. Ford, *Journals of Congress,* XI, 540.

34. Return of September 1780, *Revolutionary War Rolls,* National Archives.

35. Ford, *Journals of Congress,* XVIII, 894, 960.

36. Return of March 1781, *Revolutionary War Rolls,* National Archives.

37. Washington, *Writings,* VI, 400; VIII, 457. Ford, *Journals of the Continental Congress,* XI, 540.

38. *Ibid.,* III, 400.

39. Birkhimer, *Artillery,* p. 7. Washington, *Writings,* VII, 20.

40. Washington, *Writings,* VII, 143. Ford, *Journals of the Continental Congress,* VIII, 753.

41. Washington, *Writings,* X, 277. Ford, *Journals of the Continental Congress,* X, 147.

42. *Ibid.,* XIV, 602; XVII, 724.

43. *Ibid.,* XVIII, 854; XIX, 330.

44. Washington, *Writings,* VI, 351, 386. Ford, *Journals of the Continental Congress,* VI, 1025.

45. Washington, *Writings,* VI, 387.

46. Ford, *Journals of the Continental Congress,* VI, 1045; VII, 7.

47. *Ibid.,* VII, 178.

48. Washington, *Writings,* VI, 483.

49. Ford, *Journals of the Continental Congress,* VII, 34.

50. Washington, *Writings,* VII, 51.

51. Ford, *Journals of the Continental Congress,* XI, 540.

52. *Ibid.,* XVII, 960. Washington, *Writings,* XX, 163.

53. Return of February 9, 1778, *Revolutionary War Rolls,* National Archives.

54. Return of November 1, 1778, *ibid.*

55. Returns of July 1781 and February 1782, *ibid.*

56. *Ibid.* Burt Loescher, "Bland's Virginia Horse: The Story of the First Continental Light Dragoons," *Military Collector & Historian,* VI (Spring 1954), 1-6.

57. Ford, *Journals of the Continental Congress,* VI, 1007. Washington, *Writings,* VIII, 224.

58. Return of November 10, 1777, *Revolutionary War Rolls,* National Archives. Albert W. Haarman, "General Armand and His Partisan Corps, 1777-1783," *Military Collector & Historian,* VII (Fall, 1960), 97-102.

59. Ford, *Journals of the Continental Congress,* XI, 693. Return of August 30, 1778, *Revolutionary War Rolls,* National Archives.

60. Haarman, "Armand's Partisan Corps," p. 97.

61. *Ibid.,* pp. 98, 99. Ford, *Journals of the Continental Congress,* XIII, 143.

62. *Ibid.,* X, 315; XI, 545.

63. Return of November 1, 1778, *Revolutionary War Rolls,* National Archives.

64. Return of August 1779, *ibid.* Ford, *Journals of the Continental Congress,* XIV, 822; XVI, 164.

65. *Ibid.,* X, 29, 312. Washington, *Writings,* VI, 502.

66. Ford, *Journals of the Continental Congress,* XIII, 132, 143; XVIII, 1051.

67. *Ibid.,* XVIII, 960.

68. *Ibid.;* XIX, 9; XX, 510. Haarman, "Armand's Partisan Corps," p. 99. Return of October 1781, *Revolutionary War Rolls,* National Archives.

69. Haarman, "Armand's Partisan Corps," p. 99.

Bibliography of Sources Cited

Contemporary Sources

Bartlett, John R., ed., *Records of the Colony of Rhode Island and Providence Plantations in New England,* 10 vols., Providence, 1856-1865.

Blakeslee, Samuel, "Narrative of Colonel Samuel Blakeslee," *Buffalo Historical Society Publications,* VIII, (1905), 419-438.

Bland, Humphrey, *A Treatise of Military Discipline,* 4th ed., London, 1740.

Bouton, Nathaniel, and others, eds., *New Hampshire State Papers,* 40 vols., Manchester, N.H., 1867-1941.

Browne, William H., and others, eds., *Archives of Maryland,* Baltimore, 1884—.

Candler, Allen D., compiler, *The Revolutionary Records of the State of Georgia,* 3 vols., Atlanta, 1908.

Clinton, George, *Public Papers of George Clinton,* ed. by Hugh Hastings, 8 vols., New York, 1899-1904.

Commissary of Stores, Memorandum Book for 1782, Record Group 93, vol. 21470, National Archives.

Deane, Silas, *Deane Papers,* Charles Isham, ed., 5 vols., Collections of the New-York Historical Society, New York, 1886-1890.

Dearborn, Henry, *Revolutionary War Journals of Henry Dearborn, 1775-1783,* ed. by Lloyd A. Brown and Howard H. Peckham, Chicago, 1939.

Diderot, Denis, *Encyclopédie ou Dictionnaire Raisonné des Sciences, des Arts et des Métiers,* 17 vols., Paris, 1751-1765.

Diderot, Denis, *Recueil des Planches sur les Sciences, les Arts Libéraux, et les Arts Méchaniques Avec leur Explication,* 11 vols., Paris, 1762-1772.

Donkin, Robert, *Military Collections and Remarks,* New York, 1777.

Dundas, Col. David, *Principles of Military Movements Chiefly Applied to Infantry,* London, 1788.

Egle, William H., and others, eds., *Pennsylvania Archives*, 2nd series, 16 vols., Harrisburg, 1890.

Force, Peter, compiler, *American Archives*, 4th series, 6 vols., Washington, 1837-1846; 5th series, 2 vols., Washington, 1848-1851.

Ford, Worthington C., ed., *Journals of the Continental Congress, 1774-1789*, 23 vols., Washington, 1904-1909.

Grose, Francis, *Military Antiquities, Respecting a History of the British Army*, 2 vols., London, 1801.

Hanger, Col. George, *To All Sportsmen and Particularly to Farmers, and Gamekeepers*, London, 1814.

Hazard, Samuel, and others, eds., *Pennsylvania Archives*, 17 vols., Philadelphia, 1852-1892.

Hinde, Robert, *Discipline of the Light Horse*, London, 1778.

Historical Manuscripts in the Public Library of the City of Boston, Nos. 1-4, Boston, 1900-1904.

Hoadly, Charles J., ed., *The Public Records of the Colony of Connecticut*, 15 vols., Hartford, 1850-1890.

Hoyt, Epaphras, *Practical Instructions for Military Officers*, Greenfield, Mass., 1811.

Hoyt, Epaphras, *Rules and Regulations for Drill, Sabre Exercise, Equitation, Formation and Field Movements of Cavalry*, Greenfield, Mass., 1813.

Hoyt, Epaphras, *A Treatise on the Military Art*, Brattleborough, 1798.

Jones, John, *Plain Concise Practical Remarks on the Treatment of Wounds and Fractures*, Philadelphia, 1776.

"A Journal of Carleton's and Burgoyne's Campaigns," *Bulletin of the Fort Ticonderoga Museum*, Vol. XI, No. 5 (December 1964), 235-269; No. 6 (September 1965), 320.

Journal of the Council of Safety for the Province of South Carolina, 1775 in Collections of the South Carolina Historical Society, II, III, Charleston, 1858, 1859.

Lambert, Richard, 6th Earl of Cavan, *A New System of Military Discipline Founded upon Principle*, Philadelphia, 1776.

Lee, Henry, *The Campaign of 1781 in the Carolinas,* Philadelphia, 1824.

Lee, Henry, *Memoirs of the War in the Southern Department,* New York, 1869.

Linn, John B., and William H. Egle, *Pennsylvania in the War of the Revolution,* 2 vols., Harrisburg, 1880.

Mackenzie, Frederick, *A British Fusilier in Revolutionary Boston,* Allen French, ed., Cambridge, 1926.

Manuscript notebook of an artillery cadet at Woolwich, c. 1790, Smithsonian Institution.

McIlwaine, H. R., ed., *Journals of the Council of the State of Virginia,* 2 vols., Richmond, 1931.

Moore, Frank, compiler, *Diary of the American Revolution,* 2 vols., New York, 1860.

Moultrie, William, *Memoirs of the American Revolution,* 2 vols., New York, 1802.

Muller, John, *A Treatise Containing the Elementary Part of Fortification,* 2nd ed., London, 1756.

Muller, John, *A Treatise of Artillery,* London, 1768.

O'Callaghan, Edmund B., and others, eds., *Documents Relative to the Colonial History of New York,* 15 vols., Albany, 1853-1887.

Ogden, Matthias, *Journal of Major Matthias Ogden,* Morristown, N.J., 1928.

Orderly Book of the Siege of Yorktown from September 26th, 1781 to November 2nd, 1781, Philadelphia, 1865.

Palmer, William P., and Flournoy, H. W., eds., *Calendar of Virginia State Papers and other Manuscripts,* 11 vols., Richmond, 1875-1893.

Papers of the Continental Congress, National Archives.

Pattison, James, *The Official Letters of Maj. Gen. James Pattison,* Collections of the New-York Historical Society, New York, 1876.

Pickering, Timothy, Jr., *An Easy Plan of Discipline for a Militia,* Salem, Mass., 1775.

Porterie, M. de la, *Institutions Militaires pour la Cavalerie et les Dragons,* Paris, n.d. (c. 1764).

Roberts, Kenneth, compiler, *March to Quebec,* New York, 1940.

Robertson, John, *A Treatise of such Mathematical Instruments as are usually put into a Portable Case...with an Appendix containing the Description and Use of the Gunners Callipers...,* 3rd ed., London, 1775.

Saunders, William L., ed., *The Colonial Records of North Carolina,* 10 vols., Raleigh, 1886-1890.

Scheer, George F., and Hugh F. Rankin, *Rebels and Redcoats,* New York, 1957.

Simcoe, John G., *Simcoe's Military Journal,* New York, 1844.

Simes, Thomas, *The Military Guide for Young Officers,* 2nd ed., London, 1776.

Simes, Thomas, *The Military Medley,* London, 1768.

Smith, George, Capt., *An Universal Military Dictionary,* London, 1779.

Sullivan, John, *Letters and Papers of Maj. Gen. John Sullivan,* ed. by Otis G. Hammond, 2 vols., Concord, N.H., 1931.

Swieten, Baron van, *The Diseases Incident to the Armies with the Method of Cure,* Philadelphia, 1776.

Thacher, James, *Military Journal of the American Revolution,* Hartford, 1862.

Tielke, J. G., *The Field Engineer; or Instructions upon every Branch of Field Fortification...,* trans. by Edwin Hewgill, 2 vols., London, 1789.

Tilton, James, *Economical Observations on Military Hospitals and the Prevention of Diseases Incident to an Army,* Wilmington, 1813.

Vauban, Marshal de, *De l'Attaque et de la Défense des Places,* La Haye, 1737.

Von Steuben, Friedrich Wilhelm Ludolf Gerhard Augustin, Baron, *Regulations for the Order and Discipline of the Troops of the United States,* editions of 1779, 1794, and others.

Washington, George, *The Papers of George Washington,* Manuscript Division, Library of Congress.

Washington, George, *The Writings of George Washington,* John C. Fitzpatrick, ed., 39 vols., Washington, 1931-1944.

Wayne, Anthony, *Papers,* Revolutionary series, transcribed by Henry B. Dawson in 1860 from original manuscripts in the possession of the Wayne family. 10 bound folios, Morristown National Historical Park.

Weedon, George, *Valley Forge Orderly Book, 1777-1778;* Samuel W. Pennypacker, ed., New York, 1902.

Whitehead, William, and others, eds., *New Jersey Archives,* 39 vols., Newark, 1880-1946.

Whiting, Henry, ed., *Revolutionary Orders of General Washington,* New York, 1844.

Wilkinson, James, *Memoirs of My Own Time,* 3 vols., Philadelphia, 1816.

Windham, William, *A Plan of Discipline Composed for the Use of the Militia of the County of Norfolk,* London, 1759.

Secondary Sources

Applegate, Howard Lewis, "The American Revolutionary War Hospital Department," *Military Medicine,* April 1961, pp. 296-306.

Applegate, Howard Lewis, "The Medical Administrators of the American Revolutionary Army," *Military Affairs,* XXV, No. 1 (Spring 1961), 1-10.

Applegate, Howard Lewis, "The Need for Further Study in the Medical History of the American Revolutionary Army," *Military Medicine,* August 1961, pp. 616-618.

Applegate, Howard Lewis, "Preventive Medicine in the American Revolutionary Army," *Military Medicine,* May 1961, pp. 379-382.

Applegate, Howard Lewis, "Remedial Medicine in the American Revolutionary Army," *Military Medicine,* June 1961, pp. 451-453.

Aylward, J. D., *The Small-sword in England,* London, 1945.

Birkhimer, William E., *Historical Sketch of the Organization, Administration, Matériel and Tactics of the Artillery, United States Army,* Washington, 1884.

Blackmore, Howard L., *British Military Firearms, 1650-1850,* London, 1961.

Boatner, Mark M., III, *Encyclopedia of the American Revolution,* New York, 1966.

Bolton, Charles K., *The Private Soldier Under Washington,* New York, 1902.

Bottet, Maurice, *L'Arme Blanche de Guerre Française Au XVIIIe Siècle,* Paris, 1910.

Boudriot, Jean, *Armes à Feu Françaises, Modeles Reglementaires, 1717-1836,* 3 series, Paris, 1961, 1963, 1965.

Bright, James R., "The Rifle in Washington's Army," *The American Rifleman,* XCV, No. 8 (August 1947), 7-10.

Brown, Harvey E., *The Medical Department of the United States Army, 1775-1873,* Washington, 1873.

Calver, William L., and Bolton, Reginald P., *History Written with Pick and Shovel,* New York, 1950.

Clark, George L., *Silas Deane,* New York, 1913.

Cornwell, William S., "The Museum's Collection of Military Canteens," *Bulletin* of the Rochester Museum of Arts and Sciences, June 1964.

Doniol, Henri, *Histoire de la Participation de la France à l'Établissement des États-Unis d'Amerique,* 6 vols., Paris, 1886.

Duncan, Louis M., *Medical Men in the Revolution, 1775-1783,* Carlisle, Pa., 1931.

Farmer, Henry G., *History of the Royal Artillery Band,* London, 1954.

Farmer, Henry G., *Military Music,* London, 1950.

French, Allen, *The First Year of the American Revolution,* Boston, 1934.

Gabriel, Ralph Henry, and others, eds., *The Pageant of America,* 15 vols., New Haven, 1925-1929.

General Washington's Military Equipment, 3rd ed., Mount Vernon, Va., 1963.

Gooding, S. James, *An Introduction to British Artillery in North America,* "Historical Arms Series" No. 4, Ottawa, 1965.

Griffenhagen, George B., *Drug Supplies in the American Revolution,* U.S. National Museum *Bulletin* 225, Washington, 1961.

Holst, Donald W., and Zlatich, Marko, "Dress and Equipment of Pulaski's Independent Legion," *Military Collector & Historian,* XVI, no. 4 (Winter 1964), 97-103.

Johnston, Henry P., *The Yorktown Campaign and the Surrender of Cornwallis,* New York, 1881.

Lefferts, Charles M., *Uniforms of the American, British, French, and German Armies in the War of the American Revolution, 1775-1783,* New York, 1926.

Margerand, J., *Armement et Équipement de L'Infanterie Française du XVIe Siècle,* Paris, n.d.

Miller, Robert L., "Fredericksburg Manufactory Muskets," *Military Collector & Historian,* III, no. 3 (September 1951), 63-65.

Miller, Robert L., and Peterson, Harold L., "Rappahannock Forge: Its History and Products," *Military Collector & Historian,* IV, no. 4 (December 1952), 81-85.

Montross, Lynn, *Rag, Tag and Bobtail, the Story of the Continental Army, 1775-83,* New York, 1952.

Napoleon, Louis, and Favé, Col., *Etudes sur le Passé et l'Avenir de l'Artillerie,* 6 vols., Paris, 1846-1871.

Peterson, Harold L., *American Indian Tomahawks,* New York, 1965.

Peterson, Harold L., *American Silver Mounted Swords, 1700-1815,* Washington, 1955. This scarce booklet has also been reprinted as a supplement to Peterson, *The American Sword, 1775-1945,* rev. ed., Philadelphia, 1965.

Peterson, Harold L., *Arms and Armor in Colonial America, 1526-1783,* Harrisburg, 1956.

Peterson, Harold L., *Encyclopedia of Firearms,* New York and London, 1964.

Peterson, Harold L., "Silas Deane in France," typescript of Master of Arts thesis, University of Wisconsin, 1946.

Peterson, Mendel L., "American Epaulettes, 1775-1820," *Military Collector & Historian,* II, No. 2 (March 1950), 17-21.

Quaife, Milo M., Weig, Melvin J., and Appleman, Roy E., *The History of the United States Flag,* New York, 1961.

Quarles, Benjamin, *The Negro in the American Revolution,* Chapel Hill, N.C., 1961.

Schwartz, H. W., *The Story of Musical Instruments,* New York, 1953.

Sellers, Charles Coleman, "Portraits and Miniatures by Charles Willson Peale," *Transactions of the American Philosophical Society,* New Series, XLII, Part I (1952), 353-360.

Sonneck, Oscar, *Early Concert-life in America, 1731-1800,* New York, 1949.

Stevenson, Isobel, "Beginnings of American Military Medicine," *Ciba Symposia,* I, No. 11 (February 1940), 344-359.

Tylden, Major G., *Horses and Saddlery,* London, 1965.

Ward, Christopher, *The War of the Revolution,* 2 vols., New York, 1952.

Weller, Jac, "The Artillery of the American Revolution," *Military Collector & Historian,* Part I, Vol. VIII, No. 3 (Fall 1956), 61-65; Part II, Vol. VIII, No. 4 (Winter 1956), 97-101.

Westcott, Allan P., "For Military Merit," *Military Affairs,* V, No. 3, 211-214.

White, William C., *A History of Military Music in America,* New York, 1944.

Williams, Catherine, *Biography of Revolutionary Heroes,* Providence, R.I., 1839.

Woodward, Arthur, "Some Notes on Gun Flints," *Military Collector & Historian,* III, no. 2 (June 1951), 29-36.

Wright, John W., *Some Notes on the Continental Army,* New Windsor Cantonment Publication No. 2, Vails Gate, New York, 1963.

Index